THE HOLY EPISTLE TO THE
Ephesians

SERMONS ON A MESSIANIC JEWISH APPROACH

D. THOMAS LANCASTER

THE HOLY EPISTLE TO THE
Ephesians

SERMONS ON A MESSIANIC JEWISH APPROACH

D. THOMAS LANCASTER

Copyright © 2022 D. Thomas Lancaster. All rights reserved.
Publication rights First Fruits of Zion, Inc.
Details: ffoz.org/copyright

Publisher grants permission to reference short quotations (less than 400 words) in reviews, magazines, newspapers, web sites, or other publications in accordance with the citation standards at ffoz.org/copyright. Requests for permission to reproduce more than 400 words can be made at ffoz.org/contact.

First Fruits of Zion is a 501(c)(3) registered nonprofit educational organization.

Printed in the United States of America

ISBN: 978-1-941534-65-6 : Hardcover
ISBN: 978-1-941534-96-0 : Softcover

Scriptural quotations are from The Holy Bible, English Standard Version, copyright © 2001 by Crossway Bibles, a division of Good News Publishers. Used by permission. All rights reserved.

Cover Design: Anne Mandell

Quantity discounts are available on bulk purchases of this book for educational, fundraising, or event purposes. Special versions or book excerpts to fit specific needs are available from First Fruits of Zion. For more information, contact ffoz.org/contact.

First Fruits of Zion

PO Box 649, Marshfield, Missouri 65706-0649 USA

Phone: (417) 468-2741
Website: ffoz.org

Comments and questions: ffoz.org/contact

About the Cover

"Ascension" (1775) by John Singleton Copley. The original is in the Museum of Fine Arts in Boston, Massachusetts.

To Maria Anne

To Our Children and Grandchildren

To Beth Immanuel Messianic Synagogue

CONTENTS

Introduction. 1

Narrative Context: Paul and the Ephesians (Acts 18–28) 13

         A narrative frame for the Epistle to
the Ephesians based on Acts 18–28,
excerpted from Chronicles of the Apostles.

Sermon 1:   The Salutation and Blessing (Ephesians 1:1–23) 43

         How the pronouns in Ephesians 1 provide the key
to unlocking the meaning of Paul's message to the
Gentile disciples in Ephesus.

Sermon 2:   The Immeasurable
(Ephesians 1:18–2:13) 55

         The exaltation of Messiah and salvation through him
transcends all concerns of social status, prestige, class,
caste, nationality, and ancestry.

Sermon 3:   The Dividing Wall (Ephesians 2:14–22) 67

         Did Christ tear down the dividing wall between Jews
and Gentiles by abolishing the Torah? There's more
than one way to misunderstand the "one new man."

Sermon 4:   The Eternal Purpose of God (Ephesians 3) 77

         The "mystery of the gospel" and the "eternal purpose
of God" presented in Ephesians 3 reveal the meaning
of the redemption and the significance of the Gentile
disciples in the kingdom.

Sermon 5: Fellow Heirs (Ephesians 3:1-11) 87

What does it mean to be a "fellow heir" with Israel and part of "the commonwealth of Israel"? Paul uncovers the role of the Gentile disciples in the "mystery of Christ," which was "hidden in God" for ages past.

Sermon 6: The Fullness Who Fills All in All (Ephesians 3:11-21) 95

Paul invites Gentile disciples to find their identity in Messiah by diving into the deep waters of apostolic mysticism. A few parallels from Jewish mysticism help elucidate his ideas.

Sermon 7: A Manner Worthy of the Calling (Ephesians 4) 105

How does a disciple of Yeshua live? Paul provides a quick summary of the path of discipleship as it applies to both Jews and Gentiles, distinguishing between the old life and the new.

Sermon 8: The One Who Also Ascended (Ephesians 4:7-11)... 119

An obscure midrash about Moses is concealed behind Paul's cryptic allusion to Psalm 68 in Ephesians 4:9-10. Here's an apostolic teaching about the ascension of the Messiah that likens it to Moses ascending Mount Sinai.

Sermon 9: The Fivefold Gift (Ephesians 4:11-12) 129

It is commonly taught that Ephesians 4:11 presents fivefold gifts of ministry for leadership and service in a congregation. A post-supersessionist perspective on the passage comes to a completely different conclusion.

Sermon 10: A Lamp That Lights Many Lamps (Ephesians 4:11-14) 139

We discover how the gift of the Holy Spirit was transmitted through the disciples of Yeshua, through the apostles, the prophets, the evangelists, teachers, and pastors who first received it during the outpouring that took place on Shavu'ot.

Sermon 11:   The Children of Light (Ephesians 5:1–20) 151

Why does Paul tell the Gentile disciples in Ephesus that they must no longer live as Gentiles? In what way are Gentile disciples of Yeshua supposed to live like Jews? Paul offers his readers practical guidance for their new life with God's people.

Sermon 12:   A Profound Mystery (Ephesians 5:21–33) 163

Moving beyond the Jew-Gentile distinction, Paul considers other relationships affected by the Messiah, starting with the profound mystery of marriage.

Sermon 13:   Children, Obey Your Parents (Ephesians 6:1–4) 175

Children fall under the Torah of their parents until adulthood. There's no formula guaranteeing godly children, but here are a few pastoral tips from Ephesians 6.

Sermon 14:   Servants and Masters (Ephesians 6:5–9) 187

Apostolic directives for slaves and their owners in the Roman world have modern implications for discipleship today. Ephesians 6 teaches principles for distinction theology, discipleship, and the service of God.

Sermon 15:   Not against Flesh and Blood
(Ephesians 6:10–12) 197

Stand against the schemes of the devil and learn about spiritual warfare in Ephesus. Here's the real story behind the "armor of God" in Ephesians 6 and the meaning of "the devil's schemes."

Sermon 16:   Armageddon and the Armor of God
(Ephesians 6:13–24) 209

A discussion on the armor of God in its biblical and eschatological context: the final battle with the nations, which is called Gog and Magog and the battle of Armageddon.

INTRODUCTION

"Let's read Ephesians." That's the suggestion I made to the Messianic Jewish community of Beth Immanuel in Hudson, Wisconsin, in 2021, when we started with the first chapter of the epistle. That suggestion led to a series of Bible commentary teachings (disguised as Sabbath sermons) that now constitutes this book. Herein, I attempt to read the Epistle to the Ephesians from a Messianic Jewish perspective. As a result, these teachings assume a readership already familiar with the theology of Messianic Judaism and the Jewish approach to discipleship to Yeshua.

Messianic Judaism, as I know it, starts with the assumption that Christianity was originally Jewish. In the beginning, the community of Jesus-followers was Jewish. All its members were originally Jewish. Jesus, the apostles, and all the first disciples were practicing Jews who considered themselves part of Israel and the Jewish people. They did not envision themselves as the authors of a new religion; they considered themselves to be a sect within greater Judaism—a reformation movement inspired by the teachings of Jesus (Yeshua) of Nazareth and by their conviction that he is the long-promised Messiah King. They belonged to the sect of the Nazarenes, a first-century Jewish school of disciples centered around Yeshua. They did not hold Jesus or the gospel message in antithesis to the Law (Torah) of Moses. They upheld the words of Jesus:

> Do not think that I have come to abolish the Law or the Prophets; I have not come to abolish them but to fulfill them. For truly, I say to you, until heaven and earth pass away, not an iota, not a dot, will pass from the Law until all is accomplished. Therefore whoever relaxes one of the least of these commandments and teaches others to do the same will be

called least in the kingdom of heaven, but whoever does them and teaches them will be called great in the kingdom of heaven. (Matthew 5:17-19)

They practiced a religion that, in modern terms, can best be described as Messianic Judaism. Within a few decades, the charter members took a vote (Acts 15), and they expanded the membership to include non-Jews, but that did not, at first, alter the fundamental Jewish nature of the institution.

Messianic Judaism can be understood as a branch of Judaism that honors Yeshua of Nazareth as Messiah and as the divine Son of God. The modern Messianic Jewish movement was born from Christian missionary efforts to evangelize Jews. In the late nineteenth century, Jewish believers in Jesus began to take ownership of their faith, eschewing Gentile Christian modes of worship and interpretation and working to establish an authentic Jewish expression of their allegiance to Jesus as Messiah. In the 1960s and 1970s, the movement blossomed in the United States among young Jewish Christians of the Baby-Boom Generation. Since then, it has outgrown its original chrysalis as a Jewish missionary effort and has begun to emerge as an independent sect of Judaism, much as the communities of the original apostles did.

As was the case with those Apostolic-era Messianic communities, Messianic Judaism today includes a predominant number of Gentile participants. Many of those Gentile Christians have entered the movement seeking a more historically authentic form of Christianity. In that regard, Messianic Judaism is no longer an exclusively Jewish movement (if it ever was). Instead, it includes many "Messianic Gentiles" who, while not being Jewish, nevertheless have found a spiritual home in the Messianic synagogue. I am one of those Gentiles, but I pastor a Messianic Jewish congregation, pray in a Messianic Jewish synagogue, and teach with the Messianic Jewish ministry First Fruits of Zion. All this background information is necessary for the reader to understand the perspective from which I have written this book.

In this series of teachings on the book of Ephesians, I attempted to provide my congregation with a historical, contextual explanation of Paul's words from a Jewish perspective, but I found it difficult to do so without first dispelling common misconceptions along the way. As a result, this book challenges several long-standing Christian interpretations, many of which remain popular even in Messianic Jewish circles.

I do not intend to disparage Christian tradition; I am interested only in establishing a better Messianic Jewish reading of the text. Nevertheless, I believe that the material has the potential to engage and energize traditional Christians and Christian churches, and I hope that the book will be read outside the small circles of Messianic Judaism.

From Galatians to Ephesians

The teachings in this book follow my earlier work on Paul's epistle to the Galatians, titled *The Holy Epistle to the Galatians*. Readers familiar with that book (or at least with the school of thought that sees Paul as remaining within Judaism) will be better prepared for the discussions contained within this one. This new set of teachings on Ephesians further develops the ideas introduced in that book. But it's not strictly necessary to have read the former to understand this latter work.

Here's the basic premise set forth in *The Holy Epistle to the Galatians*: Paul did not abandon Judaism or advocate any cancellation of Jewish identity or Torah observance for Jewish followers of Jesus. However, he considered himself specially appointed to present the good news of the kingdom to the Gentiles without requiring those Gentiles to become Jewish through conversion, adopt Jewish identity, or adopt Torah observance as Jews as a prerequisite to their participation in the kingdom as disciples of Jesus. Moreover, he objected to all attempts from other Yeshua-followers to coerce Gentile disciples into undergoing conversion or adopting Jewish identity. That's Galatians in a nutshell. Ephesians follows up with several of the same themes. Needless to say, as a series of sermons transferred to print, this book is not an academic work. I have intentionally attempted to keep it on a popular reading level (even if the ideas espoused will never be popular), free of footnotes and documentation.

Nevertheless, the ideas informing the discussion have some foundation in the academic world of New Testament scholarship. Specifically, the scholarship upon which I build is the collective product of a comparatively recent stream of thought called "post-supersessionism." To understand this term, we need to understand what supersessionism is and how it came to dominate Christian theology for most of church history.

Supersessionism and Replacement Theology

Scholars date the Epistle to the Ephesians between 62 and 100 CE, giving the followers of Yeshua of Nazareth nearly two thousand years to excavate its historical, homiletical, and theological content. However, for most of that time, our reading of it has been "in a mirror dimly" (1 Corinthians 13:12). After the first-generation disciples passed away—as Polycrates put it in his letter to Victor, "great lights have fallen asleep"—non-Jewish followers of Yeshua increasingly distanced themselves from the Jewish people, from Jewish practice, and a Jewish interpretation of the Bible. R. Kendall Soulen calls this unfortunate development "a flaw in the heart of the crystal" of Christian theology, and despite the quiet murmurs of a few dissenters throughout the past few centuries, only in the last fifty years or so has this flaw become apparent to a critical mass of Jewish and Christian academics.

Traditional Christian interpretation from the time of Ignatius to the present day has held that the followers of Jesus constitute a new people of God and that this people—the "church"—has replaced or superseded the Jewish people. Consequently, everything God promised to the children of Israel in the Old Testament is now given to the church.

This, of course, includes the promises of resurrection from the dead and eternal life, but it also includes purely temporal promises—the land of Israel, agricultural success, and so forth—which have been completely reinterpreted. Sometimes they are spiritualized; sometimes they are applied literally, but to the church instead of Israel. John Piper, for example, teaches that "all followers of Christ, and only followers of Christ, will inherit the earth, including the Land [of Israel]."

This interpretive framework is often called "supersessionism" or "replacement theology" (terms that will be treated as synonymous here, despite some possible nuances in meaning), and it remains popular in many theological systems. It rests on the idea that Yeshua was the only Jewish person to fulfill the requirements of the Sinai Covenant and therefore is the only Jewish person who has any right to be a beneficiary of God's promises. Any person, whether Jew or Gentile, who wishes to inherit these promises can do so only by becoming a disciple of Yeshua and thereby joining the church, which has become a sort of reconstituted people of God—a replacement for Israel, even sometimes called the "true" or "spiritual" Israel.

In this "spiritual" Israel, the Old Testament law is abolished, as is Jewish identity. Judaism is "superseded" by Christianity, and there is no place for Sabbath observance, dietary laws, or any of the other identity markers of the Jewish people—all of which are, according to the basic tenets of traditional Judaism, essential to the continuation of Jewish identity and to the working out of the irrevocable covenants God has made with the children of Abraham, Isaac, and Jacob.

In this light, it's easy to sympathize with Jewish people who reject the Christian gospel. Jews must surely think it puzzling that we would present the New Testament, which ostensibly replaces Judaism and all Jewish religious institutions and functions, as "good news for Israel." Where's the good news in the replacement-theology gospel? Israel has been replaced, the Torah has been canceled, and God's covenant with the Jewish people is over. Is it really a mystery why most Jewish people are none too excited about this so-called "good news"?

Post-Supersessionism

Even leaving aside the understandably lukewarm Jewish response to these ideas, reading Ephesians—or any other book of the Bible—through a supersessionist lens simply presents obvious problems when it comes to interpreting the Old Testament. For example, the promises of God through the prophets ring hollow if their original recipients—the Jewish people—were not, after all, to receive them. The "new heart" of Ezekiel 36:26 and the "new covenant" of Jeremiah 31:31 provide no comfort to these prophets' original audience if this glorious inheritance was only to devolve to an entirely different group of people.

For over three hundred years, isolated writers and scholars from all walks of life have understood these problems and have questioned the standard Christian interpretation of what Yeshua's work means for the Jewish people. Gentile scholars from John Toland in the early 1700s to W. D. Davies and David Daube in the twentieth century, and Jewish scholars from Jacob Emden to Claude Montefiore and Géza Vermes all published attempts to correct some or all of the errors of supersessionism and replacement theology. Several Messianic Jewish luminaries, such as Rabbi Yechiel Tzvi Lichtenstein and Paul Phillip Levertoff, also understood the dangerous error of supersessionism. Many of them wrote treatises on Yeshua-faith from a traditional Jewish perspective and continued to live in fidelity to the Jewish way of life. Yet these scholars and their works were mostly met with derision or, more commonly, silence.

E.P. Sanders broke the dam in 1977 with the publication of *Paul and Palestinian Judaism*. While reception to his conclusions varied, the landscape of biblical studies was forever changed by his comprehensive assessment of Second Temple Judaism as a religion in which salvation was predicated not on works but on the covenant status of the Jewish people as children of Abraham and beneficiaries of the promises God made to the patriarchs.

Sanders and his contemporaries kicked off a new wave of historical Jesus research, often called the "Third Quest for the Historical Jesus," a movement that has catapulted into prominence the idea that Jesus was a first-century rabbi firmly entrenched in the Judaism of his day. Yet Paul remained an enigma—and Paul's writings are foundational for the development of the identity of the Gentile follower of the Jewish Rabbi Yeshua of Nazareth.

Paul's language about being saved by grace instead of works was in particular need of reinterpretation in light of this reassessment of Jesus and Judaism—after all, if Sanders was right, and Jews didn't believe they were saved by works, then what was Paul actually arguing against? James Dunn's *New Perspective on Paul*, published only a few years after Sanders' landmark work, offered an answer that has garnered broad acceptance and sparked considerable dialogue: The "works" by which Gentiles are not saved are the works of conversion to Judaism. Therefore, Paul's core argument in these verses was that his Gentile readers were already saved and did not need to become Jewish.

Dunn, however, continued to believe that Paul sought to break down the dividing wall (cf. Ephesians 2:14) by eradicating the markers of Jewish identity even among Jewish disciples of Yeshua, thereby creating the famous "one new man" (2:15) so prevalent in Christian ecclesiology. It was left to a relatively small contingent of the next generation of scholars to argue that Paul remained a practicing Jew and that his thought can be wholly reconciled with the continuation of the role and calling God granted exclusively to the Jewish people. It is to these scholars, now too numerous to name, but including Matthew W. Bates, Pamela Eisenbaum, Paula Fredricksen, David Flusser, Lloyd Gaston, Mark Kinzer, Amy-Jill Levine, Mark Nanos, Isaac Oliver, David Rudolph, R. Kendall Soulen, Oscar Skarsaune, Krister Stendahl, Peter

Tomson, J. Brian Tucker, Joel Willitts, Brad Young, Magnus Zetterholm, Christopher Zoccali, and their historical forbears that I owe a debt for laying the logical, historical, and theological foundation upon which today's post-supersessionist interpretation of Paul is built. I owe a special debt to Lionel J. Windsor's book *Reading Ephesians & Colossians after Supersessionism: Christ's Mission through Israel to the Nations* for his insights on Ephesians 2:14–15 and 4:11–12.

Distinction Theology

In my congregation, at First Fruits of Zion, and in this book, I use a term inspired by a post-supersessionist interpretation that is intended as a counter to the term "replacement theology." That term is "distinction theology." Distinction theology is simply the premise that Jews and Gentiles retain their respective social identities within the body of Messiah—that there is a difference between the two, even after their admittance into the school of Yeshua's disciples.

One might think, "That's obvious enough. Why do we need a whole theology called 'distinction theology'? Obviously, there's a difference between Jews and Gentiles." But it's not obvious. Most New Testament readers believe that the New Testament teaches that both Jewish disciples and Gentile disciples are homogenized into a new identity, a third race, the "one new man," and that in Messiah, there is no difference between Jews and Gentiles.

In Messianic circles, this misapprehension finds expression in two different ways. If you believe there is no distinction and that Christ has canceled the Torah, it looks like replacement theology. The new Christian free-from-the-law identity has replaced the old Jewish under-the-law identity, and there is no remaining distinction between Jews and Gentiles. If, on the other hand, you believe there is no distinction but that the Torah has not been canceled, you are liable to fall into "one law" theology. Since there's no distinction between Jews and Gentiles, both share an equal obligation to the Torah, and therefore, there is no actual difference.

If you adopt either one of those perspectives, replacement theology or one law theology, you will misunderstand the New Testament because both of them are based on the paradigm of supersessionism. Both of them assume the old definition of the people of Israel has been superseded by a new "spiritual" Israel in which the distinction between Jew and Gentile is erased.

The misapprehension is based upon a misunderstanding of New Testament passages like Galatians 3:28: "There is neither Jew nor Greek, there is neither slave nor free, there is no male and female, for you are all one in Christ Jesus." When it comes to eligibility for the kingdom and the World to Come, there is indeed no difference between Jew nor Greek, male nor female, slave nor free. However, there certainly are differences in role and responsibility and in privilege and prerogative between all of those dichotomous categories. Likewise, when Simon Peter says, "He made no distinction between us and them, having cleansed their hearts by faith" (Acts 15:9), he refers to eligibility for the kingdom. His point is that since God has not made a distinction as to eligibility for the kingdom, there is no need for non-Jews to become Jewish.

In the kingdom, Messiah will rule over both Israel and the nations. He will be the King of the Jews, but he will also be the King of kings. The messianic kingdom will be universal. The prophecies say that in the kingdom, the Jewish people will all be gathered back to the promised land, and the kingdom of Israel will be restored. The same prophecies say that in the kingdom, the nations will make pilgrimage to the Holy Land, worshiping with the Jewish people from new moon to new moon and from Sabbath to Sabbath. Their sacrifices will be received on God's altar, and his Temple will be a house of prayer for all nations, and they will say to one another, "Come, let us go up to the mountain of the LORD, to the house of the God of Jacob, that he may teach us his ways and that we may walk in his paths" (Isaiah 2:3).

In those days, under the radial arrangement of the *ekklesia* ("assembly," usually translated as "church"), the Torah will go out from Jerusalem to the nations. These prophecies about the kingdom of heaven assume a distinction between Jews and Gentiles even during the Messianic Era. For those prophecies to receive a literal fulfillment, there must be a distinction between Jews and Gentiles even after the coming of Yeshua and the establishment of his kingdom.

Both have obligations to the Torah and the commandments, but these obligations are not identical. There's only one Torah, but there are two kinds of people in Messiah's communities: Israel and the nations. The same Torah applies to both, but it has distinct roles and obligations for both groups. Some commandments apply to the Jewish people but do not apply to Gentiles, and the nation of Israel has certain privileges and prerogatives that the nations do not possess.

Rule for All the Communities

Distinction theology teaches that Gentile identity does not replace Jewish identity, and Jewish identity does not replace Gentile identity. Both Israel and the nations are part of the kingdom; therefore, both Jews and Gentiles have roles to play within the communities of Yeshua's disciples.

The key passage behind distinction theology, as pointed out by Rabbi Dr. David Rudolph, is 1 Corinthians 7:17, which Paul refers to as his rule for all the communities:

> But as God hath distributed to every man, as the Lord hath called every one, so let him walk. And so ordain I in all churches. Is any man called being circumcised? let him not become uncircumcised. Is any called in uncircumcision? let him not be circumcised. Circumcision is nothing, and uncircumcision is nothing, but the keeping of the commandments of God. Let every man abide in the same calling wherein he was called. (1 Corinthians 7:17-20 KJV)

I have used the King James translation, cumbersome as it may be, because it's a solid translation that conveys the sense of the Greek. Here is my paraphrase:

> According to whatever God allotted to every person when the Master called him, so let him walk (live out). This is my rule for all the communities of Yeshua. Was any man Jewish when the Master called him? Let him not become a Gentile. Was any man a Gentile? Let him not become Jewish. Being Jewish is irrelevant, and being Gentile is irrelevant. The important thing is to keep the commandments of God. Therefore, let every person remain in the same state as he was when he was called. (1 Corinthians 7:17-20, my translation)

Of course, there are reasonable exceptions to Paul's rule for all the communities, such as intermarriage or mixed ancestry. But the principle remains valid. There's a difference. Not everyone is alike.

Yet that difference between Jews and Gentiles is not the important thing. The important thing is to observe God's commandments as they apply to each person. The Jewish disciple observes the commandments that apply to him or her as a Jew, and a Gentile disciple observes the commandments that apply to him or her as a Gentile. Some commandments are universal (e.g., the prohibition on murder). Some commandments (e.g., circumcision as *brit milah*) apply exclusively to the Jewish people and should not be practiced by Gentile disciples. Some commandments (e.g., calendar observances) are incumbent only upon the Jewish people but are not off-limits to Gentiles.

Distinction theology maintains the unique roles of both Jews and Gentiles within the communities of Yeshua. This means that Gentiles should not feel as though they need to become Jewish or adopt Jewish identity, and likewise, Jews should not feel compelled to adopt Gentile culture and Gentile identity.

The Epistle to the Ephesians is a crucial source text for these ideas, and properly understanding Paul's arguments therein will clarify and support these concepts.

Structure of the Book

Before the series of teachings on Ephesians, I have included, as a first chapter, a narrative commentary titled "Paul and the Ephesians," which provides the context and occasion behind the Epistle to the Ephesians. I lifted this text from my much longer commentary on Acts and the Apostolic Era titled *Chronicles of the Apostles*.

- Sermon 1 deals with the salutation, in which Paul contrasts the Jewish and Gentile disciples of Yeshua, highlighting their variegated backgrounds, roles, and callings, yet including both as full-fledged members of the Yeshua movement.
- Sermon 2 outlines Paul's specific concerns for the Gentile Ephesians. They are in danger of misunderstanding what they have already attained

as followers of Yeshua and of thinking that they must become Jewish to be part of the kingdom.

- Sermon 3 explores Paul's metaphor of the dividing wall and clarifies what Paul meant by creating "one new man" from the Jewish and Gentile disciples—their respective identities remain, even in Yeshua.
- Sermon 4 explains that God's purpose in redeeming Israel was to extend his redemptive work to the nations, proving his superiority over their false gods.
- Sermon 5 details Paul's distinction theology and what it means that the Gentile disciples are "fellow heirs" with the Jewish people.
- Sermon 6 talks about the "fullness of God," with which the disciples are filled with reference to ideas drawn from Jewish mysticism.
- Sermon 7 signals a transition in Ephesians 4, where Paul begins transmitting practical advice to the Ephesian disciples in light of their calling as disciples.
- Sermon 8 explores the parallels between the grace Yeshua attained through his ascension and the Torah that Moses obtained when he ascended Mount Sinai.
- Sermon 9 explains the "fivefold ministry" of Ephesians 4:11-12 as a reference to the community of first-generation Jewish disciples in Jerusalem.
- Sermon 10 traces the Spirit's transmission from disciple to disciple, beginning on Shavu'ot and continuing through Acts and the epistles.
- Sermon 11 expounds on Paul's directive to be "children of light" (Ephesians 5:8), outlining the moral demands of discipleship.
- Sermons 12-14 explore the three dichotomous relationships to which Paul pays special attention—husbands and wives, parents and children, and masters and slaves.
- Sermons 15-16 explain the "armor of God" passage in light of Paul's goal throughout the rest of the epistle—to explain the inclusion of Gentile disciples without their taking on Jewish identity.

Acknowledgments

Thank you to the good people at Beth Immanuel who patiently endured these teachings in the first place. Thank you to my friend and colleague Boaz Michael, founder and director of First Fruits of Zion (FFOZ), who makes it possible for me to publish my thoughts. Thank you to my colleague Aaron Eby who first pointed out to me the differentiated pronouns in Ephesians 1–2, an insight that proved to be a sort of Rosetta Stone to unlock the whole epistle. Thanks to Jacob Fronczak, who provided the material with a much-needed edit and assisted with the above overview of recent Pauline scholarship. Thank you to the whole staff at First Fruits of Zion and to all the *FFOZ Friends* who provide the financial support and spiritual encouragement necessary to make a book like this possible.

Whether you agree or disagree with the conclusions I set forth in this book, I believe that you will at least find some inspiration along the way in your devotion to Jesus and your practice of the faith. Regardless of the differences, ultimately, all disciples of Jesus share the unity of faith: "One Lord, one faith, one baptism, one God and Father of all, who is over all and through all and in all" (Ephesians 4:5–6). May every disciple of our holy Master Yeshua who reads and studies Paul's Epistle to the Ephesians receive an abundant blessing for life and for peace, both in this world and in the one to come.

Maranatha!

D. Thomas Lancaster
Hudson, Wisconsin
17 Adar I 5782

NARRATIVE CONTEXT:
PAUL AND THE EPHESIANS
(ACTS 18–28)

> A narrative frame for the Epistle to
> the Ephesians based on Acts 18-28,
> excerpted from *Chronicles of the Apostles*.

> Paul, an apostle of Christ Jesus by the will of God, to the
> saints who are in Ephesus, and are faithful in Christ Jesus.
> (Ephesians 1:1)

By the time Paul composed his epistle to "the saints in Ephesus," he had already fostered a long-term relationship with those saints and with associated communities of Yeshua believers in Asia Minor. His labors in Ephesus had born significant fruit. It's likely that all seven of the communities of Yeshua followers addressed in Revelation 1-2 began with Paul's work in Ephesus. To understand his epistle to the Ephesians and unlock its meaning, we need to review the story that led to its composition. The contents of this long preliminary chapter retell that story in the form of a commentary on pertinent parts of Luke's narrative in Acts 18-28 with some additional insights from the epistles.

Arrival in Ephesus

The apostle to the Gentiles had his eye on Ephesus, the capital of Asia Minor, long before arriving there. Two years before setting foot in the city, he had intended to travel to Ephesus with Silas when they were "forbidden by the Holy Spirit to speak the word in Asia" (Acts 16:6).

After spending eighteen months or so in Corinth over the years 50–51 CE, Paul prepared to return to his home base in Syrian Antioch. He hoped to coordinate the trip in such a way that he could first arrive in Jerusalem for the Festival of Sukkot (Tabernacles). He left Corinth with his friends and colleagues, Priscilla and Aquila, Jewish believers from Rome who were moving their tent-making business to Ephesus. Timothy almost certainly went with Paul, too, even though Luke does not mention other traveling companions. Silas had either left Corinth already or chosen to remain behind. He does not appear again in the book of Acts.

Two or three days after leaving the harbor city of Cenchrea, Paul's ship sailed into the port of the great city of Diana (Artemis). Ephesus was one among many Ionian Greek settlements on the Aegean coastland. Ancient accounts praise Ephesus for its splendid beauty. Situated at the mouth of the Cayster River between the Coressus Mountains and the sea, Ephesus enjoyed notoriety as the most important city in the Roman province of Asia Minor. The proud city had a large theater, stadiums, gymnasiums, extensive libraries, luxurious bathhouses, broad, paved streets, marble roads, running fountains, a well-stocked marketplace, and multiple temples to the Caesars and the gods. The magnificent temple of Diana (Artemis), one of the celebrated seven wonders of the Roman world, overshadowed the city and attracted pilgrims and worshipers from all over the empire.

Paul's ship anchored at the mouth of the Cayster River. He and his party disembarked and followed the impressive, doublewide, and colonnaded harbor road up into the city. Paul and Timothy had only a few days to spend in the great city before their ship left. They would be spending the Sabbath. Paul wanted to take advantage of the opportunity by teaching in the synagogue. A large Jewish community made their home in Ephesus. "On the next Sabbath ... he himself entered into the synagogue" (Acts 18:19, Western Text).

To Paul's delight, the Jews of Ephesus received his message about the kingdom with interest and enthusiasm. They asked him to spend more time with them. He could not, however, because he had a ship to catch. He was making all haste to reach Jerusalem in time for the festival. He told them, "I must by all means keep the coming festival in Jerusalem, but I will come back if it is God's will" (Acts 18:20, Western

Text). As it turned out, it was God's will for Paul to return to Ephesus. Acts 19 records the story of his return to the city and his sojourn among the believers there for two years.

City of Artemis

> It happened that while Apollos was at Corinth, Paul passed through the inland country and came to Ephesus. There he found some disciples. (Acts 19:1)

The ancient city of Ephesus operated as a major urban port on the western coast of modern Turkey and enjoyed the status of principal city of the Roman Province of Asia (Minor). Although under Roman control since 133 BCE, Ephesus did not become a Roman colony; it retained its status as a free city. The Roman proconsul over Asia administered the province from Ephesus.

The city's population of two hundred thousand people made it the third-largest city in the Roman Empire. Only Rome and Alexandria were larger. The port at Ephesus received traffic from the Aegean to the west, the Bosporus and Dardanelles to the north, Syria and Israel to the east, and Egypt to the south. Two important highways intersected at Ephesus and connected the city with the distant frontiers of the Roman Empire, making it a vital communication center for Rome and a hub for all culture and commerce in western Asia.

Greek mythology associated the city's origins with the legendary Amazon warriors and the goddess Artemis (Diana). On the coins minted at Ephesus, the goddess wears a crown in the shape of the walls of Ephesus. A great Temple to Artemis at Ephesus drew pilgrims and worshipers of Artemis from all over the world. The temple also functioned as a treasury and bank for economic interests all over the Mediterranean world. In the second century BCE, Antipater of Sidon ranked the Ephesian Temple of Artemis as the greatest of the seven wonders of the world:

> I have set eyes on the wall of lofty Babylon on which is a road for chariots, and the statue of Zeus by the Alpheus, and the hanging gardens, and the colossus of the sun [at Rhodes], and the huge labor of the high pyramids, and the vast tomb of Mausolus; but when I saw the house of Artemis

that mounted to the clouds, those other marvels lost their brilliancy, and I said, "Lo, apart from Olympus, the sun never looked on anything so grand." (Antipater, *Greek Anthology* IX.58)

Likewise, Pliny the Elder rated the temple at Ephesus as the greatest work of Greek architecture:

> The most wonderful monument of Grecian magnificence, and one that merits our genuine admiration, is the Temple of Diana at Ephesus, which took one hundred and twenty years in building, a work in which all Asia joined … The entire length of the temple is four hundred and twenty-five feet, and the breadth two hundred and twenty-five. The columns are one hundred and twenty-seven in number, and sixty feet in height, each of them presented by a different king … the great marvel in this building is, how such ponderous architraves could possibly have been raised to so great a height … the lintel over the entrance doors was an enormous mass of stone, and by no possibility could it be brought to lie level upon the jambs which formed its bed [except by a miracle]. (Pliny, *Natural History* 36.21)

Artemis was the most widely worshiped and revered goddess in the ancient world. She was the twin sister of Apollo, the goddess of the hunt, the wilderness, childbirth, virginity, and chastity. Her father, Zeus, granted her the wish of perpetual virginity. Her mythological companions took vows of chastity, as did her cult followers. Like the Vestal Virgins of the Vesta cult, Artemis had worshipers sworn to celibacy.

At the same time, in seeming contradiction, images of Ephesian Artemis depict her bristling with multiple breasts, and the Ephesians looked to her as a mother-goddess and fertility goddess. The fusion of the two ideals suggests syncretism between the Greek Artemis and an older Ephesian fertility goddess. The combination worked, and the Artemis of Ephesus achieved worldwide acclaim. A second-century writer sums up the fame of Ephesus and Artemis nicely:

> All cities worship Artemis of Ephesus and individuals hold her honor above all the gods. The reason, in my view, is the

renown of the Amazons who traditionally dedicated the image, also the extreme antiquity of this sanctuary. Three other points as well have contributed to her renown, the size of the temple, surpassing all other buildings among humans, the eminence of the city of the Ephesians and the renown of the goddess who dwells there. (*Pausanias* 4.31.8)

The Synagogue in Ephesus

Paul and Timothy found lodging in the home of Priscilla and Aquila, Jewish believers from Rome whom Paul had originally encountered in Corinth. In the recent months, they had relocated to Ephesus. Paul took work again in the tent-making trade. Priscilla and Aquila were also tent-makers, and they simply expanded their enterprise to include Paul. He worked his trade the entire length of his stay in Ephesus. His labor provided for his own needs and even those of his immediate colleagues. He later boasted about his years in Ephesus, "I coveted no one's silver or gold or apparel ... these hands ministered to my necessities and to those who were with me" (Acts 20:33–34).

Priscilla and Aquila were active members of the large Jewish community in Ephesus. The Jews of Ephesus had been there since the third century BCE. Josephus describes how the Jews at Ephesus enjoyed special dispensations from Augustus that shaped Roman-Jewish policy throughout the Empire. Similarly, Marcus Agrippa's defense of the Ephesian Jewish community secured Jewish rights under Rome. A city as large as Ephesus must have had at least a dozen synagogues.

Paul returned to the one at which he had spoken on his previous visit. The synagogue welcomed him back and gave him a forum to present his teachings. He spent three months in the synagogue, every Sabbath arguing persuasively about the kingdom. When Luke says Paul was "reasoning and persuading," he refers to the standard rabbinic teaching mode. The rabbis framed their discourses as arguments. Rabbinic argumentation does not imply acrimony or hostility toward opponents. It employs a legal discussion of proof-texts with back-and-forth dialogue, questions, counterarguments, and logical deductions driving toward a conclusion. The mere fact that an Ephesian synagogue gave Paul a platform for his teaching for three months implies that the congregation received his message and respected his opinions.

Paul's first convert to discipleship was a man named Epaenetus (Romans 16:5). The God-fearing Gentiles, Tychicus and Trophimus, became disciples early on as well. A man named Onesiphorus brought his entire household into the Messianic faith and rendered many services to Paul and Timothy (2 Timothy 1:16–18).

The Study Hall of Tyrannus

After three months, opposition to Paul's message surfaced. It may have taken that long for the Jews of Ephesus to realize that Paul's gospel invited Gentiles into the fold. In Acts 21, "Jews from Asia" recognized Paul in Jerusalem with "Trophimus the Ephesian," and "they supposed that Paul had brought him into the temple" (Acts 21:29). They assumed that, since Paul had brought the Gentiles into their synagogues, he would also bring them into the Temple.

One might mistakenly assume that the Jewish community would be happy to support a teacher adept at turning the Gentiles away from idols. One man in particular, Alexander the metalworker, "strongly opposed" Paul's teaching (2 Timothy 4:15). As a Jew, he was not directly part of the idol-making trade, but his fortunes were evidently connected with the broader interests of his guild.

Alexander galvanized the opposition, and they began to denounce "The Way."

Paul had learned in his previous travels that it did little good to overstay his welcome. Rather than remain in the synagogue and see the gospel message reduced to ugly bickering, he chose to withdraw. As he had done in Corinth, he took the disciples of Yeshua with him when he left, and they found new venues in which to assemble and fellowship.

Priscilla and Aquila made their home in Ephesus available as a house-synagogue (1 Corinthians 16:19). Paul looked for a larger, more public place. In the Roman world, orators and philosophers sought venues in which to present their ideas, whether in private homes or public lecture halls. Paul wanted someplace like that where he could teach on his own terms without worrying about being chased out.

An Ephesian man named Tyrannus owned a lecture hall called "the school of Tyrannus." The name Tyrannus means "tyrant." It may have been a common name. It appears among Ephesian inscriptions from the period. The translation "school" is misleading: *schole* (σχολή) means "leisure." In the Greco-Roman world, a leisure hall was an auditorium for hearing oratory. Tyrannus owned a leisure hall.

It seems unlikely that Tyrannus was merely a wealthy Ephesian Gentile renting out his facility to the apostles. Idolatrous trappings would adorn such a facility, and these adornments would make it difficult for the apostles to use the facility as a place of Torah learning and prayer. Tyrannus may have been a member of the Jewish community. Some scholars consider the hall of Tyrannus a "private synagogue" or local *beit midrash* ("house of study") where Jewish scholars could gather to discuss Torah and access scrolls (Acts 19:9). Paul used the hall to reach "both Jews and Greeks" (Acts 19:10). This suggests that the hall functioned within the Ephesian Jewish community.

Paul rented the facility from Tyrannus, or perhaps the man was inclined to offer it to the apostle without charge. The Western Text says that Paul had the use of the hall for five hours a day: "He took the disciples with him and had discussions daily in the lecture hall of Tyrannus from the fifth to the tenth hour," i.e., from 11:00 AM to 4:00 PM (Acts 19:9, Western Text). The arrangement worked well for Paul. He spent the morning hours working as a tent-maker and the afternoons teaching. In the Greco-Roman world, the business day started at dawn, and public affairs concluded before noon. Most people took a siesta during the early afternoon. Paul and his disciples used the quiet hours for study and teaching.

The Ephesus Years

Paul taught at the lecture hall of Tyrannus for two years, operating it as a believer's study hall (*beit midrash*). He did not limit his outreach efforts to Jews. "All who lived in Asia heard the word of the Lord, both Jews and Greeks." The good news of Messiah took root among Gentiles "not only in Ephesus, but in almost all of Asia." In all those places, Paul "persuaded and turned away a great many people, saying that gods made with hands are not gods" (Acts 19:26).

Acts 19:10 indicates that Paul taught in the lecture hall of Tyrannus for two years, but the total duration of his stay in Ephesus was longer. He had already been in Ephesus three months before renting the hall. Later, when leaving Asia Minor for the last time, Paul reminded the Ephesian elders, "For three years I did not cease night or day to admonish every one with tears" (Acts 20:31). This implies that the events narrated subsequent to Acts 19:10 occurred over a period of many months after the two years in the lecture hall. The three years in Ephesus (52–55 CE) represent Paul's longest stay in any one place during his missions.

Paul taught both publicly and privately in Ephesus. His work established several small house-synagogues, like the congregation that met in the home of Priscilla and Aquila. Paul later recalled teaching in Ephesus "in public and from house to house, testifying both to Jews and to Greeks of repentance toward God and of faith in our Lord Jesus Christ" (Acts 20:20–21).

Paul's three years in Ephesus were not just one more stop on his missionary travels. Ephesus became the new base of Paul's ministry, just as Antioch had been in Syria. His farewell to the Ephesian elders in Acts 20 indicates the special significance of the Ephesus community to his work.

The apostle to the Gentiles enjoyed his golden years of effective work while based in Ephesus. From Ephesus, the gospel went out like spokes from the hub of a wheel. He sent out a steady flow of epistles and fellow workers from Ephesus to visit his other congregations.

Gentile Disciples in Ephesus

Paul planted several congregations of God-fearing Gentiles in Ephesus. The congregations in Ephesus consisted of men and women of status as well as commoners and slaves (Ephesians 6:1–9). Although Paul won disciples from both Jews and Gentiles in Ephesus, the number of Gentiles far outweighed the number of Jewish believers. Paul speaks of them as "the churches of the Gentiles" (Romans 16:4). Nevertheless, as will see in his epistle, he encouraged the Ephesian Gentiles to think of themselves as adjunct members of the Jewish people.

Paul's epistle to the Ephesians speaks about how his readers "once walked, following the course of this world, following the prince of the power of the air, the spirit that is now at work in the sons of disobedience" (Ephesians 2:2). He reminds the Ephesians that they are "Gentiles in the flesh who are called 'Uncircumcision,'" and that prior to their encounter with Messiah, they were "alienated from the commonwealth of Israel and strangers to the covenants of promise, having no hope and without God in the world" (Ephesians 2:12). All of that has changed. The Messiah abolished the enmity between Jew and Gentile, reconciling them into one new man: "the Gentiles are fellow heirs [with Jews] and members of the same body [of Messiah]" (Ephesians 3:6). Therefore the Gentile believers are "no longer strangers and aliens [to Israel], but ... fellow citizens with the saints" (Ephesians 2:19).

Magic and Extraordinary Miracles

While living and teaching at Ephesus, the LORD was pleased to perform "extraordinary miracles" through the hands of Paul. The gospel message needed extraordinary miracles to achieve credibility in a city like Ephesus. Ephesus had a reputation for the magical arts. It boasted schools of magic where sorcery could be studied and learned. Paul taught the Ephesians that they struggled not "against flesh and blood, but against the rulers, against the authorities, against the cosmic powers over this present darkness, against the spiritual forces of evil in the heavenly places" (Ephesians 6:12).

Ephesus was so well known for sorcery that it was common throughout the Mediterranean to refer to magical scrolls as *Ephesia grammata*, i.e., "Ephesus Letters." Such scrolls contained secret formulations of meaningless, magical words along the line of "hocus-pocus" and "bibbity-bobbity-boo." Those who knew how to string the meaningless syllables together and properly pronounce the words used them to cast spells and charms. Casting spells also invoked the "secret names" of spirits, demons, or deities. The power of a spell-scroll derived from the secret names it contained.

The Torah forbids occultism, but the Roman world considered Jews to have potent magic. Because Jews left the holy name of God unpronounced, the superstitious—among both Jews and Gentiles—believed that God's name must have magical properties. Some magical scrolls from the first century invoke the name of the God of Israel in their attempts to manipulate the world. First-century Jewish exorcism rituals also involved the invocation of secret names, including adjuration by the ineffable name of God.

Paul healed the sick and cast out evil spirits. He established a local reputation as a holy man, miracle worker, and exorcist. As his reputation grew, the people in Ephesus used to steal his personal articles of clothing—handkerchiefs, sweat-rags, and aprons that he wore while at work as a tent-maker—and use them to heal the sick and cast out evil spirits. Paul did not approve of the use of holy handkerchiefs and blessed aprons, but enthusiastic disciples and superstitious Ephesians found the articles of clothing efficacious for healings.

Seven Sons of Sceva

A band of Kohen brothers worked in the exorcism business at Ephesus. Luke refers to them as the seven sons of Sceva, "a Jewish chief priest." Sceva (*Sceuas,* Σκευᾶς) means "left-handed fighter" in Greek. It may be a Greek approximation for some form of the Hebrew *Sheva* ("seven," שבע), a name related to the Sabbath or the number seven. No high priest with that name served as high priest in Jerusalem, but Sceva may have simply been a family member of one of the high priestly dynasties.

Sceva's seven sons were exorcists. People hired them to exorcise demons. In a town so saturated with the occult, the sons of Sceva never lacked for business, but they regarded Paul as a competitor, and they sought to employ his power. They made careful inquiries and learned that he invoked the name of Yeshua of Nazareth.

When casting out a demon, a Jewish exorcist ordinarily invoked the name of God or the name of Solomon. The apostles did not presume to take the authority of God's name directly. The apostles believed that the Master alone wielded the authority of God's name (John 17:11-13). Yeshua, in turn, gave his apostles the authority to cast out demons in His own name, a name invested with the full weight of his Father's name (Philippians 2:9-10). The apostles demonstrated the efficacy of prayer and healing in Yeshua's name. Even during the Master's lifetime, some non-disciples began to use the name of Yeshua for exorcism (Mark 9:38-40).

A variant in the Western Text implies that the sons of Sceva used the name of Yeshua in conjunction with the name of God and the name of Paul to attempt an exorcism:

> They were accustomed to exorcize such people, and entering into the demon-possessed man they began to invoke the Name [HaShem], saying, "We charge you by Yeshua whom Paul preaches, to come out!" (Acts 19:14 Western Text)

The Western Text also indicates that more exorcists than just the sons of Sceva employed the name of Yeshua in their exorcism rituals. Gentile spell-casters were soon to follow. One spell scroll contains the exorcism formula, "I adjure you by Jesus, the God of the Hebrews."

Rabbinic literature also reluctantly admits the reality of the miracles performed in Yeshua's name but forbids it all the same. Some sages maligned the Master as a sorcerer, and they accused him of using a secret name of God to perform his miracles. By the second century, the sages forbade using the Master's name for healing. They also forbade Jews from accepting the prayers of Yeshua's disciples (Talmud, b.*Avodah Zarah* 27b).

Failed Exorcism

The seven sons of Sceva decided to try to employ the name of Yeshua in their exorcism business. Yeshua was a common Jewish name, so to specify, they adjured the evil spirits saying, "I adjure you by the Jesus whom Paul proclaims" (Acts 19:13). Apparently, the initial results of this formula were encouraging. The seven sons continued to command evil spirits by the name of the LORD, in the authority of "Yeshua whom Paul preaches." On one occasion, however, the evil spirit responded, "I recognize Yeshua, and I know about Paul, but who are you?" The question implies, "You do not have the right to be wielding that authority." To punctuate his point, the possessed man gave the seven brothers a sound thrashing. The demon-possessed sometimes exhibit superhuman strength, particularly in the course of exorcism. The demoniac tore the clothes from the men's bodies and sent them fleeing from the house, cut, bruised, and bleeding.

An Open Door of Effective Work

Word about the incident and the flight of the seven naked men traveled rapidly throughout the Ephesian Jewish community. Even the Gentiles heard about what had happened. Thanks to the buffoonery of the seven sons of Sceva, the city of Ephesus feared and reverenced the name of Yeshua.

The story shook up the believers as well. Those who had already believed confessed their involvement with occult practices. Both Jews and Gentiles who had dabbled in magic and sorcery came to Paul, confessing their sin and renouncing their secret practices. They sought deliverance from the evil spirits that their occultism had invoked. On one occasion, Paul and the apostles hosted a public burning of "Ephesian Letters" and magical spell scrolls. They estimated the value of burned scrolls at 50,000 silver drachmas. One drachma was the average daily wage. In modern terms, they committed millions of dollars' worth of magic scrolls to the fire.

This might be the incident Paul mentioned to the Corinthians when he told them that he planned on lingering in Ephesus, where "a wide door for effective work has opened" (1 Corinthians 16:9).

Wild Beasts at Ephesus

Jews and Gentiles of Ephesus spoke of Paul as the Jewish holy man, and "the name of the Lord Jesus was extolled" (Acts 19:17). "The word of the Lord continued to increase and prevail mightily" (Acts 19:20), but at the same time, Paul told the believers in Corinth, "There are many adversaries" (1 Corinthians 16:9). Among those adversaries, Alexander the metalworker continued to forge new plots against Paul.

Luke skips most of the stories from the three years that Paul stayed in Ephesus. When saying farewell to the Ephesian elders, Paul recalled the tears and trials of living in Ephesus and the many "plots of the Jews" (Acts 20:19). Luke does not elaborate on the tears and trials Paul suffered in Ephesus, and he does not tell his readers any details about the plots of the Jews.

Elsewhere, Paul made a cryptic reference to fighting wild beasts at Ephesus:

> If the dead are not raised at all ... Why are we in danger every hour? I affirm, brethren ... I die every day! What do I gain if, humanly speaking, I fought with beasts at Ephesus? If the dead are not raised, let us eat and drink, for tomorrow we die. (1 Corinthians 15:29–32)

Dethroning Artemis

All this while, Paul and his co-laborers continued to preach Jewish monotheism and faith in Yeshua to the Gentiles of Ephesus. As Paul's reputation grew, he attracted the attention of the local silversmiths' guild. The silversmiths in Ephesus manufactured Artemis (Diana) shrines for tourists. One could visit Ephesus, purchase a little replica of Artemis or her temple, bring it to her priesthood for a blessing, and then bring it back to one's own place and worship the goddess from the comfort of one's home. The many-breasted Ephesian Artemis made a truly unique addition to one's collection of gods and goddesses.

Demetrius the silversmith was no fool. He recognized where all the Jewish talk about monotheism had to lead. If Gentiles started embracing the Jewish religion, they would abandon the old gods. When that happened, no one would buy little silver idols any longer. He would go out of business.

Demetrius gathered his fellow craftsmen and roused them with an impassioned speech. He reminded them that their prosperity depended on people worshiping the idols, and he warned them that in Ephesus and "almost all of Asia," Paul was persuading people to turn from the gods, "saying that gods made with hands are not gods at all."

A precipitous drop in the sale of idols would be bad enough, Demetrius argued, but far worse was the insult to the great goddess Artemis and her temple in Ephesus. The silversmith exclaimed, "She whom all of Asia and the world worship will even be dethroned from her magnificence!"

Demetrius' words had their desired effect. Whipped into a fury, the idol-makers of Ephesus began to chant, "Great is Artemis of the Ephesians!" The silversmiths' guild took to the streets with their angry mantra and quickly assembled a crowd. Nothing riles a crowd faster than shouting a catchy slogan.

Riot in Ephesus

The shouting crowd grew. Pilgrims and Ephesians joined them. The situation escalated rapidly.

The silversmiths tried to find Paul, but they could locate only two of his disciples: Gaius and Aristarchus, disciples from the congregations in Macedonia. Gaius and Aristarchus happened to be in the wrong place at the wrong time.

Aristarchus was a God-fearer from Thessalonica who accompanied Paul on his travels from Ephesus all the way to Rome (Acts 20:4, 27:2;

Colossians 4:10; Philemon 24). The identity of Gaius is less certain. He probably is not the same as Gaius Titius Justus of Corinth, who lived next door to the Corinthian synagogue and hosted the assembly in his home (Acts 18:7; 1 Corinthians 1:14; Romans 16:23). This was more likely Gaius of Derbe, who is mentioned a few verses later (Acts 20:4).

The angry crowd of Ephesians seized Gaius and Aristarchus and dragged them off to the city's enormous theater. Carved into the side of Mount Pion and nearly five hundred feet in diameter, the three-tiered theater could seat more than 24,000 spectators.

Paul heard about what was happening. He wanted to go directly to the theater to address the crowd, but the disciples would not allow him. They feared for his life.

The streets filled with people, and everyone rushed to the theater to find out what the commotion was all about. As the city spun out of control, some "Asiarchs who were friends of his" sent Paul repeated messages warning him not to venture into the theater.

The provincial "archs" represented Roman interests abroad, regulating the imperial cult, imperial games, honors, statuary, and so forth on behalf of the empire. Rome elected wealthy Roman aristocrats to fill the offices for one-year terms. The men sponsored functions like the imperial games from their own purses and promoted imperial patriotism abroad. All the provinces had them. In Bithynia they were called Bythyniarchs; in Syria they were the Syriarchs, and so forth. The Asiarchs of Ephesus were responsible for overseeing the worship of the goddess Roma and the emperors and for securing allegiance to the empire.

Luke omits the story of how Paul of Tarsus became friends with certain Asiarchs. It seems like an unlikely alliance. Paul's promotion of monotheism among God-fearers did not support the imperial cult. At the same time, Jews were already exempt from the cult. The Asiarchs might have viewed the clash between Paul and the Ephesians as a conflict between Roman law (which exempted Jews) and local religious enthusiasm. The relationship between Paul and the Asiarchs probably formed at some point during his stay in Ephesus on the basis of his Roman citizenship.

People from all over the city heard the uproar and left what they were doing to join the fun. They poured into the theater. Caught up in the crowd frenzy, most of them did not even know what the uproar was about. "Some were shouting one thing and some another."

Alexander of Ephesus

One group of people in the assembly did know why they were there. The Jews of Ephesus knew that the angry Artemis-zealots would make no distinction between Paul's disciples and the Jewish community. The riot placed the whole Jewish population in serious danger.

The Jewish community leaders acted quickly. They needed to pacify the angry crowd. They chose a man known as Alexander to speak on their behalf. Luke's narrative uses his name as if his readers should already know who he was, but Alexander was a common name. He may have been a local synagogue official or an important political person in Ephesus. It seems likely that he was "Alexander the coppersmith":

> Alexander the coppersmith did me great harm; the Lord will repay him according to his deeds. Beware of him yourself, for he strongly opposed our message. (2 Timothy 4:14-15)

Was Alexander a member of the metalworker's guild with Demetrius? Had he warned Demetrius about Paul's teachings and encouraged him to take action? If so, his plot against Paul had gone awry, and now the threat of pogrom hovered over the whole Jewish community.

Alexander tried to silence the crowd in order to speak to them. He wanted to tell them that, as a rule, Jews attempt to live at peace with all peoples. Jews living among Gentiles abide by a long-standing policy against blaspheming other peoples' gods. Alexander wanted to distinguish between the local Jewish community and the renegade work of Paul of Tarsus.

The crowd did not allow him to make his case. When they saw that he was a Jew, they identified him with Paul and the believers. (Note that nearly three years after Paul had left the Ephesian synagogue, the believers of Ephesus still appeared to outsiders simply as Jews.) The crowd in the theater shouted in unison for about two hours: "Great is Artemis of the Ephesians!"

The Assembly Dismissed

The city clerk entered the theater and calmed the crowd. He was, in essence, the town's registrar, a local Ephesian official in charge of keeping records, recording deposits to the temple, and filing notes and reports on city assemblies.

When he had silenced the crowd, he scolded them for their rash and irresponsible behavior.

The city clerk dismissed the crowd's concern that Artemis might be dethroned from her place of magnificence in Ephesus. After all, no one could deny that her image had fallen from heaven and now stood in her temple at Ephesus. Some speculate that the Ephesians fashioned an idol of Artemis from a meteorite. Her temple at Taurus contained a meteorite worshiped as an image of the goddess, and the practice of worshiping meteorites was not unusual. The clerk referred Demetrius and the idol-makers to the city forum where they could bring their complaint to the proconsul, and then he warned the crowd that the Roman government would call the city to account for the riot.

Finally, he dismissed the assembly. The Ephesians left the theater somewhat sheepishly, perhaps embarrassed at all the commotion.

Gaius and Aristarchus left, thanking God for a narrow escape. The Jewish community of Ephesus also sighed in relief as the city went back to normal. Paul knew he could no longer stay in Ephesus. As soon as he felt it safe to do so, he summoned his closest disciples and bid them farewell. In the spring or early summer of 55 CE, he took a few companions (Gaius and Aristarchus?) and left Ephesus.

Miletus

In the spring of 56 CE, Paul and his companions booked passage on a ship that could carry them to Caesarea. Paul intended to arrive in Jerusalem before Pentecost. Traveling with him were delegates from communities of Yeshua-believers he had planted in Asia Minor and Achaia. He intended to present Gentile disciples to James and the other elders and apostles in Jerusalem to make a case for their inclusion within the broader Yeshua community. He also carried a sizable amount of money collected from those same communities, which he intended to donate to the poor among the disciples in Jerusalem.

While en route, their ship entered one of the harbors of the ancient Ionian city of Miletus. The city of Miletus occupied a position on the western coast of Anatolia near the mouth of the Maeander River. Miletus had a long, proud history as one of the most important cities in the ancient Greek world. Under the Romans, the city experienced a resurgence of prosperity and success. Miletus had four harbors, a thriving economy, and magnificent Roman-era architecture. A massive theater looked out on the Theater Harbor. Two marble lions flanked the entrance to the Lion Harbor. A proud temple to Apollo capped the city. (The Maeander River has long ago silted in the city, moving the shoreline five miles out from the old harbors. The gulf on which the city once sat survives today only as an inland lake.)

Paul had almost certainly visited Miletus during his years living in nearby Ephesus. The city had a strong Jewish community that had fought for and won the right to observe the Sabbath, send the half-shekel to Jerusalem, and live according to Torah (Josephus, *Antiquities* 14:244–246/xiv.21). The remains of the synagogue can be seen today. An important inscription from the Miletus theater reads, "For the Jews and the God-fearers." Jews and God-fearing Gentiles sat together in the public theater.

Since the ship was to remain at Miletus for more than a day, Paul sent for the elders of the Ephesus community (thirty miles to the north). He asked them to travel to Miletus immediately so that he could see them one last time before leaving. Luke explains, "For Paul had decided to sail past Ephesus so that he would not have to spend time in Asia; for he was hurrying to be in Jerusalem, if possible, on the day of Pentecost." Moreover, Ephesus was no longer safe for Paul to enter.

The elders of the Ephesus community must have traveled through the night. By the time they arrived, Paul had only a few hours left before his ship was to put out to sea. Paul assembled the small group of men at the harbor. Memories came flooding back as he looked into their faces. They were a mixed group of Jewish and God-fearing Gentile disciples. He had placed each one in a position of authority over the assemblies at Ephesus.

Luke records Paul's short farewell to the Ephesian elders in Acts 20:18–37. Luke must have written the speech from his own eyewitness recollection of the occasion; it sounds like the authentic voice of Paul the letter-writer. He touches on many themes common in his epistles. Readers of his epistles recognize genuine Pauline sentiments and turn-of-phrase.

He reminded the elders about his time among them and how his teaching had met resistance in the Jewish community. He had served the Master "with all humility and with tears and trials." The trials had come upon him through the plots of adversaries. "I fought with wild beasts at Ephesus," Paul once told his readers (1 Corinthians 15:32).

He remembered Alexander the metalworker who "did me great harm … for he strongly opposed our message" (2 Timothy 4:14-15). He remembered the riot that had forced him to leave the city. Despite the constant opposition, he boldly taught, both in public and private, even from house to house.

In the farewell speech, Paul summarized his teaching in Ephesus. He said, "I have gone about proclaiming the kingdom" (Acts 20:25), "testifying both to Jews and to Greeks of repentance toward God and of faith in our Lord Jesus Christ" (Acts 20:21). Paul's gospel message was the same message proclaimed by the Master and the rest of the apostles: "Repent, the kingdom of heaven is at hand." His message differed from that of the other apostles only in that that he proclaimed the message of repentance to both Jews and Gentiles.

Uncertainty and Unconcerned about Himself

Paul explained to the elders that he was on his way to Jerusalem, "bound in spirit." He had no choice. The Spirit of God compelled him to make the trip. He anticipated trouble ahead. In every city and assembly he had visited, the Spirit had warned him about the road ahead. Moreover, the Spirit of God indicated to Paul that he would never again see Ephesus or the believers there. This was his last farewell to them.

Paul did not know if he was going to survive the trip to Jerusalem, but he assured the elders of Ephesus that whether he lived or died mattered nothing to him. He said, "I do not consider my life of any account as dear to myself, so that I may finish my course and the ministry which I received from the Master Yeshua, to testify solemnly of the gospel of the grace of God." This is authentic Pauline language. The statement evokes similar passages from his writings where he used the metaphor of running a race or completing a course:

> To make sure I was not running or had not run in vain. (Galatians 2:2)

> Do you not know that those who run in a race all run, but only one receives the prize? Run in such a way that you may obtain it … So I do not run aimlessly. (1 Corinthians 9:24-26)

> In the day of [Messiah] I may be proud that I did not run in vain or labor in vain. (Philippians 2:16)

I have finished the race, I have kept the faith. (2 Timothy 4:7)

Innocent of the Blood of All Men

Paul publicly testified, "I am innocent of the blood of all men" because he had not hesitated to declare "the whole purpose of God" to everyone, both Jews and Gentiles. The statement of innocence alludes to the words in Ezekiel 33:6 about the guilt of a watchman who fails to issue a warning to the people. Paul made a similar statement when exiting the synagogue in Corinth: "Your blood be on your own heads! I am innocent" (Acts 18:6).

He did not mean that he had testified to every person he had ever met. He meant that he had testified to everyone impartially, warning both Jews and Gentiles to repent. He referred to his message of the gospel to both Jews and Gentiles as "the whole purpose of God." A few years later, while imprisoned in Rome and writing to the same group of men from prison, he expanded upon the "the eternal purpose" and "mystery of God's will," explaining it to mean the inclusion of the Gentiles (Ephesians 1:9, 3:3–11).

Shepherd the Flock

Paul charged the overseers of Ephesus to diligently shepherd the flock and feed the assembly of the Master. The shepherding metaphor goes back to Moses and David, Israel's shepherd-leaders. The prophets often depicted Israel as the flock of God, and they referred to their kings and religious leaders as the shepherds. The Master referred to himself as the Good Shepherd who laid down his life for the flock, and he instructed his disciple Simon Peter to feed and care for his sheep. The apostles spoke of their community leaders as shepherds. The word pastor (*poimen*, ποιμήν) literally means "shepherd." Simon Peter exhorted elders over a community to shepherd their congregations on behalf of the "Chief Shepherd."

Shepherds must protect their flocks from predators. Paul warned that after his departure, wolves would attack the flock. He urged the shepherds to be ready. The wolves are heretics, false teachers, and false prophets. Our Master warned his disciples, "Beware of false prophets, who come to you in sheep's clothing but inwardly are ravenous wolves"

(Matthew 7:15). Paul foresaw that many of the wolves and predators would come from within the flock: "From among your own selves will arise men speaking twisted things, to draw away the disciples after them" (Acts 20:30). This gloomy prediction is similar to the words of Moses, who, while saying his farewells to Israel, predicted that they would fall into apostasy and idolatry:

> For I know that after my death you will surely act corruptly and turn aside from the way that I have commanded you. And in the days to come evil will befall you, because you will do what is evil in the sight of the LORD, provoking him to anger through the work of your hands. (Deuteronomy 31:29)

Paul often warned about a coming apostasy: "For three years I did not cease night or day to admonish every one with tears" (Acts 20:31). In his epistle to the Thessalonians, he predicted a coming time of apostasy during which the "man of lawlessness" would be revealed because "the mystery of lawlessness is already at work" (2 Thessalonians 2:3-7). In another place, Paul wrote, "The Spirit expressly says that in later times some will depart from the faith by devoting themselves to deceitful spirits and teachings of demons" (1 Timothy 4:1). He had seen some of the future.

Commended to God

Paul commended the Ephesian elders to God's keeping and "to the word of his grace," that is, the message about Yeshua. He promised that if they remained in God's care and in the message of Messiah, the LORD would build them up to spiritual maturity and grant them the inheritance of "all those who are sanctified."

He reminded them that, while working among them, he provided for himself and his colleagues by toiling with his own hands. He had not financially burdened anyone in the community, nor had he at any time coveted anyone's money or belongings. Paul frequently made similar disavowals in his epistles (E.g., 2 Corinthians 11:6-10). Though he taught that teachers should be compensated for their efforts, he himself refused any contributions from the people among whom he ministered. In reminding them of his self-sufficiency he alluded to similar declarations made by Moses and Samuel (Numbers 16:15; 1 Samuel 12:3).

The mariners called Paul's party to board the ship. The apostle drew the Ephesian elders close around him on the beach, and they all fell to their knees to pray. Paul prayed over them, laid hands on them, embraced them, blessed them, and wept. The elders wept as well; pained by the prediction that they would not see him again, they kissed him and embraced him. They were still clinging to him and saying their farewells as he made his way to the docks. They never saw him again.

The Prison Epistles

Five years later, Paul awaited trial in Rome. How did it happen? His association with Gentile disciples precipitated a riot in Jerusalem that led to his trial before the Sanhedrin, subsequent trials before Felix, Festus, Agrippa II and Bernice, and finally, a transfer to Rome, where he hoped to receive a fair trial before the emperor.

He had to wait two full years for that trial, all the while confined to his own rented quarters under a sort of house-arrest status. During those years, he was free to receive visitors. Most scholars assume he composed the "prison epistles" of Ephesians, Philippians, Colossians, and Philemon while incarcerated as a prisoner there. Some scholars speculate that Paul's prison letters might have been composed during his imprisonment in Caesarea or, perhaps, even during a brief imprisonment in Ephesus. The oldest, most reliable traditions assign the prison epistles to his first imprisonment in Rome.

Paul fills the prison epistles with frequent references to his chains. He spoke of himself as "a prisoner of Christ Jesus on behalf of you Gentiles" (Ephesians 3:1) and "the prisoner for the Lord" (Ephesians 4:1, cf. Philemon 1, 9, 23). He called himself an "ambassador in chains" for the sake of the "mystery of the gospel" (Ephesians 6:19-20). He asked the readers of his epistles to remember his chains and pray on his behalf.

In his prison epistles, Paul referred to his court trials and defenses. He told the Philippian believers, "For you are all partakers with me of grace, both in my imprisonment and in the defense and confirmation of the gospel" (Philippians 1:7). He boasted that his "imprisonment in the cause of the Messiah" had become known in the elite circles of Rome and that this had the effect of encouraging other Roman believers "to speak the word without fear" (Philippians 1:13-14).

Timothy arrived in Rome a few months after Paul. He brought Paul reports about various communities. Timothy might have brought news from Galatia. Timothy's arrival gladdened Paul's heart. Timothy helped Paul with his correspondence by co-writing several epistles. According to the salutations, Timothy co-wrote the prison epistles with Paul.

Paul told the Philippians that he would send Timothy to visit them in Macedonia, but he wanted Timothy to remain with him in Rome at least until he could be certain about the outcome of his trial before Caesar:

> I hope in the Lord Jesus to send Timothy to you soon, so that I too may be cheered by news of you.... I hope therefore to send him just as soon as I see how it will go with me, and I trust in the Lord that shortly I myself will come also. (Philippians 2:19, 23-24)

The apostle had a special affection for his number-one disciple. In his epistle to the Philippians, he praised Timothy: "I have no one like him ... for they all seek their own interests" (Philippians 2:20-21). He knew that Timothy would be "genuinely concerned" for the welfare of the Macedonian believers.

The others around Paul might not have been as selfless as Timothy, but Paul did have a few other kindred spirits with him in Rome. His faithful companions Luke and Aristarchus had stayed with him during the two years of his incarceration in Caesarea, and they traveled with him all the way from Caesarea to Rome. They shared his shipwreck on Miletus, and now they lived with him in the capital city. In all, they demonstrated their loyalty to their teacher by devoting more than five years of their lives to serving him like personal servants. Paul referred to both of them as his fellow workers. Aristarchus was also his "fellow prisoner." Luke was "the beloved physician" (Colossians 4:10, 4:14; Philemon 24).

Tychicus of Ephesus arrived seeking Paul. Tychicus was one of the original delegates that Paul brought with him to Jerusalem. He almost certainly carried greetings, letters, gifts, and news from the congregation in Ephesus and other communities around Asia Minor. Tychicus remained with Paul in Rome for a short while before returning to Asia with letters for the believers in Ephesus and the Lycus Valley.

News about Paul's imprisonment in Rome reached the congregation at Philippi through Paul's co-worker Epaphras (Epaphroditus) of Colossae. The wealthy household of Lydia and the other disciples at Philippi loaded Epaphras with a generous financial contribution and care package for the apostle. Paul thanked the Philippian believers: "It was kind of you to share my trouble ... I have received full payment, and more. I am well supplied, having received from Epaphroditus the gifts you sent, a fragrant offering, a sacrifice acceptable and pleasing to God" (Philippians 4:14, 18).

Epaphras arrived in Rome in bad health from the hazards of the journey, sick and near death. Paul said, "Indeed he was ill, near to death. But God had mercy on him, and not only on him but on me also, lest I should have sorrow upon sorrow" (Philippians 2:27). Paul further wrote, "Honor such men, for he nearly died for the work of Christ, risking his life to complete what was lacking in your service to me" (Philippians 2:29-30).

As Epaphras recovered from his illness, he cheered Paul and Timothy with news about the formation of congregations at Colossae and Laodicea. He also expressed his concerns about the new proto-Gnostic teachings that he had encountered in Colossae. Paul decided to compose epistles to the Lycus Valley congregations, but he elected not to send Epaphras with them. Instead, he wanted Epaphras to travel directly to the Macedonian congregations with the epistle to the Philippians:

> I have thought it necessary to send to you Epaphroditus my brother and fellow worker and fellow soldier, and your messenger and minister to my need, for he has been longing for you all and has been distressed because you heard that he was ill. (Philippians 2:25-26)

Others joined Paul in Rome as well. Paul's epistles mention a Jewish believer named Yeshua, who went by the Roman name Justus and another disciple named Demas. To Paul's surprise, John Mark, the cousin of Barnabas, arrived in Rome and sought him out. Two decades had passed since John Mark first left Jerusalem in the company of Barnabas and Paul. On their first journey into the interior of Anatolia,

John Mark abandoned the apostles at Perga. When Barnabas later wanted to take John Mark along again, Paul objected sharply, and the two apostles went separate ways.

That was all a long time ago. The years had matured John Mark and knocked off Paul's sharp edges. All was forgiven. In Philemon 24, Paul lists Mark as one of his fellow workers. He made plans to dispatch Mark to the congregations in Anatolia. (Perhaps to see if Mark would go into the interior this time? Perhaps a sharp edge remained?) He told the Colossian brethren to receive him: "If he comes to you, welcome him" (Colossians 4:10). Later, during his last imprisonment, Paul described John Mark as "useful to me for ministry" (2 Timothy 4:11).

The Fugitive

In the same year that Paul arrived in Rome, a powerful earthquake shook the Lycus Valley, and Onesimus fled from his master, Philemon. Escaped slaves posed a common problem in the Roman world. An escaped slave had little chance of finding refuge in normal society. They were easy to single out. Roman law punished those who might harbor them, and their owners typically offered a bounty for the return of a slave. A papyrus fragment from two hundred years earlier provides an example of the type of circulars and wanted posters upon which Onesimus could expect to be featured:

> A slave belonging to Aristogenes, son of Chrysippus, an envoy from Alabanda, has run away. His name is Hermon; he is also called Nilus. He is by birth a Syrian of Bambyce, eighteen years old, of middle height, smooth face, strong calves, cleft chin, mole to the left of his nose, scar over the left corner of his mouth, two foreign letters tattooed on his right wrist. He has three minas in gold coin, ten pearls, and an iron collar with an oil-flask and shaving tools on it, and is wearing a short cloak and apron.
>
> Whoever brings him back will receive two talents of copper; if he reports him at a temple, one talent; if with a responsible and law-abiding person, three talents. Anyone so desiring, give information to the governor's representatives.

With him ran away Bion, a slave of Callicrates, one of the chief officers at the court; short, broad-shouldered, thin-legged, with light-blue eyes; when he ran away he wore a cloak and slave's leathern girdle, and took a woman's cosmetic box worth six talents, and five thousand copper drachmas.

Whoever brings him back will receive the same reward as for the above-mentioned. Inform the governor's representatives about this one also. (A. S. Hunt and C. C. Edgar, trans., *Selected Papyri, Loeb Classical Library*, Cambridge, MA: Harvard University Press, 1934, 2:135, 139)

Somehow, Onesimus ended up in Rome. He may have come to Rome to seek out Epaphras—the godly man who had shown him kindness and taught him about the one true God. Perhaps he had come to Rome with hopes of disappearing into the anonymity of a large, urban center far from home. If so, Epaphras ruined his hopes by recognizing his friend's slave in the streets. However it happened, Epaphras brought the escaped slave to Paul.

Paul spoke to Onesimus about the gospel and introduced him to his Master. Onesimus exchanged his hopeless freedom for the hope of service to King Messiah. Paul adopted the escaped slave as one of his own disciples.

A Difficult Problem

The situation with Onesimus created a difficult problem for Paul and Epaphras. The solution required a delicate strategy. On the one hand, they had a biblical obligation to protect Onesimus. The Torah forbids returning an escaped slave to his master:

> You shall not give up to his master a slave who has escaped from his master to you. He shall dwell with you, in your midst, in the place that he shall choose within one of your towns, wherever it suits him. You shall not wrong him. (Deuteronomy 23:15–16)

On the other hand, Roman law forbade them from aiding and abetting a fugitive slave. Furthermore, Philemon would certainly find out that they had his slave. What would he say when he learned that the Apostle Paul harbored that thief and fugitive? The situation might breach Paul's relationship with Philemon and the assembly at Colossae that met in his home. It could damage the integrity of the gospel.

Paul thought the matter through carefully and discussed the dilemma with both Onesimus and Epaphras. He explained that he did not want to jeopardize his pending trial and the potential growth of the congregation in Colossae by association with a fugitive. At the same time, he could not and would not turn Onesimus over to the authorities or force him to go back to Colossae. The Torah did not allow for that option. Nevertheless, the Torah did not prohibit Onesimus from voluntarily returning to his master. Paul urged the fugitive to return and repair the relationship. He said that, for his part, he would compose a letter to Philemon, beseeching him to pardon Onesimus and to give him his liberty. Paul explained that Onesimus could travel back to Colossae, not as a returning slave, but as a disciple of Paul, traveling along with Paul's messenger Tychicus of Ephesus.

Epistle to Philemon

In his letter to Philemon, Paul explained that Onesimus had come to him, repented, and become a disciple. Paul admitted that he felt reluctant about sending Onesimus back to Colossae. He considered keeping the young man in Rome where Onesimus could serve him as a disciple in the ministry of the gospel. However, he did not want to do that without Philemon's consent. He told Philemon to receive the escaped slave back, not as a returning slave, but as a beloved brother in the Master. Paul wrote, "I appeal to you for my child, Onesimus, whose father I became in my imprisonment. (Formerly he was useless to you, but now he is indeed useful to you and to me)" (Philemon 10-11).

Paul pressured Philemon to grant him a favor by giving Onesimus his freedom. He said, "If you consider me your partner, receive him as you would receive me. If he has wronged you at all, or owes you anything, charge that to my account. I, Paul, write this with my own hand: I will repay it—to say nothing of your owing me even your own self" (Philemon 17-19).

The first-century Roman writer and politician Pliny the Younger wrote a strikingly similar letter to a friend named Sabinianus on behalf of an alienated freedman:

> The freedman of yours with whom you said you were angry has been with me, flung himself at my feet, and clung to me as if I were you. He begged my help with many tears, though he left a good deal unsaid; in short, he convinced me of his genuine penitence. I believe he has reformed, because he realizes he did wrong. You are angry, I know, and I know too that your anger was deserved, but mercy wins most praise when there was just cause for anger. You loved the man once, and I hope you will love him again, but it is sufficient for the moment if you allow yourself to be appeased. You can always be angry again if he deserves it, and will have more excuse if you were once placated. Make some concession to his youth, his tears, and your own kind heart, and do not torment him or yourself any longer—anger can only be a torment to your gentle self. I'm afraid you will think I am using pressure, not persuasion, if I add my prayers to his—but this is what I shall do, and all the more freely and fully because I have given the man a very severe scolding and warned him firmly that I will never make such a request again. (Pliny, *Epistles* 9.21)

In addition to his requests on behalf of Onesimus, Paul also told Philemon that he anticipated receiving Nero's pardon soon. After that, he planned on visiting. He told Philemon to prepare a guest room. He hoped to follow up on the work of Epaphras in Colossae, Laodicea, and Hierapolis. He closed the letter to Philemon with greetings from John Mark, Aristarchus, Demas, and Luke.

Mail Call

In the same mailbag, Paul sent letters to the congregations at Ephesus, Colossae, and Laodicea. The letter to the Ephesians summarized Paul's teachings about the relationship between Jewish believers and God-fearing Gentiles. Some scholars believe that Paul used the letter to the Ephesians as a generic epistle for general circulation among his congregations.

The letter to the Colossians attempted to deflect the influence of the proto-Gnostic heresy, which Epaphras had recently encountered in those congregations. Paul refuted the hierarchical angelology and asceticism taught by the mystics, and he warned the Colossian believers against accepting the hollow philosophical ideas of men. He told the believers in Colossae to also read the letter he sent to Laodicea. Likewise, he told the Laodiceans to read the letter he wrote to the Colossians: "When this letter has been read among you, have it also read in the church of the Laodiceans; and see that you also read the letter from Laodicea" (Colossians 4:16). He told both congregations about Epaphras' concern for them: "For I bear him witness that he has worked hard for you and for those in Laodicea and in Hierapolis" (Colossians 4:13). Unfortunately, the letter to Laodicea does not survive.

Tychicus and Onesimus set out from Rome carrying Paul's letters to their destinations. We do not know how the story ended. Did Philemon agree to grant Onesimus his freedom?

Onesimus of Ephesus

In the early second century, Ignatius of Antioch addressed an epistle to the Ephesians in which he three times referred to their bishop by the name of Onesimus. Might he have been the same Onesimus?

The bishop Onesimus might be the reason that Paul's letters appear in our New Testament. It seems reasonable to believe that, after Philemon freed him, he gave Onesimus the letter to keep with his papers of manumission. Perhaps Onesimus continued to travel with Tychicus and began to collect copies of Pauline letters. How else could such a personal letter as Philemon have entered the ecclesiastical collection—unless Onesimus himself was the one who put the collection together?

The thought invites further speculation. If Onesimus became an elder over the community in Ephesus—perhaps taking up that mantle after the death of John—then he stood in a position to encourage the public reading of Paul's letters in the assemblies of Asia Minor. Philemon's "useless" fugitive slave might have been responsible for both the preservation and the elevation of Paul's letters. The story of Onesimus might be the story of how Paul's letters, including the "Epistle to the Ephesians," ended up in the Bible in the first place.

Proposed Timeline (Acts 18–28)

51 CE
- Paul leaves Corinth
- First visit to Ephesus
- Pilgrimage to Jerusalem

52 CE
- Paul's Third Missionary Journey
- Paul settles in Ephesus (52–55 CE)
- Lecture Hall of Tyrannus

55 CE
- Riot in Ephesus
- Paul leaves Ephesus
- Paul in Macedonia
- 2 Corinthians 1–9
- Paul in Illyricum

56 CE
- Paul winters in Corinth
- Epistle to the Romans

57 CE
- Paul's delegates rendezvous in Troas
- Paul's farewell to Ephesian elders at Miletus
- Paul and delegates sail to Judea
- Paul arrested in Jerusalem at Pentecost
- Trial before Sanhedrin
- Paul before Felix and Drusilla
- Paul imprisoned in Caesarea

59 CE
- Felix deposed
- Festus procurator
- Paul before Festus
- Paul before Agrippa II and Bernice
- Paul's voyage to Rome
- Paul shipwrecked on Malta

60 CE
- Paul arrives in Rome
- Earthquake in Lycus Valley
- Onesimus flees from Philemon

61 CE
- Paul imprisoned in Rome
- Epistle to the Ephesians
- Epistle to the Philippians
- Epistle to the Colossians
- Epistle of Philemon

SERMON ONE:
THE SALUTATION AND BLESSING
(EPHESIANS 1:1–23)

How the pronouns in Ephesians 1 provide the key to unlocking the meaning of Paul's message to the Gentile disciples in Ephesus.

> Paul, an apostle of Christ Jesus by the will of God, to the saints who are in Ephesus, and are faithful in Christ Jesus. (Ephesians 1:1)

We reckon Ephesians to be among Paul's so-called "prison letters," a series of communications he sent out from Rome during his first imprisonment there. He addresses it to "the saints who are in Ephesus," a large community of Gentile disciples spread across several assemblies that met in houses and synagogues in the large city of Ephesus. From the stories in the book of Acts, we know more about Paul's work in Ephesus and the believers in Ephesus than in almost any other city.

Paul himself could not visit Ephesus even if he were not in chains. He became a *persona non grata* during the Ephesian riots, during which a crowd of idolaters took to the streets, shouting, "Great is Diana of the Ephesians" (Acts 19:21–41). He bade the elders of Ephesus farewell on his way to Jerusalem before his arrest, but he did so at Miletus because he could not return to Ephesus (Acts 20:17). Other Jews who once labored for the gospel in Ephesus were also absent. Apollos, who used to teach there, had moved on. Priscilla and Aquila, who, for some time, lived in Ephesus and hosted a community of disciples in their home, had also returned to Rome.

Paul's disciple Timothy continued to steward the disciples of Ephesus in Paul's absence. Around this time, John the apostle also made his way toward Asia Minor and would soon be in residence in Ephesus. All these teachers were Jews, but most of the disciples in Ephesus were Gentiles. The letter to the Ephesians is addressed specifically to the Gentile disciples in the communities: "the saints who are in Ephesus, and are faithful in Christ Jesus."

The word "saints" means "holy ones." Paul considered them set apart from the rest of humanity because of their allegiance to the Messiah Yeshua. To be "faithful in Christ Jesus" means to be loyal to Yeshua, believing that he is the Messiah King and living under his authority and rule, obeying his commandments, and heeding his words. That's what it means to be "faithful in Christ Jesus."

Salutation

> Grace to you and peace from God our Father and the Lord Jesus Christ. (Ephesians 1:2)

The apostle sends salutations in the form of a blessing that the disciples in Ephesus should enjoy God's abundant favor (grace) and a blessing of peace dispatched from God. According to Yeshua's instructions, Paul refers to God as "our Father." The favor of God that the apostle wishes upon these disciples is that same favor obtained through the Master Yeshua the Messiah, God's favored Son who obtained such abundant favor through his righteousness and his suffering that it is of sufficient quantity to share with his disciples. Likewise, Paul bestows a blessing for peace by the same means and in the same authority, namely, through the authority of the name of the Prince of Peace.

The Long Blessing

> Blessed be the God and Father of our Lord Jesus Christ, who has blessed us in Christ with every spiritual blessing in the heavenly places, even as he chose us in him before

> the foundation of the world, that we should be holy and blameless before him. In love he predestined us for adoption to himself as sons through Jesus Christ, according to the purpose of his will, to the praise of his glorious grace, with which he has blessed us in the Beloved. (Ephesians 1:4-6)

After the salutation, Paul opens the epistle with a blessing formulated according to the traditional liturgical pattern for a *berachah*: *Blessed be God who has done such and such.* In this case, God is titled the "God and Father of our Master Yeshua the Messiah." Of all God's many titles, this one is the most precious to us as disciples of Yeshua. Ordinarily, a *berachah* refers to God as "King of the Universe," which is a universal truth that applies to everyone and everything; it expresses everyone's relationship to God. However, Paul chooses a much more personal title, which applies only to our Master Yeshua and to those of us who are privileged to know God through our relationship with him. He is not just the creator of heaven and earth and the King of the universe; he is the God and Father of our Master Yeshua.

However, as the epistle continues, it now becomes critically important to pay attention to the pronouns. Paul says that God has "blessed us in Messiah with every spiritual blessing in heavenly places" and that "he chose us in him before the foundation of the world." Who is "we"? Who is "us"?

Most readers assume that the first-person common plural forms here refer to all Christians as if Paul is speaking generally about what God has done for every disciple of Yeshua. However, it becomes evident just a few verses later that he is differentiating himself and those included with him in this designation from the Ephesian disciples, who he refers to in the second-person pronoun as "you." That begins in 1:13 when he says, "In him you also, when you heard the word of truth ... believed in him."

So it is evident that Paul is distinguishing between two different groups: those to whom he refers as "we" and those to whom he refers as "you." This distinction is critically important to understanding the entire epistle to the Ephesians and, for that matter, all the writings of Paul. The distinction Paul is making is between Jewish disciples and Gentile disciples. Paul speaks of the Jewish disciples, including the apostolic community, the apostles, and all the Jewish believers in Yeshua, as "we." He speaks to the Gentile disciples as "you."

Scholars have long observed that the epistle to the Ephesians does not necessarily address any specific local issues. Instead, it conveys a theological message that could apply to any of Paul's assemblies in any place where he had been active teaching. For that reason, scholars speculate that this may have been a generic letter that Paul composed to be read not just in Ephesus but also in other assemblies in Asia Minor as Tychicus delivered the mail. It neatly summarizes Paul's theology of distinction and the place of the Gentile disciple in the kingdom.

At least in these opening chapters, the pronouns are deliberately distinguishing between Jewish disciples of Yeshua and Gentile disciples. Paul speaks as a member of the Jewish community of disciples; specifically, he speaks as an apostle, one of the Jewish disciples of Yeshua charged with the responsibility of testifying to the resurrection of Yeshua and transmitting his teaching. But in a broader sense, he also speaks on behalf of all the Jewish people because, as we know from Paul's theology, he considers the Jewish disciples of Yeshua merely to be the leaven that leavens the whole lump and to be the holy root that sanctifies the whole tree. According to Paul's theology, it's only a matter of time until the rest of the Jewish people join him and the Jewish disciples in their convictions about Yeshua. Accordingly, he and the apostles speak on behalf of the whole nation of Israel, assuming an identity in juxtaposition to that of the Gentile disciples.

What Advantage Has the Jew?

In his opening blessing, Paul makes a series of claims on behalf of the Jewish disciples of Yeshua—claims that, in his broader theology, ultimately extend to the entire nation of Israel. The first three claims he makes about Israel are as follows:

1. He has blessed the Jewish people in Messiah with every spiritual blessing in heavenly places.

2. He has chosen the Jewish people from before the foundation of the world to be holy and blameless.

3. In love, he has predestined the Jewish people for adoption to himself as sons through Yeshua the Messiah.

We might argue that these three sweeping statements do not apply to all Jews or all Israel, but instead only to Jewish believers. Surely, it is the Jewish disciples of Yeshua who are blessed with every spiritual blessing, chosen before the foundation of the world, and predestined for adoption as sons through Yeshua. Yet if we seek to understand Paul's worldview as one that is tenable within the context of first-century Judaism, we find it more likely that all three statements apply to all Israel, even if their more specific messianic quality currently adheres only to the early adopters—namely, the apostles and Jewish disciples.

1. The spiritual blessings are the blessings God promises Israel in the Torah. As of yet, they have not been fully realized in this world as material blessings because the redemption has not yet come, but Paul maintains that they are already spiritually realized in Messiah in heavenly places.

2. The Jewish people are called the chosen people because God chose them from all nations. Jewish theology teaches that before creating the heavens and the earth, God chose Abraham. He chose the Jewish people to be holy, which means to be sanctified, as it says in the *Kiddush*, "he has chosen us and sanctified us," and he chose them to be blameless through the forgiveness of sins, as it says, "Their sins and lawless deeds I will remember no more" (Jeremiah 31:34).

3. The Jewish people were predestined for adoption through Yeshua. It was, in fact, for this purpose that the Messiah was sent to Israel, as Yeshua said, "I was sent to the lost sheep of Israel," and as Peter said, "the promise is for you and for your children" (Acts 2:39). For this reason, the Jewish people are called "sons," as God said, "Out of Egypt I called my son," and "Say to Pharaoh, 'Israel is my firstborn son ... Let my son go that he may serve me'" (Exodus 4:22-23), "for he avenges the blood of his children" (Deuteronomy 32:43).

In other words, Paul is saying that all these blessings belong to Israel—to the Jewish people—and not to the Gentiles. He has "blessed us in the Beloved"; that is, he has blessed Israel in the merit of the

Messiah. Israel receives the blessings. Israel is selected from before the foundation of the world to be the chosen people. Israel is predestined to be adopted as sons of God. Paul doesn't ordinarily engage in this type of aggrandizement, but in this opening passage, he is rhetorically flaunting his privileged position in Messiah as a Jew, as a Jewish disciple, and as an apostle. The following verses only serve to heighten this exalted status.

Redemption of Israel

Paul continues his discourse concerning the Jewish people:

> In him we have redemption through his blood, the forgiveness of our trespasses, according to the riches of his grace, which he lavished upon us. (Ephesians 1:7–8)

Paul is indeed speaking of the Jewish disciples of Yeshua; nevertheless, the disciples are merely the first fruits of the fulfillment of the eschatological promises of the prophets, who state that all Israel is to be redeemed. The word translated as "redemption" refers to both a personal spiritual redemption and national redemption, which will occur when the Messiah comes again. Who is it that the Messiah comes to redeem? He comes to redeem Israel. How will he redeem Israel? By the merit of his suffering, which accrued sufficient grace and favor from God to effect the forgiveness of Israel's sins and trespasses, bringing an end to all punishments, including the exile, the curses, and all subjugation to foreign powers.

The blood of the Messiah is the life of the Messiah, which he laid down on behalf of the nation to die on a Roman cross that he might purchase the redemption through the forgiveness of sins. This is why Peter was able to say to his countrymen, the Jewish people, "Repent and be baptized every one of you in the name of Jesus Christ for the forgiveness of your sins, and you will receive the gift of the Holy Spirit. For the promise is for you and for your children" (Acts 2:38–39). Paul says that the death of the Messiah obtained so much extra favor with God that there is sufficient quantity to lavish the riches of his grace upon Israel.

The Mystery of His Will

> In all wisdom and insight making known to us the mystery of his will, according to his purpose, which he set forth in Christ as a plan for the fullness of time, to unite all things in him, things in heaven and things on earth. (Ephesians 1:8–10)

Here in Ephesians 1:8–10, Paul mentions the mystical trifecta of *chochmah, binah,* and *da'at* ("wisdom, insight, and knowledge"). Through wisdom, insight, and knowledge, the three spheres in which God's Spirit intersects human consciousness, God has revealed his mysterious will "according to his purpose, which he set forth in Messiah as a plan for the fullness of time." Again, this will has been revealed to the same "us" as in the previous verses—that is, Israel.

This plan has been in the works since the beginning, and it's a universal plan "to unite all things in him [Messiah], things in heaven and things on earth." This refers to the very Jewish concept of the ultimate consummation of the unity of all things in God. Everything is connected; everything has a purpose; nothing is random; nothing is accidental; everything is united today, albeit in a hidden way, and will be united in a visible way in the future through the work of the Messiah. Since the beginning of creation, this has been the plan, and even since before creation.

Again, to whom has this plan been revealed in wisdom, insight, and knowledge? To the Jewish people. Through the Spirit of God in *chochmah, binah,* and *da'at,* and through the power of the prophetic word, which is the Torah and the Scriptures of Israel, all of which foretold the momentous events of Yeshua's ministry, this plan was revealed to Israel, to the Jewish people. As representatives of Israel, Paul and the rest of the apostles and Jewish disciples of Yeshua have become the stewards of that revelation.

The Inheritance of Israel

> In him we have obtained an inheritance, having been predestined according to the purpose of him who works all things according to the counsel of his will, so that we who

were the first to hope in Christ might be to the praise of his glory. (Ephesians 1:11-12)

Paul says that in the Messiah, "we"—the Jewish people—have obtained an inheritance. This inheritance consists of God's covenantal promises to Abraham, Isaac, and Jacob. These are the promises that are recorded in the Torah and were amplified by the prophets: the land, the redemption, the kingdom, and even eternal life. This is the inheritance passed down from the fathers to the sons.

Paul says that this inheritance was predestined, according to the will and purpose of God, to come through the Messiah "so that we who were the first to hope in the Messiah might be to the praise of his glory." "The first to hope in Messiah" is another unambiguous reference to Israel, the Jewish people, who had been anticipating the arrival of an eschatological king long before the events of the New Testament. However, Paul must also have had in mind the Jewish disciples and the apostles, who had placed their hope more specifically in the person of Yeshua.

These Messianic Jews, the Jewish disciples, were the first to hope in the Messiah so that they, as representatives of Israel, "might be to the praise of his glory"—in other words, that they might validate Messiah's identity, vouching on his behalf.

Paul's doxological introduction sets the stage for the rest of his letter. It defines a grammatical in-group—"we," the Jews, and more specifically, Jewish disciples of Yeshua—and a grammatical out-group, "you," the Gentiles who have attached themselves to Israel through their allegiance to Yeshua, the Messiah of Israel. In the later chapters of his letter, Paul takes great pains to prove that the in-group and the out-group are not actually "in" or "out" of the kingdom of God at all—that there is "one body and one Spirit... one Lord, one faith, one baptism, one God" (Ephesians 4:4-6). This unification of discrepant groups mirrors the Pauline dichotomies in, for example, Galatians 3:28: "There is neither Jew nor Greek, there is neither slave nor free, there is no male and female, for you are all one in Christ Jesus." Yet, despite the spiritual unification of Jew and Gentile, Paul's initial framing of the discussion—in which the two are discussed separately—provides critical context for these later assertions and gives the reader insight into his theology of distinction.

What About Gentile Disciples?

> In him you also, when you heard the word of truth, the gospel of your salvation, and believed in him, were sealed with the promised Holy Spirit, who is the guarantee of our inheritance until we acquire possession of it, to the praise of his glory. (Ephesians 1:13-14)

The phrase "you also" here indicates a change in subject; now Paul is speaking to and of Gentile disciples of Yeshua. While his immediate audience is undoubtedly the Gentile disciples in Ephesus, his status as the "apostle to the Gentiles" (Romans 11:13) and the general nature of his theological and practical observations here broadens the audience to the broader community of non-Jewish followers of Yeshua.

The "word of truth" that Paul's Gentile audience had heard was the gospel of their salvation, the good news of how they, too, stood to be rescued by Yeshua. When they heard this good news, they "believed in him," which is to say, they transferred their allegiance to him, accepted him as King and Lord, and placed their hope in him in trust and obedience—a stark contrast to their previous political allegiance, which was most probably to the Roman emperor Nero.

When they shifted their allegiance to the Messiah of Israel, they received the "promised Holy Spirit," a down payment and a deposit on the future Messianic Era. Paul doubtless has in mind Joel 2:28: "I will pour out my Spirit on all flesh"—not just upon Israel, not just upon the Jewish people, but upon all flesh. This promise of the kingdom applies to all nations. The Gentile disciples of Yeshua are the first fruits of that future universal era of spiritual enlightenment, and this they share with the Jewish disciples.

Both the Gentile disciples and the Jewish disciples of Yeshua have received and been sealed by the same Holy Spirit. Paul says that the receiving of this Spirit by both Jews and Gentiles "is the guarantee of our inheritance until we acquire possession of it, to the praise of his glory." The complete inheritance is the kingdom on earth, the Messianic Era, a reality yet future in our day as it was in the days of Paul. But we have both—Jew and Gentile—received a token of it, a pledge and a down payment, in the form of the Holy Spirit, "to the praise of his glory." Again, this phrase means, essentially, "to validate Messiah's identity, and vouch on his behalf." The Jewish disciples first received this pledge at the time of the outpouring of the Spirit in Acts 2, on the day of Shavu'ot in the Temple. The Gentile disciples first received this pledge at the time of the outpouring of the Spirit in Acts 8, in Samaria, and Acts 10, in the home of Cornelius the Centurion. Since then, the Spirit has been poured out continuously on the disciples of Yeshua.

A Prayer for Gentile Disciples

> For this reason, because I have heard of your faith in the Lord Jesus and your love toward all the saints, I do not cease to give thanks for you, remembering you in my prayers, that the God of our Lord Jesus Christ, the Father of glory, may give you the Spirit of wisdom and of revelation in the knowledge of him, having the eyes of your hearts enlightened. (Ephesians 1:15-18)

The Gentile disciples express their allegiance to Yeshua through their "love toward all the saints." Paul's prayer for Gentile disciples is one of gratitude: "I do not cease to give thanks for you." But he also asks God to open the eyes of their hearts. He asks him to bestow, through the Spirit of God, an additional measure of wisdom, revelation, and knowledge (*chochmah*, *binah*, and *da'at*) upon the Gentile disciples so that the eyes of their hearts will be enlightened. "Eyes of your hearts" refers to insight and understanding; in Hebrew idiom, the heart is the mind. With this phrase, Paul implies that there is something the Gentile disciples are not understanding, something they are failing to see. Paul wants them to see it, so he asks God to open their eyes so they can see it. What exactly are they failing to see and understand?

> That you may know what is the hope to which he has called you, what are the riches of his glorious inheritance in the saints, and what is the immeasurable greatness of his power toward us who believe, according to the working of his great might that he worked in Christ when he raised him from the dead and seated him at his right hand in the heavenly places, far above all rule and authority and power and dominion, and above every name that is named, not only in this age but also in the one to come. And he put all things under his feet and gave him as head over all things to the church, which is

his body, the fullness of him who fills all in all. (Ephesians 1:18-23)

Paul gives three distinct answers to this question:

1. The hope to which he has called you.
2. The riches of his glorious inheritance in the saints.
3. The immeasurable greatness of his power toward all of us (Jews and Gentiles) who believe.

Paul is concerned for the Gentile disciples. Apparently, despite their faith in Messiah, their love for all the saints, their good works, and their devout loyalty to Yeshua, Paul's audience is missing some big pieces of the redemptive picture. They have yet to fully understand three things: the hope to which God has called them, the riches of their inheritance, and the greatness of God's power.

Paul spends the rest of the book of Ephesians unpacking these three ideas. He aims to inform his readers—people who, as Gentiles, have spent their entire lives up until then as idolaters, estranged from the God of Israel—of the magnificence of God's redemptive plan and their specific role therein.

SERMON TWO:
THE IMMEASURABLE
(EPHESIANS 1:18–2:13)

The exaltation of Messiah and salvation through him transcends all concerns of social status, prestige, class, caste, nationality, and ancestry.

In the previous chapter, we saw that Paul was concerned for the Ephesian disciples; despite their faith in Messiah, their love for all the saints, their good works, and their devout loyalty to Yeshua, they were missing some big pieces of the picture. So he prayed for them, asking God to open the eyes of their hearts, so that they might know

> ... what is the hope to which he has called you, what are the riches of his glorious inheritance in the saints, and what is the immeasurable greatness of his power toward us who believe, according to the working of his great might that he worked in Christ when he raised him from the dead and seated him at his right hand in the heavenly places, far above all rule and authority and power and dominion, and above every name that is named, not only in this age but also in the one to come. And he put all things under his feet and gave him as head over all things to the church, which is his body, the fullness of him who fills all in all. (Ephesians 1:18-23)

To recap, the Gentile disciples in Ephesus lacked understanding of these three things:

1. The hope to which he has called you.
2. The riches of his glorious inheritance in the saints.
3. The immeasurable greatness of his power toward all of us (Jews and Gentiles) who believe.

Rule for All the Communities

Over the following chapters of the epistle, Paul does his best to communicate to the disciples in Ephesus the extraordinary ramifications of their position as non-Jewish followers of Jesus. His concern for them seems to be that they have not taken hold of their new spiritual identity. He spends most of the first chapter describing the privilege of being Jewish and therefore having an incomparable heritage in Israel through Messiah. However, he subsequently manifests his concern for the Gentile disciples. Apparently, they felt as if none of God's promises applied to them and that, therefore, to be part of the team, to truly belong, they needed to leave behind their Gentile identity and become Jewish. Paul addresses the same problem in Galatians. In fact, this is Paul's battle in all of his congregations. Everywhere he planted the gospel, his Gentile disciples decided they would rather be Jewish disciples. They ended up coveting Jewish identity and feeling jealous of the Jewish members of the community. Consequently, Paul was always on a mission to persuade them to remain Gentiles and understand their own identity. He called it his rule for all the churches:

> This is my rule in all the churches. Was anyone at the time of his call already circumcised? Let him not seek to remove the marks of circumcision. Was anyone at the time of his call uncircumcised? Let him not seek circumcision. (1 Corinthians 7:17-18)

When Paul writes "circumcision," he isn't just talking about surgery; he's using a well-established first-century shorthand for Jewish identity. If we want to capture his meaning, we should translate it this way:

> Was anyone at the time of his call already Jewish? Let him (or her) not seek to remove their Jewish identity. Was anyone at the time of his call non-Jewish? Let that person not seek to become Jewish. (1 Corinthians 7:17-18, my translation)

There are at least two exceptions to this rule: intermarriage and reconciling a mixed Jewish identity. Intermarriage requires conversion for the non-Jewish spouse. That's Jewish law based on biblical principles. Disciples with Jewish ancestry or who have been raised assuming they were Jewish should be given the opportunity to reconcile that identity. Outside of those reasons, Paul says, "No, Gentiles should not become Jewish."

The Messianic Jewish movement finds itself in a unique social situation that mirrors that of the early church more directly than any other modern-day expression of faith. While the apparent desire to become Jewish on the part of many of Paul's first-century readers makes little sense within the traditional Christian theological framework, the struggles of Gentiles fitting into a Jewish environment—which is precisely the situation everywhere Paul went—have been reproduced in Messianic Jewish congregations today. It's the same fundamental sociological problem: the feeling of disenfranchisement under which Gentile disciples seem to labor.

Non-Jewish Christians in most churches never experience this feeling because replacement theology "solved" the problem in the second century by teaching that Christian identity erases and replaces former identities and nationalities with a new identity—namely, that of being a Christian. Therefore, Jewish Christians are no longer really Jewish; Gentile Christians are no longer Gentile; both are homogenized into a third race that replaces the former identities.

That wasn't Paul's message. Replacement theology is a distortion of Paul's message that has held the church captive for most of two thousand years.

Paul's solution to the sense of Gentile disenfranchisement was not replacement theology. He did not seek to erase the difference between Jews and Gentiles. Instead, he asked God to open the eyes of the hearts of the Gentile disciples so that they might see these three things:

1. The hope to which he has called you.

2. The riches of his glorious inheritance in the saints.

3. The immeasurable greatness of his power toward all of us who believe.

I want to discuss each one briefly before moving on because these describe for us—that is, for both Jewish and Gentile disciples—the ultimate end of salvation in Yeshua. Here's a quick summary of the three points Paul was laying down.

1. *The hope to which he has called you.*

This language of being "called" is typical Pauline language that hearkens back to the Master calling disciples to follow him. He called Simon Peter and his brother Andrew, saying, "Follow me." He called James and John the sons of Zebedee, saying, "Follow me." He called each of his disciples with that personal invitation to surrender their lives to a life of discipleship. In Paul's opinion, Yeshua continues to do so every time anyone, Jew or Gentile, is presented with the good news and the call to discipleship. This explains why he says in 1 Corinthians 7:18, "Was anyone at the time of his call already circumcised? ... Was anyone at the time of his call uncircumcised?"

Accordingly, to be "called" means to be called to be a disciple of Yeshua. The "hope to which he has called you" then means "the hope" of the redemption, the kingdom, the resurrection of the dead, and a share in the World to Come.

Yeshua said, "All that the Father gives me will come to me, and whoever comes to me I will never cast out ... and this is the will of him who sent me, that I should lose nothing of all that he has given me, but raise it up on the last day" (John 6:37-39). That's the hope of the calling.

2. *The riches of his glorious inheritance in the saints.*

This refers specifically to the inheritance promised to the children of Abraham, Isaac, and Jacob—God's covenant promises to the forefathers. One would naturally assume this inheritance to be the sole purview of the Jewish people, the children of Israel. In the following chapters, Paul will explain that Gentile disciples of Yeshua, by virtue of their connection to Yeshua, have become "fellow heirs" with Israel and thereby also inherit these promises.

These promises begin in Genesis 12. They include blessing: "I will bless those who bless you and curse those who curse you." They include the land and the promise of a great nation—to be fully realized in the Messianic Era. They include all nations: "I will make you a father of many nations." They include the city of New Jerusalem that Abraham glimpsed from a distance. These promises undergird the whole Torah, and they are the promises upon which the prophets expand through the whole Tanach. This is your heritage, your biblical inheritance. It's no longer exclusive to the Jewish people but also now to those called from the nations. This is the glorious inheritance we share with his holy ones—the holy people.

3. *The immeasurable greatness of his power.*

This refers to the resurrection of the dead. God's power (*gevurah*) is manifested with the resurrection of the dead. We make that association every time we recite the second blessing of the *Amidah*—the prayer recited during the daily times of prayer in the synagogue.

To illustrate the extent of this power, the apostle goes on to describe the Messiah's resurrection, ascension, and enthronement. By means of God's immeasurably great power, he resurrected Yeshua from the dead, raised his corporeal human body into heavenly places, and seated him at his right hand, giving him authority above everything and everyone, above spirits and physical beings, above angels and demons, above everything in this universe, both in this age (as we will see when his kingdom is revealed during the Messianic Era) and also in the World to Come.

This is how the apostles interpret the words of the Prophet Isaiah when he describes the Messiah as "high and lifted up, and ... exalted" (Isaiah 52:13). In this exalted position, Yeshua has become "the fullness of him who fills all in all," which is to say, he has been filled with "the fullness of God."

The immeasurable greatness of God's power is mighty enough to raise high, lift up, and exalt mortality to immortality, the finite to the infinite, and the mundane to the divine, to become the fullness of God. The result will be, as Paul said earlier in the chapter, "to unite all things in him, things in heaven and things on earth" (Ephesians 1:10). The whole universe gets absorbed into this union, which is "the fullness of him who fills all in all"—the fullness of God in the risen Messiah.

God has infused the physical creation, matter and energy, time and space, with his own being through Yeshua—uniting all things in him, in his physicality, until he fills all things in every way. We can't even begin to comprehend what that means, but it implies that the whole nature of reality as we know it is being subsumed under Yeshua.

"Even though we once regarded Messiah according to the flesh, we regard him thus no longer" (2 Corinthians 5:16). God has taken that high, uplifted, and exalted being, his Son, which according to the flesh we knew as Yeshua of Nazareth, and he has "put all things under his feet and given him as head over all things" to the community of Yeshua's disciples, "which is his body."

He has united the whole universe in Yeshua and subjected it under Yeshua, and he has given Yeshua to us.

Not According to the Flesh

Here we encounter a part of the picture that Paul was afraid his Gentile readers might be missing—especially if we are moping around worried about whether or not we are Jewish. The apostle to the Gentiles was frustrated to see this flesh-level obsession with status and prestige, this never-ending navel-gazing and handwringing about feeling like a second-class citizen. That's why he prayed that the eyes of their hearts should be opened and that they should not just see and comprehend these things, but that they should *know* the hope to which God has called them, the riches of their inheritance in the saints, and the immeasurable greatness of God's power.

With the apostle's permission, allow me to paraphrase his thought here. "If you understood the full implication of your salvation through Yeshua, you would not be concerned with your status, your prestige, your social class or caste, or your nationality or ancestry because who you are as a disciple of Yeshua transcends all of that."

This can be compared to the teaching in the Talmud that if Israel had not sinned with the golden calf, they would have attained immortality and divinity, as it says in Psalm 82:6: "I said, 'You are gods, sons of the Most High, all of you.'" But when Israel sinned, they forfeited that status, and divinity was stripped from them. Thus it says, "Nevertheless, like men you shall die, and fall like any prince" (Psalms 82:7). So too, our Master. When they said to him, "We are going to stone you for blasphemy, because you, being a man, make yourself God" (John 10:33), he replied, "Is it not written ..., 'I said, you are gods'? If he called them gods to whom the word of God came [at Mount Sinai]—and Scripture cannot be broken—do you say of him whom the Father consecrated and sent into the world, 'You are blaspheming,' because I said, 'I am the Son of God'?" (John 10:34-36). Likewise, God has predestined all Israel "for adoption to himself as sons" (Ephesians 1:5), and the Gentile disciples are to participate equally in this destiny.

If I'm talking over your head, don't worry about it. Paul didn't worry about talking over our heads either. It's not possible to reduce this type of mystical departure to a mundane level where it can be easily grasped, quantified, or contained. It is sufficient to understand the rhetorical point that our spiritual identity is so much higher than petty concerns of pride and self-importance, lifted up so much further than prestige, class, or social caste, and exalted so far beyond the need for the human ego to be affirmed and gratified, that the distinction between Jewish and Gentile disciples seems irrelevant.

It's certainly not irrelevant, and it still exists, just as the distinction between male and female still exists. The apostle dedicated most of the first chapter to making the distinction between Jew and Gentile explicit. But if we grasp the scope of our salvation that culminates in the unification of all things in the Messiah, distinctions in this current age should seem inconsequential.

This does not mean the Gentile disciples have become Jewish or the distinction between Jews and Gentiles has been erased. If that were the case, Paul wouldn't have had cause to write much of what we see in his epistles. It does, however, mean that the Gentile disciples needed to quit thinking of themselves as "just Gentiles." They needed to have the eyes of their hearts opened to know the meaning of their salvation.

The Prince of the Power of the Air

Prior to their salvation, the Gentile disciples were spiritually dead and destined for an even more final death:

> You were dead in the trespasses and sins in which you once walked, following the course of this world, following the prince of the power of the air, the spirit that is now at work in the sons of disobedience. (Ephesians 2:1-2)

This sums up the human condition. To be dead in trespasses and sins means to be separated from God—a lost human soul that has incarnated and forgotten God, now living an egocentric existence, like an animal, living only for the self, living only to feed the appetites, "following the course of this world." The people of the nations belong to Satan, unknowingly "following the prince of the power of the air." They follow the evil inclination and the tempter, which is the spirit at work in the sons of Belial. That's how Paul characterizes the Gentile world.

However, he admits that the same can be said of any and every unenlightened human being, including the Jewish people who follow the course of this world, "a wicked and adulterous generation," "among whom we all once lived in the passions of our flesh, carrying out the desires of the body and the mind, and were by nature children of wrath, like the rest of mankind" (Ephesians 2:3).

Despite his elevated discourse on Jewish identity in the first chapter, Paul now cautions anyone who has predicated their eternal destiny solely on that identity. If someone believes that being Jewish grants them some sort of automatic exemption from judgment or imbues them with some higher spiritual nature, a higher grade of *neshamah* (spirit), or a more refined spiritual essence than other human beings, Paul disagrees. He throws his countrymen into the same box as the nations: "We were by nature children of wrath, like the rest of mankind."

God's Trophies

> But God, being rich in mercy, because of the great love with which he loved us, even when we were dead in our trespasses, made us alive together with Christ—by grace you have been saved—and raised us up with him and seated us with him in the heavenly places in Christ Jesus, so that in the coming ages he might show the immeasurable riches of his grace in kindness toward us in Christ Jesus. (Ephesians 2:4–7)

By an act of mercy and condescension, God resurrects the spiritually dead with the Messiah. A dead person cannot resurrect himself. That's how Paul characterizes the sinner. The sinner cannot stop himself from sinning, cannot lift himself up, cannot enlighten himself or liberate himself. God is the one who raises the dead, and he has raised the community of Yeshua's disciples, both Jews and Gentiles, from that spiritual state of slumber likened to death, resurrecting them with the Messiah, and raising them with the Messiah's ascension to seat them with the Messiah at the right hand of the Father, bringing them also into that unfathomable mystical union, raised high, lifted up, and exalted.

Why? To be his trophies. This is the same reason he liberated Israel from Egypt—to make his name known "so that in the coming ages [i.e., the kingdom and the World to Come], he might show the immeasurable riches of his grace in kindness toward us in the Messiah Yeshua."

By Grace You Have Been Saved

God chose to accomplish this through sharing the favor (grace) that the Messiah Yeshua obtained by merit of his righteousness and suffering. He shares that favor with his disciples and ultimately with the entire nation of Israel and with members of the nations who cleave to him. The story of the golden calf in Exodus 32 illustrates the process of sharing in another's favor. After Israel sinned with the golden calf, breaking the covenant, God turned away from them, wanted to destroy them, and offered to start over with Moses alone. Moses, however, realized that he himself remained in God's good graces, that he had found favor in God's eyes. So to save the nation, he leveraged that favor. He identified himself with the nation so that he could share the favor he obtained from God with the people, despite the sin they committed. He said to God, "This people has sinned. But you said I have found favor in your eyes. If I have found favor in your eyes, have mercy on us your people, and go with us, and take us as your people."

"By favor you have been saved." This does not imply that Paul's readers had found favor in God's eyes; they hadn't. They were dead in their trespasses. However, Yeshua did find favor in God's eyes, and he shares that favor with his disciples by identifying with them:

> For by grace you have been saved through faith. And this is not your own doing; it is the gift of God, not a result of works, so that no one may boast. (Ephesians 2:8–9)

This is one of the most often quoted verses in the Bible today (at least within evangelicalism), but it's also one of the least understood.

That's because there are four key words in this verse, and all four of them are commonly misinterpreted.

- "Grace." People assume that "grace" means "an unmerited gift." It actually means "merited favor."
- "Faith." People assume that "faith" means "believing." It actually means "pledging allegiance, loyalty, and faithfulness."
- "Saved." People assume that "saved" means "going to heaven when you die." It actually means "to be rescued," and in this context, to be rescued from the wrath assigned to the nations by being granted a share with Israel.
- "Works." People assume that "works" means "good deeds and righteousness." It actually means "undergoing conversion (circumcision) to become Jewish."

If I were to interpret these two verses according to these common misunderstandings, I would paraphrase them to say, "For by an unmerited gift you have been saved from hell through belief in a dogma ... not a result of godly behavior or obedience, so that no one may boast."

In contrast, here's how it should be understood: "For by the favor Yeshua found in God's eyes, you have been saved from the fate of the nations on account of your allegiance to Yeshua. And this favor is not something that you obtained, it is the gift of God, not something you can obtain by becoming Jewish so that no one can boast that they deserve it on the basis of having become Jewish."

Created for Good Works

This interpretation explains what follows:

> For we are his workmanship, created in Christ Jesus for good works, which God prepared beforehand, that we should walk in them. (Ephesians 2:10)

The "workmanship" in Ephesians 2:10 refers not to the idea that God fashions every human being but rather back to the "work of conversion." Disciples are saved not by their works but by God's. God has wrought a "circumcision of the heart," as Paul explains elsewhere. So we should understand Ephesians 2:10 to mean that "God circumcised our hearts, granting us a new nature in Messiah Yeshua so that we should do good works of godliness and righteousness, which God spells out in the Torah, that we should walk in them."

The Far and the Near

> Therefore remember that at one time you Gentiles in the flesh, called "the uncircumcision" by what is called the circumcision, which is made in the flesh by hands—remember that you were at that time separated from Christ, alienated from the commonwealth of Israel and strangers to the covenants of promise, having no hope and without God in the world. But now in Christ Jesus you who once were far off have been brought near by the blood of Christ. (Ephesians 2:11-13)

Paul refers to the Gentile disciples as "Gentiles in the flesh," meaning that physically speaking, as pertains to this world, they are members of the nations. They are called "the uncircumcision"—that is, "non-Jews"—by what is called "the circumcision," a category that includes people who were born to Jewish parents and people who have undergone conversion ("made in the flesh by hands") to become part of the Jewish nation. But Paul would have these disciples from the nations remember that prior to their calling as disciples, they were separate from the Messiah, excluded from citizenship in the nation of Israel. They were strangers to the covenants God made with the Patriarchs and strangers to the new covenant God makes with the house of Judah and the house of Israel. They were without hope for life after death, and they were without the revelation of God in this world. All of that belongs to the Jewish people, not to the nations. As Peter said to the Jewish people in the Temple on the day of Pentecost, "the promise is for you and for your children" (Acts 2:39).

Prior to their calling, the disciples from the nations were excluded from:

- Messiah
- The commonwealth of Israel
- The covenants

- Hope for resurrection
- The revelation of God in this world

Such was their pitiable condition before their calling to take up the yoke of discipleship and follow after Yeshua before they cast their allegiance with him. But now, "in the Messiah Yeshua, you who once were far off have been brought near by the blood of the Messiah."

The Gentile disciples have been brought near to the Messiah, to identity with Israel, to the covenants, to hope for the resurrection, and to the revelation of God in this world. They have been brought near by the blood of the Messiah (i.e., by the merit of his suffering).

As Peter said to the Jewish people in the Temple on the day of Pentecost, "the promise is for you and for your children and for all who are far off, everyone whom the Lord our God calls to himself" (Acts 2:39).

"'Peace, peace, to the far and to the near,' says the LORD" (Isaiah 57:19).

SERMON THREE:
THE DIVIDING WALL
(EPHESIANS 2:14–22)

Did Christ tear down the dividing wall between Jews and Gentiles by abolishing the Torah? There's more than one way to misunderstand the "one new man."

Exodus 35 and 36 record that the community of Israel came together in a remarkable show of solidarity to contribute toward the construction of the Tabernacle. All the people participated in the effort to make a dwelling place for God. They contributed fabrics, precious stones, gold, silver, ram skins, acacia wood, oil, spices, and everything necessary for the effort. Moreover, God's Spirit inspired the people of the community with the wisdom, insight, and knowledge for all types of craftsmanship. They contributed their talents, working together to build a holy Sanctuary as a dwelling place for God's presence in the midst of Israel.

In the second chapter of Ephesians, Paul seizes upon this story as a metaphor to illustrate the community of Yeshua's disciples joining together in one effort to build a dwelling place for God by the Spirit.

What's more, Exodus describes the construction of the Tabernacle's courtyards: the outer court, the inner court (called the "holy place"), and the place behind the curtain, which is called the holy of holies. In the second chapter of Ephesians, Paul employs the layout of the Temple's courtyards to illustrate the idea of Gentile disciples, who previously were far from God, being brought near through the Messiah.

In Paul's day, the largest of all the Temple's courts was the great Court of the Gentiles. Men and women from all nations, some of them tourists and visitors to Jerusalem and others God-fearers who revered the God of Israel, routinely ascended the Temple Mount and assembled in the Court of the Gentiles. There they could worship the God of Israel and pay their respects to the Jewish God, even if they themselves were polytheists. However, they could not proceed from the Court of the Gentiles into the Temple proper. A dividing wall stood between the Gentile worshiper and the inner courts of the Temple. Jews were allowed to go in as far as the altar of burnt offering. Gentiles could not enter the holy courts.

Josephus wrote about the dividing wall of partition:

> There was a partition made of stone all around, whose height was three cubits; its construction was very elegant; upon it stood pillars, at equal distances from one another, declaring the law of purity, some in Greek, and some in Roman letters, that "no foreigner should go within that sanctuary." (*Jewish War* 5.5.2)

In another place, he says it was "a stone wall for a partition, with an inscription, which forbade any foreigner to go in under pain of death" (*Antiquities* 15.11.5). Archaeologists excavating around the ruins of the Temple have discovered pieces of these signs with these inscriptions.

In Acts 21, Paul was bringing sacrifices for purification and the completion of a vow. To do so, he had to enter the Temple up to the very Court of Israel. As he passed from the Court of the Gentiles and into the Court of Israel, several pilgrims from Asia Minor recognized him. They had earlier seen Paul around Jerusalem with Trophimus the Ephesian—a Gentile from Ephesus.

The Jews from Asia Minor knew Paul. They knew that his message was flooding the synagogues all over Asia Minor with Gentiles because those were their own synagogues. They knew something of his theology regarding Gentiles, if not the details of it. They at least knew enough to be certain that they did not like him. Naturally, they assumed that Paul was there in Jerusalem, bringing his beloved Gentiles past the dividing wall and into the Court of Israel, just as he had brought so many Gentiles into their synagogues. They tried to accost him:

"Men of Israel, help! This is the man who is teaching everyone everywhere against the people and the law and this place. Moreover, he even brought Greeks into the temple and has defiled this holy place." For they had previously seen Trophimus the Ephesian with him in the city, and they supposed that Paul had brought him into the temple. Then all the city was stirred up, and the people ran together. They seized Paul and dragged him out of the temple, and at once the gates were shut. (Acts 21:28–30)

None of the statements they made about Paul were true. Paul did not bring Trophimus the Ephesian into the Temple. He did not teach against the Jewish people, against the Torah, or against the Temple, and he did not bring Greeks into the Temple or defile the holy place. He taught that Gentile disciples do not, and should not, become Jewish. He taught that Gentile disciples are not "under the law" as Jewish people. He taught that the Temple would, in the future, be a house of prayer for all nations—the geographic and religious center of the world for both Jews and Gentiles.

Paul did not bring Gentiles past the Temple's dividing wall, but he did transgress the metaphoric wall separating Israel from non-Israel. He had obscured the sharp lines of who was in and who was out by bringing non-Jews into the Jewish religion to worship the Jewish God through allegiance to the Jewish Messiah. He had transgressed a social and religious boundary. His disregard for the metaphoric wall between Jew and Gentile led to his arrest, imprisonment, and eventual trial in Rome.

Breaking Down the Wall

While imprisoned in Rome, Paul wrote the epistle to the Ephesians. In the epistle, he was deliberately clear about his readers' identity as Gentiles. He makes it evident that they were excluded from Israel. He said, "You were separate from Messiah, excluded from citizenship in Israel and foreigners to the covenants of the promise." They were foreigners to the covenants of Israel. They had no claim to the covenants of the forefathers.

After casting their lot in with the Messiah, however, they had undergone a change in status. While they were formerly aliens and strangers to the nation of Israel, somehow, through some mystery, their identity had changed: "But now in Christ Jesus you who once were far off have been brought near by the blood of Christ" (Ephesians 2:13).

This new status and identity did not depend on becoming Jewish. "Not by works lest any man boast," Paul said, and by "works," he meant the conventional conversion ritual, complete with the works of circumcision, immersion, and sacrifice—the "works" of the Pauline Epistles.

The spiritual transformation Paul spoke of was "not by works" but "by grace ... through faith." It came by the grace of God bestowed simply and purely through allegiance to Yeshua. He explains the mechanics of the process in Ephesians 2:14: "For he [Yeshua] himself is our peace, who has made us both one and has broken down in his flesh the dividing wall of hostility."

The image of a dividing wall of hostility between Jew and Gentile alludes directly to the wall of separation between the Court of the Gentiles and the Court of Israel. The wall of separation, which forbade Gentiles on pain of death from entering the Court of Israel and the Temple of God, was a potent metaphor for the theological exclusion of Gentiles from the kingdom and the hope of the World to Come. According to Paul, the wall of separation—the barrier between the people of the nations and the people of God—is destroyed by Messiah.

Abolishing the Torah

As we read through Ephesians 2, we hit a speed bump at 2:14-15, which seems to affirm the replacement theology view that Christ canceled the Law. Here's how it reads in the English Standard Version:

> For he himself is our peace, who has made us both one and has broken down in his flesh the dividing wall of hostility by abolishing the law of commandments expressed in ordinances, that he might create in himself one new man in place of the two, so making peace. (Ephesians 2:14-15)

Compare the paraphrase in the New International Version:

> For he himself is our peace, who has made the two one and has destroyed the barrier, the dividing wall of hostility, by abolishing in his flesh the law with its commandments and regulations. (Ephesians 2:14-15)

The translators of the ESV and the NIV, like most translators of English versions of the Bible, have rendered the Greek to say that Messiah's death not only brought peace between Jewish and Gentile disciples but also abolished the Torah. According to this interpretation, the death of the Messiah erased the distinction between Jews and Gentiles along with the whole Torah of Moses. By this reading, Jew and Gentile are thus made alike because, with the law abolished, Jews no longer have any obligations to remain Jewish or practice Judaism. Obviously, this is a problem in that it conflicts with the rest of the Bible—including, importantly, the Master's explicit prohibition on supposing that he intended to abolish the Torah.

I understand the passage differently. I do not read it as stating that Messiah abolishes the Torah; rather, he abolishes the enmity engendered by Torah. For clarity, I believe it should read, "For he himself is our peace, who has made the two one and has destroyed the barrier, the dividing wall, by abolishing in his flesh the enmity." Specification of the source of this enmity follows immediately: "The Torah with its commandments and regulations." It is the Torah's commandments and regulations that have caused the enmity between Jew and Gentile, but it is the enmity, not the Torah, that has been abolished.

The King James Version, which is a more literal rendering of the Greek, does a better job of translating the verse:

> For he is our peace, who hath made both one, and hath broken down the middle wall of partition between us; having abolished in his flesh the enmity, even the law of commandments contained in ordinances; for to make in himself of twain one new man, so making peace. (Ephesians 2:14-15)

It's not completely clear what Paul means by the odd phrase "law of commandments contained in ordinances," but I believe the statement refers to a halachic argument over Jew-Gentile interaction within the assembly of Messiah—an argument we see coming up frequently in Acts and the Epistles. It has to do with the boundaries of table fellowship and purity concerns.

The Torah indeed engenders a sort of "enmity" between Israel and the idolatrous Gentile world. Every command and ordinance marks out the parameters of who Israel is and who Israel is not. Israel belongs to God as his chosen people, his treasured possession, while the nations belong to "the prince of the power of the air" (Ephesians 2:2). The Torah creates a dividing wall that keeps the two types of people separated. The Torah determined who was in and who was out. The commandments of the Torah are directed to the children of Israel, not to the children of Adam—and not even to the children of Noah, except for the broadest strokes of ethical monotheism. In that regard, the Torah itself created the wall of separation that kept Jews and Gentiles separate.

But what if the Gentiles were to abandon idolatry and cast their allegiance with the King of Israel? In that case, the enmity between the two and the need for separation is abolished. From this perspective, Ephesians 2:14–15 does not contradict the Master's words in Matthew 5:17 ("Do not think I have come to abolish the Law [i.e., the Torah]"). Instead, it indicates that the Gentile disciples of Yeshua have been brought past the metaphoric dividing wall that once kept Jewish people and non-Jewish people on opposite sides of the fence. It says, "For he himself is our peace."

The Temple of the Future

In first-century Judaism, the dividing wall of hostility was more than just a metaphor. It was a literal wall in the Temple's outer courts that kept Gentiles at a distance. In the Messianic Era, I don't believe there will be a wall of division in the Temple.

The Prophet Isaiah declares that the stranger who keeps the Sabbath and holds fast to God's covenant will be received in the innermost courts of the Temple. His sacrifices will be received on the altar, and the Temple will be a house of prayer for all nations. Paul probably had this very passage in mind as he wrote of Messiah abolishing the dividing wall. The dividing wall, which would forbid the Gentile from entering the Temple to offer sacrifice, seems to be completely absent in Isaiah's Messianic-age prophecy:

> The foreigners who join themselves to the LORD, to minister to him, to love the name of the LORD, and to be his servants, everyone who keeps the Sabbath and does not profane it, and holds fast my covenant—these I will bring to my holy mountain, and make them joyful in my house of prayer; their burnt offerings and their sacrifices will be accepted on my

altar; for my house shall be called a house of prayer for all peoples. (Isaiah 56:6–7)

One New Man

Messiah creates in himself one new man from the two. The Greek of Ephesians 2:15 can literally be rendered to say, "to make in himself out of two, one new man, so making peace."

Under the influence of replacement theology, the English Standard Version subtly rewords it to say, "That he might create in himself one new man in place of the two." Replacement theology does not get much more explicit than that. According to that translation, a Jewish Christian is no longer Jewish, and a Gentile Christian is no longer Gentile; their "new man" identity has replaced those former identities. In other words, once a Jew becomes a disciple of Yeshua, he or she is no longer Jewish.

That's not at all Paul's intention. His intention is that, while retaining their distinct identities, the Jewish people and the people from the nations are brought together, like complementary parts of a puzzle, to create a third entity. A friend of mine, Rabbi Michael Schiffman, has been known to complain, "Why is the 'one new man' always uncircumcised?" His point is that this passage has been misinterpreted to negate Jewish identity by homogenizing it with Gentile identity. That's a huge error. Messiah did not come to abolish Jewish identity or abolish Gentile identity. Instead, he brings them together into a new thing called the kingdom of heaven, "so making peace [that he] might reconcile us both to God in one body through the cross, thereby killing the hostility" (Ephesians 2:15–16).

Paul's theology looks toward the future resurrection. We die with Messiah on the cross and rise to new life with him, and in the resurrection, these distinctions of Jew and Gentile really will be abolished. They are utterly irrelevant to the resurrected, just as they are irrelevant to the spirit. Of course, in practical terms, we aren't actually dead and resurrected yet. Distinction still remains, but that's just for a short while, a brief transitionary period, until the resurrection. In the meantime, we have already attained this new identity—the new creature—in spiritual communion between the two.

The Far and the Near

"He came and preached peace to you who were far off [i.e., the Gentiles] and peace to those who were near [i.e., the Jews]" (Ephesians 2:17). We see here an allusion to Isaiah 57:19: "Peace, peace, to the far and to the near," as Simon Peter said to the Jewish people in the Temple on the day of Shavu'ot: "The promise is for you and for your children and for all who are far off, everyone whom the Lord our God calls to himself" (Acts 2:39).

This unity does not come through the elimination of distinction. It comes through the fact that we both draw near to God through the same portal—namely, the Messiah: "For through him we both have access in one Spirit to the Father" (Ephesians 2:18). Salvation in Messiah opens that portal for both Jewish people and Gentiles from the nations.

The Saints and Household of God

In conclusion, Paul can say to the Gentiles in Ephesus, "So then you are no longer strangers and aliens, but you are fellow citizens with the saints and members of the household of God" (Ephesians 2:19).

This does not mean that they have become Jewish or that Jewish identity has been neutralized. The phrase "fellow citizens" refers to our citizenship in the kingdom of heaven under the King of Israel, King Messiah. The Gentile disciples in Ephesus are made fellow citizens with the Jewish people in the kingdom, not fellow citizens in the Jewish nation ("Israel according to the flesh"), since both retain their respective national identities.

Paul says that the Gentiles in Ephesus have become fellow citizens with the saints and the household of God, which I take to mean the community of Yeshua in the nation of Israel—that is, the Jewish believers who represent Israel to the Gentiles. Paul speaks here on behalf of "the saints and the household of God." He describes this household of God as "built on the foundation of the apostles and prophets, Christ Jesus himself being the cornerstone, in whom the whole structure, being joined together, grows into a holy temple in the Lord" (Ephesians 2:20-21). He is describing Israel. Israel is built upon the foundation of the Torah and the Prophets and is now further established upon the foundation of the apostles, who testify to the resurrection of the

Messiah. The Messiah himself is the chief cornerstone, a reference to Psalm 118:22: "The stone that the builders rejected has become the cornerstone."

Let's make sure we see the picture; the metaphors are changing quickly. At this point in the epistle, Paul depicts the nation of Israel as the saints and household of God, "a structure, being joined together, [which] grows into a holy temple in the Lord." In so doing, he alludes to the Exodus narrative in which the whole community of Israel contributes toward the construction of the Tabernacle as they create a holy Temple and dwelling place for the Spirit of God. The metaphor invokes the image of Moses assembling the various parts of the Tabernacle to create the dwelling place of God. Far from replacing Israel, the picture is of the Jewish people as the saints and the household of God, built upon the prophets, the apostles, and the Messiah himself, as a holy temple.

You Also

Where do the Gentile disciples in Ephesus fit into this picture? Are they to be left behind the dividing wall again? No. The chapter concludes with another direct address to the Gentile readers: "In him you also are being built together into a dwelling place for God by the Spirit" (Ephesians 2:22). Not only has the metaphoric dividing wall that once separated us been broken down, but both peoples are being built together into this spiritual temple. The structure is not yet complete, but when it is, we will see an end analogous to that of the Torah's account of the construction of the Tabernacle: "So Moses finished the work. Then the cloud covered the tent of meeting, and the glory of the LORD filled the tabernacle" (Exodus 40:33-34).

SERMON FOUR:

THE ETERNAL PURPOSE OF GOD
(EPHESIANS 3)

The "mystery of the gospel" and the "eternal purpose of God" presented in Ephesians 3 reveal the meaning of the redemption and the significance of the Gentile disciples in the kingdom.

> God has taken his place in the divine council; in the midst of the gods he holds judgment. (Psalm 82:1)

The seventh day of Passover is the anniversary of the day that the children of Israel crossed the Red Sea, which the sages liken to their immersion into a mikvah. Through the Red Sea, the children of Israel passed through a purification, washing away the filth of Egypt, and they underwent a transformation, a change in status, from slavery to freedom. On the far side of the water, they sang praises to God most high who had revealed himself in such manifest glory, and they declared, "Who is like you among the gods, O LORD? Who is like You, majestic in holiness, awesome in glorious deeds, doing wonders?" (Exodus 15:11).

In the daily liturgy of the Jewish people, this declaration is repeated twice a day, in conjunction with the blessing of redemption that comes between the *Shema* and the *Amidah*. This pride of place reflects the importance of these ideas in Jewish thought.

The question, "Who is like you among the gods, O LORD? Who is like You, majestic in holiness, awesome in glorious deeds, doing wonders?" is a rhetorical question with an obvious answer: There is none among the gods like the LORD. There is none majestic in holiness like the LORD. There is none so fearsomely worthy of praises and acclamation. None works such powerful wonders.

That's the point of the entire story of the exodus from Egypt. That's what the whole affair was all about: God demonstrating his supremacy over the so-called gods of the nations.

God Declares His Name

Perhaps that wasn't clear to the common Hebrew slave suffering in Egypt. I imagine that if we were enslaved people in Egypt, we wouldn't see the big picture of a contest between the gods. We'd be more concerned about our own situation and how the world-shaking cataclysm of the ten plagues affected us personally.

As individuals in the middle of this unfolding drama, concerned only with our own little lives, our personal redemption, and our personal salvation, we might not see the bigger picture of what is happening around us. We might never stop to ask ourselves, "Why should God Almighty care to redeem us from Egypt anyway?" Though we, as mere escaping slaves, might not have the wherewithal to ask the question, God answers it anyway. It is a matter of reputation—his reputation.

The exodus from Egypt was God's opportunity to "declare his Name." He used the redemption of Israel to establish his reputation:

> The Egyptians shall know that I am the LORD. (Exodus 7:5)

> That you many know that there is no one like the LORD our God. (Exodus 8:10)

> That you may know that I am the LORD in the midst of the earth. (Exodus 8:22)

> To show you my power, so that my name may be proclaimed in all the earth. (Exodus 9:16)

> That you may tell in the hearing of your son and of your grandson ... that you may know that I am the LORD. (Exodus 10:2)

> On all the gods of Egypt I will execute judgments: I am the LORD. (Exodus 12:12)
>
> I will get glory over Pharaoh and all his host, and the Egyptians shall know that I am the LORD. (Exodus 14:4)

Why did God do all this in Egypt? Why the big display of power? Why the contest? Why did he redeem Israel? To show his power and to proclaim his name through all the earth.

Judging the Gods of Egypt

For the LORD, the contest of the gods is a demonstration of his sovereignty. Through the events of the Exodus story, God is establishing his name in the earth. He is making his entrance onto the stage of world history. In redeeming Israel, God sends a clear message to the whole world: "I exist; I am God; there is none like me!" He sends a message to the false gods of the world. He demonstrates that he alone is God, and there is none other:

> I will pass through the land of Egypt that night, and I will strike all the firstborn in the land of Egypt, both man and beast; and on all the gods of Egypt I will execute judgments: I am the LORD. (Exodus 12:12)

The Jewish people are his victory trophies, as he says, "You shall be my treasured possession among all peoples" (Exodus 19:5). The word translated as "treasured possession" is *segulah*, a word that refers to the trophy treasure a conqueror takes from his vanquished foe.

God's Reputation

The redemption from Egypt serves God's purpose, which is to establish his name. The redemption of the Jewish people is part of something much bigger than just getting out of making bricks; it's part of a plan to reveal God's eternal glory to "gods" and men. The Jewish people are to be like trophies of victory in the banquet hall of the King as a testimony to the nations.

For example, consider the reaction of Moses' father-in-law Jethro. This man was considered the high priest of Midian. The midrash says he worshiped all the gods. He was a connoisseur of deities. He put the "poly" in polytheism. But when he heard about how God had delivered the Jewish people from Egypt, he said, "Blessed be the LORD, who has delivered you out of the hand of the Egyptians and out of the hand of Pharaoh and has delivered the people from under the hand of the Egyptians. Now I know that the LORD is greater than all gods" (Exodus 18:10-11). Jethro becomes the first convert.

Rahab, the Canaanite innkeeper of Jericho, also converts and for the same reason. She says, "The fear of you has fallen upon us, and that all the inhabitants of the land melt away before you. For we have heard how the LORD dried up the water of the Red Sea before you when you came out of Egypt" (Joshua 2:9-10).

Any Other God?

Moses summarizes the entire matter with another rhetorical question:

> Has any god ever attempted to go and take a nation for himself from the midst of another nation, by trials, by signs, by wonders, and by war, by a mighty hand and an outstretched arm, and by great deeds of terror, all of which the LORD your God did for you in Egypt before your eyes? (Deuteronomy 4:34)

Again, it's a rhetorical question. He supplies the answer: "To you it was shown, that you might know that the LORD is God; there is no other besides him" (Deuteronomy 4:35).

According to this idea, the declaration of monotheism is the central thrust of the story of the exodus from Egypt and the whole redemption. The entire drama was intended to bring us to the realization that God alone presides over heaven and earth, that he transcends all other spiritual beings, that he is the one God, that "the LORD is God; there is no other besides him." That's the purpose of the redemption.

When the Scriptures tell us "there is no other," this is true on more than one level. Understand it this way. One might object by saying, "There certainly are other gods—those that the nations worship." However, though they call themselves gods, those spiritual entities are not at all on the level of the LORD. They are lower beings, part of the created order, and in comparison with the LORD, they are as if they are nothing—nonexistent. Ultimately, God is the Aleph and the Tav, the beginning and the end; from him, all things have come into being, and ultimately, all things will be reconciled into him, and apart from him, there is nothing that exists. Currently, that reality of the universal oneness of God is necessarily concealed within this world so that "others" like ourselves can exist. However, that concealment creates the illusion that other gods also exist and that we ourselves are independent of God, as Satan said to Eve, "You will be like God" (Genesis 3:5).

The Future Redemption

The ultimate redemption of the future will be like the first redemption. In the future redemption, God will again rescue his people from the nations:

> Therefore say to the house of Israel, Thus says the LORD God: It is not for your sake, O house of Israel, that I am about to act, but for the sake of my holy name, which you have profaned among the nations to which you came. And I will vindicate the holiness of my great name, which has been profaned among the nations, and which you have profaned among them. And the nations will know that I am the LORD, declares the Lord GOD, when through you I vindicate my holiness before their eyes. (Ezekiel 36:22-23)

The LORD declares that he will redeem Israel from exile for the sake of his reputation. The prophecy goes on to explain that he is going to gather his people from the four winds, spiritually purify them with the sprinkling of clean water, invest into them a new spirit and a new heart, resurrect them from the dead, unite them in the land of Israel, rebuild his Temple, and shepherd them as one flock under the Davidic Messiah King in the Messianic Kingdom. That is the future redemption. All this he summarizes by saying, "I will sanctify my great name."

When we pray the Master's prayer, "Our Father in heaven, may your name be sanctified (hallowed be thy name)," we are supposed to have this prophecy in mind. We are asking God to bring the final redemption and establish the Messianic Kingdom so that "the nations will know that I am the LORD."

The Gods of the Nations

In the days of the Bible, there were only two types of people in the world: the Jewish people and the nations. The Jewish people belonged to God. The nations belonged to the other gods. Every nation had its gods. You didn't choose your gods the way we choose a religion in today's world. Instead, you were born into a people, and your people had certain gods. Or rather, the gods owned your people.

Jewish angelology explains the situation like this. God presides over a Sanhedrin of seventy angels. Each of the seventy nations has its own specific guardian angel. The angels are called "princes," and their domains are the principalities. For example, in the book of Daniel, the angels Gabriel and Michael contend with the Prince of Persia, the angelic prince over the Persians (Daniel 10:13, 20). These angelic entities present themselves to the nations as divine beings, as gods, and they enjoy the adoration of their subjects.

The Midrash Rabbah explains that the angelic prince over the Egyptians was called Mitzrayim (the Hebrew word for Egypt) and that when the Torah says in Exodus 14, "Mitzrayim pursued the people of Israel" and "the people of Israel lifted up their eyes, and behold, Mitzrayim was marching after them," it refers to this angelic prince, of whom Pharaoh was an agent, just as Moses was an agent of the LORD. So the contest between the gods (between God and Mitzrayim) was finally settled at the Red Sea. God prevailed, defeated the angel Mitzrayim, and took the Hebrews away from him. "For they are my slaves, whom I brought out of the land of Egypt; they shall not be sold as slaves" (Leviticus 25:42).

The name of the God of Israel is profaned among the nations when his people fall into the possession of other gods. It looks like the other gods are more powerful than him. After all, if he were more powerful, why couldn't he protect his people? To rectify this misconception, God redeemed his people, and in so doing, he sanctified his name.

He didn't do it merely for the sake of the Jewish people. He did it for the sake of his name and the sake of the nations so that "the nations will know that I am the LORD." Or, to put it in our Master's words, "That the world may know" (John 17:23).

Mystery of the Gospel

So when we are asked whether or not it is appropriate for a Gentile disciple to participate in the Jewish Passover, we should remember that it was specifically for the sake of the nations that the Jewish people were redeemed in the first place, and it will be specifically for the sake of the nations that the Jewish people will be redeemed in the future.

This is what Paul refers to in Ephesians 3 as "the mystery of the gospel." To put it another way, "the mystery of the gospel" is the hidden secret behind the good news about the kingdom of heaven. Paul says he received insight into this mystery through a revelation. The revelation to which he refers occurred when, in the Temple in Jerusalem, he was caught up to the third heaven and saw a vision of the Master, who said to him, "Go, for I will send you far away to the Gentiles" (Acts 22:21). The mysterious secret behind the good news of the gospel, Paul explains, is the redemption of the nations.

The Eternal Purpose

In Ephesians 3, he explains that the mysterious hidden secret behind the good news about the kingdom of heaven was according to God's eternal purpose, which is to say that the redemption of the nations was the whole plan all along:

> To me, though I am the very least of all the saints, this grace was given, to preach to the Gentiles the unsearchable riches of Christ, and to bring to light for everyone what is the plan of the mystery hidden for ages in God who created all things, so that through the church the manifold wisdom of God might now be made known to the rulers and authorities in the heavenly places. This was according to the eternal purpose that he has realized in Christ Jesus our Lord. (Ephesians 3:8-11)

By redeeming the nations along with Israel, God intended to sanctify his name before the nations and before their gods, "the rulers and authorities in the heavenly places," which Paul refers to a few chapters further on as "the rulers ... the authorities ... the cosmic powers over this present darkness ... the spiritual forces of evil in the heavenly places" (Ephesians 6:12).

In the coming messianic redemption, God will sanctify his name by taking the nations away from the gods of the nations. This is the "eternal purpose," the redemption of humanity. Not just Israel but all of humanity will be swept up into this final redemption. Then the adversary will be chained, thrown into a pit, and sealed in it for a thousand years "so that he might not deceive the nations any longer" (Revelation 20:3). Then God's name will be sanctified, and all the nations will know that there is no god like the LORD, the God of Israel.

This is what we declare through the days of the Counting of the Omer (the fifty days between Passover and Shavu'ot) in the recitation of Psalm 67:

> That your way may be known on earth, your saving power among all nations. (Psalm 67:2)
>
> Let the nations be glad and sing for joy, for you judge the peoples with equity and guide the nations upon earth. Selah (Psalm 67:4)
>
> God shall bless us; let all the ends of the earth fear him! (Psalm 67:7)

That's the sweeping drama of redemption: a universal redemption, the mystery of the gospel, and the eternal purpose of God. The Messiah comes not just for Israel but for all the sons and daughters of Adam. This inspiring revelation drove the Apostle Paul to reach out to the nations. He saw Gentile disciples of Yeshua as the first fruits of this final redemption, just as the Jewish disciples were the first fruits of the redemption of Israel.

Paul's Epistle to the Ephesians reveals a plan for universal dominion, a plan by which God intends to take over the world. Gentile believers are God's tokens and trophies of victory in an ancient struggle against darkness and concealment. The eternal purpose of God is the redemption of the whole world.

Pattern of Redemption

The exodus from Egypt set the pattern. When God took the Israelites out of Egypt and away from Pharaoh and the gods of Egypt, he established his superiority over all those gods. Israel was his trophy of victory. He used the exodus from Egypt to establish his name. It foreshadowed a second, greater exodus—an exodus begun under the blood of a greater lamb. This second exodus is the redemption of the nations. As he redeems the nations, God is repeating the exodus from Egypt over and over again, and there is nothing Pharaoh or the gods of Egypt can do about it. The spiritual powers and principalities of the Gentile nations can only watch in dismay as their brick-makers slip away through the Red Sea.

Our salvation is a demonstration of God's wisdom and sovereign power to rulers and authorities in the heavenly realms. Which of them, what other god, has ever tried to take for himself every nation? Which god of the nations has done anything like it? Which god of the nations can do anything to stop it? To Paul, the mystery of the gospel is the salvation of the whole world. "For God so loved the world, that he gave his only Son" (John 3:16). That's what we are talking about when we speak about the kingdom of heaven being revealed on earth and when we ask God to sanctify his name and bring his kingdom.

Too Small a Thing

The point of the redemption is God's final victory over the so-called gods of this world. It's the revelation of his name as one within this world of concealment in which it appears that he is not one and not sovereign. The picture is much bigger than just the individual disciple and his or her personal salvation. It is bigger than the liberation from Egypt. It is bigger than the salvation of the Jewish people. God's eternal purpose is that his wisdom should be made known to the rulers and authorities in heavenly realms by means of taking away their people and their property and redeeming a people out of every tribe, tongue, and nation on earth.

Before the foundation of the earth, the LORD said to the soul of King Messiah:

> It is too light a thing that you should be my servant to raise up
> the tribes of Jacob and to bring back the preserved of Israel;
> I will make you as a light for the nations, that my salvation
> may reach to the end of the earth. (Isaiah 49:6)

The scope of Messiah's work is not limited to the restoration of the tribes of Israel. That purpose is too small when compared with the greater purpose God has in mind. The eternal purpose of God is that Messiah should carry the LORD's salvation to the Gentiles, even to the ends of the earth.

The Gentiles Isaiah spoke of are the same Gentiles to whom Paul was writing in the book of Ephesians. They were formerly strangers and aliens, far off, strangers to the promises, without God and without hope. They were the ones upon whom God intends to shine the light of Messiah. This is in keeping with God's eternal purpose—that the manifold wisdom of God should be made known to the rulers and authorities in the heavenly realms. God's salvation must go to the ends of the earth so that through the seed of Abraham, all the families of the earth should be blessed.

Then all humanity will declare, "There is none like you among the gods, O LORD." In that day, the idols will be cut off and toppled down, as it says in the *Aleinu* prayer: "Every knee will bend and every tongue confess. And in that day, the LORD will be one, and his name will be one" (cf. Zechariah 14:9).

Psalm 82, the psalm that begins with the words "God has taken his place in the divine council; in the midst of the gods he holds judgment," then concludes with the hopeful petition, "Arise, O God, judge the earth; for you shall inherit all the nations!"

SERMON FIVE:
FELLOW HEIRS
(EPHESIANS 3:1–11)

What does it mean to be a "fellow heir" with Israel and part of "the commonwealth of Israel"? Paul uncovers the role of the Gentile disciples in the "mystery of Christ," which was "hidden in God" for ages past.

God redeemed the Jewish people from Egypt not for their own sake but to make known his name and reputation—that the Egyptians might know, that the Israelites might know, and the ends of the earth might know that he is God and that there is none else. He used the redemption from Egypt to discredit the false gods of the world's greatest superpower, showing himself to be supreme above the powers and principalities and spiritual forces of this present darkness.

When the Jewish people fall into the hands of foreign powers, it profanes his name because it appears that the gods of the nations are more powerful than he is. For this reason, he says to the exiles of Egypt, "You have profaned my name among the nations." In the final redemption, he will again redeem his people from the nations, spiritually cleanse them, resurrect the dead, bring the exiles back to the land of Israel, give them a new spirit, unite them under the government of King Messiah, rebuild his Temple in their midst, and restore his presence among them to sanctify his name. He says, "Then the nations will know that I am the LORD" (Ezekiel 37:28).

In the process of redeeming Israel, he will turn the tables on the false gods of the nations by taking their people away from them. The cosmic heist of the nations has been his secret objective the entire time.

Apostle to the Gentiles

> For this reason I, Paul, a prisoner of Christ Jesus on behalf of you Gentiles—assuming that you have heard of the stewardship of God's grace that was given to me for you, how the mystery was made known to me by revelation, as I have written briefly. (Ephesians 3:1-3)

Paul looked for a day when God's kingdom would include not just Israel but also all nations as a universal revelation to humanity. That's why Paul insisted on distinction between Jews and Gentile disciples and dissuaded Gentile disciples from becoming Jewish. Every Gentile who confessed faith in the God of Israel and allegiance to the Messiah of Israel was a step closer to realizing that vision, but every Gentile disciple who forsook his nation and converted to become Jewish was a step further from realizing that vision. If all the Gentile disciples were to become Jews, then the Messianic redemption would not reach to all nations; it would be limited to Israel. Such a prospect ran counter to the whole eternal purpose of God's redemptive work. Hence Paul's rule of distinction for all the churches (1 Corinthians 7:18-20).

James, the brother of the Master, made the same argument when he handed down the Apostolic Decree in Acts 15. When the apostles decided that Gentile disciples need not become Jewish, James justified the decision by quoting a prophecy from Amos 9 about how in the kingdom, the nations would also be called by God's name:

> With this the words of the prophets agree, just as it is written, "'After this I will return, and I will rebuild the tent of David that has fallen; I will rebuild its ruins, and I will restore it, that the remnant of mankind may seek the Lord, and all the Gentiles who are called by my name,' says the Lord, who makes these things known from of old." (Acts 15:15-18)

Paul spoke to the Gentile disciples in Ephesus with authority because he considered himself the official "apostle to the Gentiles." He had been imprisoned in Rome solely on account of his association with Gentile disciples. That's what got him in trouble with the authorities, and that's how he ultimately ended up waiting for a trial before Nero in Rome. He considered himself the official apostle to the Gentiles because the Messiah himself commissioned him through a revelation he received while worshiping in the Temple. Caught up to the third heaven in a state of altered consciousness, he saw a vision of Yeshua saying to him, "Go, for I will send you far away to the Gentiles" (Acts 22:21). That revelation sent him on a quest to understand God's purpose for the nations and how the good news of the gospel might apply to them. This is the "mystery ... made known to me by revelation."

The Mystery of Christ

> When you read this, you can perceive my insight into the mystery of Christ, which was not made known to the sons of men in other generations as it has now been revealed to his holy apostles and prophets by the Spirit. (Ephesians 3:4–5)

The apostle spoke of his "insight into the mystery of Christ." On the surface, this sounds like some sort of theological or Christological idea—penal substitutionary atonement through Christ's blood, the efficaciousness of his vicarious suffering, the fellowship of the eucharist, or some other sacramental language. However, these ideas are not in view. Instead, Paul refers to the same topic the rest of the epistle is about—namely, Gentile inclusion. The "mystery" is the redemption of the nations, something concealed from previous generations but now revealed through the apostolic authorities. The "mystery" is that the Gentile disciples are fellow heirs, members of the same body, and partakers of the promise of the kingdom and the World to Come by means of the good news of the Messiah Yeshua. The "mystery," now revealed, is that this is what the Messiah was meant to accomplish all along.

Fellow Heirs

> This mystery is that the Gentiles are fellow heirs, members of the same body, and partakers of the promise in Christ Jesus through the gospel. (Ephesians 3:6)

The Gentile disciples are to be considered fellow heirs with Israel. However, an overly broad interpretation here can lead to confusion.

To be a fellow heir does not mean that one attains identical status or sameness. It does not mean that the Gentile disciples share the same calling, responsibilities, and privileges as the Jewish people. It does not mean "*equal* heir."

To be a fellow heir with Israel does not mean that I, as a Gentile disciple, share the same biblical obligations and privileges as Israel. But it does mean that I share in Israel's inheritance. The image is that of a father dividing his estate among his sons. According to the Torah's inheritance laws, all of his sons receive a single portion in the same inheritance except the firstborn, who receives a double portion.

What is the inheritance? Paul explained it in the first chapter of the epistle as the hope of the Jewish people:

> In him we [the Jewish people] have obtained an inheritance, having been predestined according to the purpose of him who works all things according to the counsel of his will, so that we who were the first to hope in Christ might be to the praise of his glory. (Ephesians 1:11-12)

In the Messiah, the Jewish disciples obtained the inheritance that God promised to the children of Abraham, Isaac, and Jacob. The inheritance consists of the promises that came through the Torah and were amplified by the prophets: the blessings and promises of Abraham, the land, the redemption, the kingdom, and even eternal life in the resurrection and the World to Come. This is the inheritance passed down from the fathers to the sons. Paul explained that this inheritance was predestined according to the will and purpose of God to come through the Messiah so that the Jewish people "who were the first to hope in the Messiah might be to the praise of his glory."

The idolatrous Gentile nations, on the other hand, were at the time "separated from Christ, alienated from the commonwealth of Israel and strangers to the covenants of promise, having no hope and without God in the world" (Ephesians 2:12). In Messiah, however, individuals from those nations who were formerly "far away" have been brought near and receive a portion in the same inheritance along with the people of Israel. They are no longer strangers to the covenants of the forefathers, separated from the Messiah, and without hope or God in the world. Instead, they have been brought into the commonwealth of Israel.

The Commonwealth of Israel

At this point, we should discuss the concept of the "commonwealth of Israel." In the previous chapter, Paul states that the Gentiles outside of a relationship with the Messiah are "alienated from the commonwealth of Israel." Gentile disciples of Yeshua, however, are no longer alienated from the commonwealth. As with the concept of "fellow heirs," there are wrong ways to understand a Gentile disciple's inclusion in the commonwealth of Israel. The replacement-theology interpretation understands this to mean that the church has replaced Israel. The one-law interpretation goes so far as to say that since Gentile disciples are included in the commonwealth of Israel, that makes them Israelites, giving them the same status as proselytes, that is, Jews not of Jewish birth. That's not what it means.

Paul's concept of "commonwealth" is undoubtedly based on his experience within the Roman Empire as a Roman citizen. The Greek word translated as commonwealth (*politeia*) could be understood as "a citizenship." It's closely related to the word for citizen (*polites*). Paul himself was a Roman citizen and therefore was part of the commonwealth (citizenship) of Rome, though he was neither Roman nor Italian. He was a Jew from Tarsus who had never been to Italy until his arrest.

As the Roman Empire expanded to encompass most of the known western world, it became evident that they could not control all their holdings by sheer military force. Revolutionary wars on multiple fronts would quickly overtax the Roman legions and spread them too thinly. Instead of ruling by sheer brute force, the Romans introduced the concept of obtaining Roman citizenship, giving their subjects something to aspire toward other than independence from Rome. *What's even better than throwing off the Roman yoke? Becoming a Roman!*

The Romans extended the privilege of being a Roman citizen to loyalists and sold it to the wealthy. One's children could inherit the coveted status. It was also possible to become a Roman citizen through manumission. This was by far the most common way to acquire citizenship in the empire. If you served as a slave in a Roman citizen's household and your owner granted you freedom, he could adopt you into his household and thereby grant you citizenship. Paul's forefathers in Tarsus might have obtained their citizenship in that manner, as did many other Diaspora Jews, who took on the title "freedmen."

Elsewhere, Paul explains to the Gentile disciples, "So you are no longer a slave, but a son, and if a son, then an heir through God" (Galatians 4:7).

Roman citizens had political privileges and protections that non-citizens did not, but they were not the same as Romans. In the analogy, Paul spoke of Gentile disciples obtaining kingdom citizenship in Israel. The citizenship Paul sees for non-Jews is not citizenship in the nation of Israel proper, which he elsewhere refers to as "Israel according to the flesh," just as he refers to his readers as "you Gentiles in the flesh." The citizenship enjoyed by the Gentile disciples remains tied to the future kingdom of Israel, which is the kingdom of God. That "commonwealth of Israel" extends to all disciples of King Yeshua.

With this kind of language, Paul intended to communicate the distinction between Israel and the nations in a physical sense while indicating inclusion through Messiah in the spiritual sense and in the future political reality. The commonwealth of Israel belongs to the future when King Messiah will annex all nations under the empire called the kingdom of God. The Gentile disciples will be citizens of the kingdom, not just vanquished and conquered peoples. The disciples of Yeshua will rule along with him, occupying positions of spiritual authority, judging angels, presiding over principalities and authorities, and replacing the corrupt spiritual government of the prince of this present darkness.

Paul's Gospel

Paul summarizes all these concepts as "my gospel," a term he uses to differentiate it from the good news proclaimed only to Israel. He considered himself called by God to steward and transmit this good news for Gentiles:

> Of this gospel I was made a minister according to the gift of God's grace, which was given me by the working of his power. To me, though I am the very least of all the saints, this grace was given, to preach to the Gentiles the unsearchable riches of Christ, and to bring to light for everyone what is the plan of the mystery hidden for ages in God, who created all things, so that through the church [*ekklesia*] the manifold

wisdom of God might now be made known to the rulers and authorities in the heavenly places. (Ephesians 3:7-10)

Paul considered himself to be the vessel of enlightenment to the world on this matter of Gentile citizenship in the kingdom. Throughout the Epistle to the Ephesians, he presumed himself to represent Israel, the Jewish people, the "apostles and prophets," as he transmits revelation to the nations. The special revelation that he had received pertained to the destiny of the nations, namely, that they, too, will be swept up in the final redemption under King Messiah. Paul's Gentile disciples are the first fruits of that future redemption: "This was according to the eternal purpose that he has realized in Christ Jesus our Lord" (Ephesians 3:11). This was God's plan from the outset.

Sometimes when describing our relationship with Israel, the Gentile disciples use the self-deprecating term "second-class citizen," implying that while the Jewish people are first-class, our citizenship is more of an honorary status. That's actually true if we are talking about citizenship in the nation of Israel. But it's not at all true if we are talking about citizenship in the kingdom. In either case, we have learned that the nations are not second-string in God's arrangements or an afterthought on his agenda. Instead, the objective behind Israel's redemption is the redemption and salvation of the nations. The objective behind Messiah's mission is not just the redemption of Israel. Rather, that objective can be rightly understood as a means toward an end, that end being the redemption of humanity, as the Gospel of John says, "For God so loved *the world*, that he gave his only Son, that whoever believes in him should not perish but have eternal life. For God did not send his Son into *the world* to condemn *the world*, but in order that *the world* might be saved through him" (John 3:16-17, emphasis mine).

Such was the eternal purpose of God.

SERMON SIX:
THE FULLNESS WHO FILLS ALL IN ALL
(EPHESIANS 3:11-21)

Paul invites Gentile disciples to find their identity in Messiah by diving into the deep waters of apostolic mysticism. A few parallels from Jewish mysticism help elucidate his ideas.

In the previous chapter, while working through Ephesians 3, we discovered the eternal purpose of God. That seems significant. We learned that Paul brought the world a revelation that for ages past had remained concealed. He called it the "mystery of Christ" and the "mystery of the gospel." He referred to it as the "manifold wisdom of God" and the "eternal purpose of God." He differentiated it from the gospel proclaimed exclusively to the Jewish people by referring to it as "my gospel" because he believed God had commissioned him to transmit this revelation to the world. What was the revelation? That God is redeeming the nations through Yeshua the Messiah and salvaging the human race to reveal his glory and discredit the false gods of the world. Paul said that this was the plan all along, but only now has the plan been made public. The Gentile disciples from the nations are the first fruits, the forerunners, of the full redemption of the nations.

Over-familiarity with the New Testament makes it easy to read over a passage like Ephesians 3 and miss the main point about the redemption of the nations. It's also normal to read through a passage like this and take for granted the amount of deep Jewish mysticism at work in apostolic theology. As we conclude our commentary on Ephesians 3, we should slow down enough to appreciate the vastness of thought that Paul marshals to express his ideas. The best way to do that will be to compare his statements with similar concepts in Jewish mysticism.

Boldness and Confidence

> This was according to the eternal purpose that he has realized in Christ Jesus our Lord, in whom we have boldness and access with confidence through our faith in him. (Ephesians 3:11-12)

In the previous chapter, we saw how Paul used an analogy from Roman life to illustrate the relationship between Yeshua and his disciples. Roman laws concerning the manumission of slaves, adoption into a family, and consequent inheritance of citizenship are still in view. He compared the disciples to household slaves in a Roman home. In this analogy, Yeshua is the owner of the slaves. The disciples are compared to household slaves set free by the Son and adopted into the family as children.

Under Roman law, a Roman citizen had the legal right to grant his slaves freedom. This was called manumission. But doing so was no great favor because a freed slave had no rights, status, money, place, or standing. Therefore, the Roman householder who wanted to grant his trusted slave his freedom would often adopt that slave into his family, lending him his family name. This is how the prisoner of war Joseph ben Matthias became Flavius Josephus. The Flavian family of Vespasian, Titus, and Domitian adopted him into their household and gave him their name. When a Roman citizen adopts a child (that is, an adult child), that child is eligible for Roman citizenship. In Paul's analogy, Yeshua is the householder who frees his slave, elevates him to the status of a son, and grants him citizenship. You who were previously alienated from the commonwealth of Israel (i.e., citizenship) have now been elevated to the level of sons who inherit citizenship in the kingdom: "If the Son sets you free, you will be free indeed" (John 8:36).

Elsewhere, Paul says to his Gentile readers, "Because you are sons, God has sent the Spirit of his Son into our hearts, crying, 'Abba! Father!' So you are no longer a slave, but a son, and if a son, then an heir through God" (Galatians 4:6-7), and, "For you did not receive the spirit of slavery to fall back into fear, but you have received the Spirit of adoption as sons, by whom we cry, 'Abba! Father!'" (Romans 8:15). Yeshua enjoys a unique and unprecedented relationship with God, intimately knowing the Father as only the Son knows him. For this reason, the disciple of Yeshua enjoys access to God, confidently approaches him as a loving father, and prays with boldness in the manner of a child speaking with a father.

Do Not Lose Heart

> So I ask you not to lose heart over what I am suffering for you, which is your glory. (Ephesians 3:13)

Having heard about Paul's imprisonment, the Gentile disciples in Asia Minor might have felt discouraged and disheartened. Their faith, practice, and self-identity depended on his gospel message. They might have feared that without Paul to reinforce their identity and represent their interests in the apostolic community, they would lose their participation in the community of Yeshua. Paul encourages them to consider his tribulations on their behalf to be a badge of honor. He did not hesitate to suffer for the sake of his message to the nations.

Every Family in Heaven and on Earth

> For this reason I bow my knees before the Father, from whom every family in heaven and on earth is named. (Ephesians 3:14-15)

He concludes these thoughts about the revelation of the eternal purpose of God with a prayer and doxology, addressing God as "the Father, from whom every family in heaven and on earth is named." Biblical Hebrew sometimes refers to a family unit as a *beit av*, i.e., "house of a father." Paul's language implies a vast universalism in which God is presented as the First Cause. We might paraphrase, "The Father who is the origin of every category of things in the universe." God seeks to redeem not just Israel but every family. Everything has its source in God, and all things belong to God, so there should be no objection to the redemption of the Gentiles who are called by God's name.

The Indwelling Messiah

What is the petition that Paul presents in prayer on bended knee before the Father of all families? Here's his prayer on behalf of the Gentile disciples in Ephesus:

> That according to the riches of his glory he may grant you to be strengthened with power through his Spirit in your inner being, so that Christ may dwell in your hearts through faith. (Ephesians 3:16–17)

Paul prayed that they would be strengthened in their inner being, that is to say, that God's Spirit should strengthen their spirits (*neshamot*) so that the Spirit of Messiah "may dwell in your hearts," much as the *Shechinah* (God's Dwelling Presence) took up its dwelling in the Tabernacle and the *Logos* (Word) of God was made flesh and tabernacled in the physical person of Yeshua of Nazareth. Paul wants the Holy Spirit to quicken our transcendent inner being (the *neshamah*) so that we might become a receptacle for the Spirit (*neshamah*) of the Messiah.

This is not the only place the apostle speaks of this concept of the Messiah taking residence within the consciousness and within the person of his disciples. In Galatians 2:20, he says, "It is no longer I who live, but Christ who lives in me." In Romans 8, he says, "The Spirit of God dwells in you. Anyone who does not have the Spirit of Christ does not belong to him. But if Christ is in you ... he who raised Christ Jesus from the dead will also give life to your mortal bodies through his Spirit who dwells in you" (Romans 8:9–11).

This is in keeping with our Master's prayer, "I in them and you in me, that they may become perfectly one, so that the world may know that you sent me and loved them even as you loved me" (John 17:23).

Ibbur

Let's dwell on this point for a moment because it comes at the conclusion of this entire discussion about the status of the Gentile disciple, the redemption of the nations, and the eternal purpose of God. We should ask ourselves, "What's the connection between the redemption of the nations and this mystical and utterly personal experience of Messiah's being, which, in some ineffable spiritual sense, is taking up dwelling within the individual?" How does Paul's discussion of the eternal purpose of God connect to Jesus in my heart?

When I was a kid growing up under the Evangelical worldview, we often spoke of having "Jesus in your heart." We referred to conversion as "accepting Christ" and praying to "invite Jesus to come into our hearts." To be "born again" meant to "receive Jesus into your heart." My Swedish grandmother expressed her dismay over the medical innovation of heart-transplant surgery lest she receive a used heart without Jesus in it. In all honesty, I never really understood the concept of having Jesus in my heart until I encountered a similar idea in Jewish mysticism.

The teaching of the Jewish mystics transmits a similar idea called *ibbur*, which literally means "impregnation" or "pregnancy." It's one of the genuinely spooky ideas that, when misunderstood, give Jewish mysticism and kabbalistic literature a bad name. It can be misconstrued to sound like some creepy occult thing. The idea is that the soul of a deceased person might be sent to assist a living person in the performance of a mitzvah (good deed or commandment) or to complete a task, especially if it is a task that this particular soul has a personal interest in completing.

For example, suppose you were an orphan and raised without parents and therefore never had the opportunity to fulfill the mitzvah of honoring your father and mother. Judaism considers it a personal tragedy never to have an opportunity to fulfill a mitzvah. After death, you might receive the opportunity to go as an *ibbur* to assist someone who is having difficulty with that particular mitzvah. By doing so, you participate with the person in the mitzvah and accrue some of the merit for the mitzvah. You would accomplish this in the form of an *ibbur*, that is, a spiritual impregnation of a small and subtle portion of your soul's identity incarnated into the person performing the mitzvah so as to assist in the effort.

It's an idea.

I'm not vouching for whether or not there is any substance to that concept whatsoever, nor am I endorsing Lurianic mysticism. But one could certainly describe the living Messiah's relationship with his living disciples in similar language. The apostles teach that the Spirit of the Messiah dwells within his disciples in order to continue his work—the work of the kingdom and the will of the Father on earth. This happens through the agency of the Holy Spirit—that same anointing Spirit of

God that rested upon Yeshua and now rests upon his disciples and impregnates them (so to speak) with a portion of the Spirit of Messiah, as the angel Gabriel said to Miriam, "The Holy Spirit will come upon you, and the power of the Most High will overshadow you; therefore the child to be born will be called holy—the Son of God" (Luke 1:35).

Ibbur means impregnation. Spiritually speaking, the identity of the Messiah is planted within his disciples like a pregnancy (i.e., a person within a person), whether they are Jewish or Gentile, to carry out his work on earth. This is why Paul could say, "It is no longer I who live, but Christ who lives in me. And the life I now live in the flesh I live by faith in the Son of God, who loved me and gave himself for me" (Galatians 2:20).

The apostles believed that this spiritual *ibbur* of Messiah within us should transform our lives—at least, this is how it is supposed to work. There is supposed to be a new life in us, a resurrected life in us, such that we are no longer pursuing our own interests but the interests of the Messiah. We no longer rely on our own sense of self, ego, and identity. Instead, we are supposed to have died to that identity, finding our identity instead in the indwelling Messiah.

What has this got to do with the Jewish-Gentile questions Paul has addressed? It goes back to the concern he raised at the end of chapter 1 when he prayed that the eyes of his readers' hearts might be enlightened to know the hope of our calling and the immeasurable greatness of God's power toward us with Messiah as the head over the *ekklesia*, "which is his body, the fullness of him who fills all in all" (Ephesians 1:23).

The Body of Adam Kadmon

Because each disciple of Yeshua is invested with this identity (*ibbur* of Messiah), the disciples share membership in a larger corporate messianic identity. Corporately, the disciples of Yeshua form a collective entity that the apostles refer to as "the body of the Messiah." This is probably Paul's favorite metaphor to describe the relationship between Israel and the Gentile disciples. Earlier in the chapter, Paul alluded to the "body of Messiah" metaphor when he said, "This mystery is that the Gentiles are fellow heirs, members of the same body, and partakers of the promise in Christ Jesus through the gospel" (Ephesians 3:6).

He will return to the concept in the next chapter, where he says, "We are to grow up in every way into him who is the head, into Christ, from whom the whole body, joined and held together by every joint with which it is equipped, when each part is working properly, makes the body grow so that it builds itself up in love" (Ephesians 4:15-16).

He invokes the image of the body of Messiah in several places in his epistles. Like the concept of *ibbur,* it also has an analog in Jewish mysticism, specifically, the description of the Heavenly Adam (*Adam Kadmon*). According to that idea, every human spirit, every *neshamah,* has its origin in a single human being, the original prototype. Together, all human beings comprise that single human being who was made in the image of God.

The Bible tells us that Adam was made "in the image of God" (Genesis 1:27), but what is the image of the transcendent and unseen God? Before creating Adam, God first created an image of himself, a reflection of himself, so to speak. According to this idea, all humanity comprises a single human being—a divine human being—who should be the image and reflection of God. Sin obscures and corrupts that image, but if we knew who we truly were on the soul level, we would realize that there is no real separation between us. We are all of the same stuff, differentiated only for the sake of this lifetime, but ultimately destined to be reunited in perfect love for one another, which is God's own love. That's one explanation of the mystical idea of the Heavenly Adam.

Paul elsewhere compares the Master to Adam (Romans 5:12-19; 1 Corinthians 15:42-49), referring to the Master as a sort of heavenly Adam or spiritual Adam. Paul's teaching about the "body of Messiah" is similar. In his metaphor, Yeshua is at the head of the body, and all his disciples comprise various body parts. The parts are different, and they have different functions in the body, but all of them are essential components of the body. It would be inappropriate for one body part to be jealous of another. Thus there can be distinction and differentiation within the body of Messiah. The eye is not jealous of the foot, nor is the foot jealous of the ear. We all belong to the same body:

> He put all things under his feet and gave him as head over all things to the church, which is his body, the fullness of him who fills all in all. (Ephesians 1:22-23)

I would summarize the thrust of the argument like this. The idea that the Messiah dwells within each person and that together we corporately form the body of the Messiah should utterly transcend our simple ideas of who is who, of human labels and egoic identity, of gender, rank, caste, clan, national standing, prestige, and honor in the eyes of men. It should make the question of who is Jewish and who is from the nations irrelevant. (It is relevant in the flesh and in this current world, but not on the level of true spiritual identity.) Our spiritual rebirth as Messiah on earth is so much more significant than those things that they should be as if they were of no account to us. God's Spirit should be quickening our inner person, the spirit within us, to the end that the Messiah himself dwells in us in this sacred union and sacred bond that brings us into the fellowship Yeshua shares with the Father. Ultimately, this process draws us into union with the one God where we discover the truth that has eluded us, namely, that God is love—love that transcends all boundaries.

The Fullness of God

Thus, Paul prayed for the disciples in Ephesus that the eyes of their hearts would be opened to apprehend the immeasurable:

> That you, being rooted and grounded in love, may have strength to comprehend with all the saints what is the breadth and length and height and depth, and to know the love of Christ that surpasses knowledge, that you may be filled with all the fullness of God. (Ephesians 3:17-19)

The apostle prayed that we "may be filled with all the fullness of God," echoing his statement at the end of the first chapter:

> ... which is his body, the fullness of him who fills all in all. (Ephesians 1:22-23)

We find a similar turn of phrase used to describe Yeshua in Colossians:

> For in him all the fullness of God was pleased to dwell. (Colossians 1:19)

In this verse, the term translated "fullness" is the Greek word *pleroma*. We can't be sure what Paul intended to imply by referring to the "fullness of God" that was pleased to dwell in Yeshua and that Paul desired to see fill Yeshua's disciples. I can tell you that it implies the sense of totality, meaning that all the "parts" (so to speak) are present. The fullness of God means God is fully present, with nothing missing. Later Christian mysticism (i.e., Gnosticism) used the term *pleroma* to describe the divine attributes of the Aeons (the Emanations) of the transcendent God through which the utterly unknowable and unrevealed limitlessness of God reveals itself above the lower worlds. This concept is, more or less, the Gnostic version of the Sephirot described in Kabbalistic literature, and there's every likelihood that the original Gnostic idea has its source in the type of apostolic mysticism we see hinted at in Ephesians and Colossians.

A similar idea exists in Jewish mysticism today in the so-called "Tree of Life (*Etz Chayim*)" which purports to chart the component attributes of God. One need not endorse the schema to see the parallels in early Christianity's esoteric ideas. According to Jewish mysticism today, the *Ein Sof* (the infinite, transcendent God) reveals himself and continuously creates the worlds below him, including this universe, through ten Emanations (*Sephirot*): Wisdom (*Chochmah*), Insight (*Binah*), Knowledge (*Da'at*), Loving Kindness (*Chesed*), Power (*Gevurah*), Splendor (*Tiferet*), Eternality (*Netzach*), Glory (*Hod*), Foundation (*Yesod*), and Kingdom (*Malchut*). Above all of them sits Crown (*Keter*), the source of all the rest. At the end of the chain is Kingdom (*Malchut*), which manifests in this physical world and receives the fullness of those above it.

The entire system is a juggling of abstraction and metaphor to try to measure the immeasurable God, to translate the ineffable into human language, and understand how the infinite God can enter the world of three dimensions and interact with human beings. Likewise, Paul earlier prayed that the eyes of our hearts might be opened to know "what is the immeasurable greatness of his power toward us who believe" (Ephesians 1:19). Now he prays that we might measure the immeasurable in "the breadth and length and height and depth, and to know the love of Christ that surpasses knowledge, that you may be filled with all *the fullness of God.*" In the apostolic scheme of the *pleroma*, whatever it might have been, love sits in the place of *Keter* (Crown) above *Da'at* (Knowledge):

> If I have prophetic powers, and understand all mysteries and all knowledge, and if I have all faith, so as to remove mountains, but have not love, I am nothing. (1 Corinthians 13:2)

So, once again, we find Paul to be speaking in the language of Jewish mysticism when he says, "For in him all the fullness of God was pleased to dwell" (Colossians 1:19). This same fullness (which in Jewish mysticism finds one expression in the Tree of Life) is the *pleroma*, the fullness of which Paul speaks when he prays for us, "that you may be filled with all the fullness of God."

The fullness of God is pleased to dwell in the Messiah, incarnated as if impregnated into the physical body of Yeshua of Nazareth. The spirit of Yeshua, a portion of his being, is pleased to dwell in his disciples, incarnated as if impregnated into each one. Together, his disciples comprise one corporate body, the body of the Messiah, which contains the fullness of God.

Compared with these thoughts and meditations on the significance of being a disciple of Yeshua, concerns over flesh-level prestige based upon who is Jewish and who is of the nations should feel petty and irrelevant.

Paul concludes this discussion on the identity of the Gentile disciple in Yeshua with a brief doxology:

> Now to him who is able to do far more abundantly than all that we ask or think, according to the power at work within us, to him be glory in the church and in Christ Jesus throughout all generations, forever and ever. Amen. (Ephesians 3:20–21)

Fake Ending

Is that the end? The "Amen" at the end of Ephesians 3:21 seems like a perfect place to end the epistle. After a breathtaking and sweeping flight through the mind of the Spirit of God, this is a good place to land. But it's not the end. From this point on, Paul comes down from the spiritual heights to explain the practical legal implications of his theological treatise. Ephesians 4 begins a discourse on how Yeshua's disciples should live.

SERMON SEVEN:
A MANNER WORTHY OF THE CALLING
(EPHESIANS 4)

How does a disciple of Yeshua live? Paul provides a quick summary of the path of discipleship as it applies to both Jews and Gentiles, distinguishing between the old life and the new.

The first three chapters of Paul's Epistle to the Ephesians should be considered the foundation of Pauline theology by which the rest of his epistles are interpreted.

He began in chapter 1 by laying out the terms of distinction between Israel—the Jewish people as represented by the apostles of the Jewish community of disciples—and the nations—strangers to the covenants of promise, without hope and without God in the world. He then demonstrated how the Gentile disciples of the Messiah had crossed over from that hopeless and godless place to be brought near, past the dividing wall of partition that once separated Israel from the nations, to become fellow heirs with Israel, like redeemed slaves, set free by the Son and elevated to the status of sonship to share in the citizenship of the kingdom.

Moreover, he indicated that this redemption of people from the nations was actually God's whole plan all along. From the beginning, God's eternal purpose was the redemption of the nations. The redemption and calling of Israel was only a necessary precursor to this ultimate objective—the redemption of humanity. As Paul delivered this discourse, he presented deep, spiritual, esoteric ideas that have close analogs in Jewish mysticism. He spoke of the indwelling of the Messiah within each of his disciples; the body of Messiah of which each disciple is a member, forming a collective entity; and the fullness of God, which is vested into the Messiah and thereby into the body of the Messiah. These inspiring and cosmic ideas about the spiritual realities involved in Yeshua-faith should utterly transcend human concerns over caste, class, status, prestige, rank, race, and gender. We are all members of one body, each body part has a different purpose, the Messiah dwells in each individual, and God fills the Messiah, all in all.

After having presented an entire discourse on Jewish and Gentile identity in Messiah, which concludes at the end of chapter 3, the Epistle to the Ephesians makes an abrupt shift, moving away from the realm of the theological and the mystical to start a new discussion on the practical ramifications of the first three chapters. It reminds me of something a disciple of Rabbi Levi Yitzchak of Berditchev once said when asked why he had become a Chasid. He said, "Rabbi Levi teaches halachah as if it is mysticism, and he teaches mysticism as if it is musar." Likewise, beginning in chapter 4, Paul's epistle descends now from the lofty and ethereal to the practical and the personal.

What Would a Disciple Do?

> I therefore, a prisoner for the Lord, urge you to walk in a manner worthy of the calling to which you have been called, with all humility and gentleness, with patience, bearing with one another in love, eager to maintain the unity of the Spirit in the bond of peace. (Ephesians 4:1-3)

Paul referred to himself as "a prisoner for the Master" because he wrote the epistle while in chains awaiting trial, presumably in Rome. He asked the Gentile disciples in Ephesus to "walk in a manner worthy of the calling to which you have been called." This refers to the "calling" to follow Yeshua as a disciple, even as he said to his first disciples, "Follow me, and I will make you fishers of men." The "calling" language also reminds us of Paul's rule for all the assemblies:

> Was anyone at the time of his call already circumcised? Let him not seek to remove the marks of circumcision. Was anyone at the time of his call uncircumcised? Let him not seek circumcision ... So, brothers, in whatever condition each was called, there let him remain with God. (1 Corinthians 7:18, 24)

At this point, however, Paul urges us to conduct our lives in a manner worthy of a disciple of Yeshua. This verse is a good rule of thumb for life, similar to the oft-invoked maxim, "What would Jesus do?" In this case, the question we should ask ourselves, in every decision, large and small, and in every interaction with one another and with other human beings, is simply, "What would a disciple of Yeshua do?" That's the manner worthy of your calling, and it's primarily about how we interact with one another, exhibiting a spirit of humility, gentleness, patience, putting up with the failings of others "in love," and being concerned about keeping the peace with one another, which he refers to as "the unity of the Spirit."

What does he mean by "the unity of the Spirit"? This refers to the unity of the spiritual bond that disciples of Yeshua share with one another as members of the spiritual body of Messiah, a unity created by the investment of God's Spirit within us. When we divide from one another, we separate ourselves from that spiritual unity. When there are factions and discord among the disciples of Yeshua, "the unity of the Spirit" is broken.

One Body, One Spirit

> There is one body and one Spirit—just as you were called to the one hope that belongs to your call—one Lord, one faith, one baptism, one God and Father of all, who is over all and through all and in all. (Ephesians 4:4-6)

With these words, Paul reminded the Gentile disciples that they were no longer polytheists going in different directions. Instead, they had all joined the same club and were following the same Master and worshiping the same God—"the one God."

Let's look at each one of these items in turn.

The "one body" is the spiritual body of the Messiah, which Paul described in the previous chapter as "one new man." Each disciple is like a single body part. Together, we combine to make the body of the Messiah. Yeshua himself is the head of the body.

The "one Spirit" is the Spirit of God, which connects all the disciples of Yeshua into the one body, as we have already learned.

The term "one Lord" should be read not as a circumlocution for God's name but rather as "one Master." This alludes to Yeshua's teaching to his disciples: "You are not to be called rabbi, for you have one teacher, and you are all brothers. And call no man your father on earth, for you have one Father, who is in heaven. Neither be called instructors, for you have one instructor, the Christ" (Matthew 23:8-10).

"One faith" refers to the disciple's confession and conviction that Yeshua is the promised Messiah, who was crucified and rose on the third day and will return to bring the final redemption. For that reason, the disciple casts his allegiance with King Yeshua and submits to his authority.

"One baptism" refers to immersion in the name of Yeshua, which means "in the authority of Yeshua." Immersion was a ritual to ceremonially mark entrance into the school of Yeshua's disciples. Elsewhere, Paul explains the symbolism as that of death and resurrection. When a person becomes a disciple, he or she surrenders his or her life, dying with the Messiah, so to speak, and then rising to newness of life with the Messiah. It symbolizes a spiritual transformation that happens when a person becomes a disciple of Yeshua.

The "one God and Father of all" is "the God and Father of our Lord Jesus Christ" (Ephesians 1:3).

The Apostolic Leaders

> But grace was given to each one of us according to the measure of Christ's gift. Therefore it says, "When he ascended on high he led a host of captives, and he gave gifts to men." (In saying, "He ascended," what does it mean but that he had also descended into the lower regions, the earth? He who descended is the one who also ascended far above all the heavens, that he might fill all things.) And he gave the apostles, the prophets, the evangelists, the shepherds

> and teachers, to equip the saints for the work of ministry, for building up the body of Christ. (Ephesians 4:7-12)

This passage will be explored more fully in a later chapter as it pertains to the ascension of Yeshua and deserves its own treatment. Suffice it to say that while many have understood the terms at the end of this passage to refer to offices and ministries that might exist in any local church, Paul here refers exclusively to the community of the Jewish believers, particularly the apostles and the first generation of Yeshua's disciples in Jerusalem. These are the "apostles, the prophets, the evangelists, the shepherds and teachers" who are equipping the saints for the work of ministry and for the building of the body of Messiah.

Full Stature

> Until we all attain to the unity of the faith and of the knowledge of the Son of God, to mature manhood, to the measure of the stature of the fullness of Christ. (Ephesians 4:13)

Paul says that the Jewish Yeshua community is building the body of Messiah toward the objective that the whole body of Yeshua's disciples—Jew and Gentile together—will "attain to the unity of the faith and of the knowledge of the Son of God." In other words, he's talking about his job as an apostle and what he's trying to accomplish among the Gentiles. The "unity of the faith" is their common confession about Yeshua and allegiance to him as King. "The knowledge of the Son of God" is to know the Messiah—not just knowing about him, but knowing him as one person knows another. The "mature manhood" refers back to the image of the body of the Messiah and the idea that we are all members of one metaphysical body.

However, the body of Messiah is not yet an adult. It's a child, and it has a lot of growing to do. As each member of the body grows into spiritual maturity, the metaphysical body of the Messiah on earth will do so also, as it says regarding the Master in the Gospel of Luke, "Jesus increased in wisdom and in stature and in favor with God and man" (Luke 2:52). As each disciple in the body of the Messiah develops and matures, the whole body develops and matures toward "the measure of the stature of the fullness of the Messiah."

No Longer Children

> So that we may no longer be children, tossed to and fro by the waves and carried about by every wind of doctrine, by human cunning, by craftiness in deceitful schemes. (Ephesians 4:14)

Paul warned the Ephesians against falling under the influence of teachers from outside the apostolic community, those he elsewhere referred to as "false apostles, deceitful workmen, disguising themselves as apostles of Christ" (2 Corinthians 11:13) and as "fierce wolves" (Acts 20:29). He refers to the work of ascetics, mystics, and proto-gnostics in Colossae as those who "delude you with plausible arguments" (Colossians 2:4), teaching "philosophy and empty deceit, according to human tradition, according to the elemental spirits of the world, and not according to Christ" (Colossians 2:8).

Until we obtain spiritual maturity, we remain vulnerable to the excitement of the new and the novel. Young people are notorious for trying out all sorts of things and experimenting their way through life, like the college student who changes his major three times in just as many years and burns through twice that many relationships. However, you expect a young person to grow up, mature, and settle down at a certain point.

It's not surprising to find Paul expressing frustration over the influence of other teachers on his disciples. The message of the gospel has disrupted the lives, belief systems, and worldviews of the Gentile disciples. They are still rebuilding. It reminds me of what happens when people encounter Messianic Jewish teaching. It's disruptive to the established status quo, forcing people to rethink what they thought they knew. All their assumptions are up for review. As a result, they become open to other new ideas and continue reshuffling the deck for a while. They become vulnerable to theological quackery and conspiracy theories. But you can't live like that forever. At some point, we need to grow up and take ownership of who we are and what we believe, no longer carried away by the next charismatic speaker or persuasive teacher or the next sensationalist idea.

Paul wanted his disciples to continue building their lives and communities on the foundation of the apostles and the prophets of the Jerusalem assembly, the community of disciples he represented, which to us, is the equivalent of the authority and testimony of the New Testament.

Each Part Working Properly

> Rather, speaking the truth in love, we are to grow up in every way into him who is the head, into Christ, from whom the whole body, joined and held together by every joint with which it is equipped, when each part is working properly, makes the body grow so that it builds itself up in love. (Ephesians 4:15-16)

Rather than falling into the trap of following every new sensational teacher and trend, Paul points his disciples back to apostolic authority, which, to them, represents the authority of Israel and the Jewish people in their role as a holy priesthood to the nations. The apostles are "speaking the truth in love," and in that truth, the whole body of Messiah finds nourishment for growth. Again, each individual is compared to a body part. When the body is acting according to the truth they receive from the apostles, the prophets, the evangelists, the shepherds, and the teachers of the apostolic community, it can grow together into Messiah, who remains at the head of this metaphysical body. When each part knows its job and understands its function, working properly, the body is healthy, and it grows to maturity in the love of God.

No Longer Walk as the Gentiles Do

> Now this I say and testify in the Lord, that you must no longer walk as the Gentiles do, in the futility of their minds. (Ephesians 4:17)

Since the Gentile disciples in Ephesus were part of this body and shared in this new identity in Messiah, they were obligated to separate themselves from their former way of life when they lived as idolaters. We aren't supposed to be like everybody else. Disciples of Yeshua are not supposed to be ordinary people who fit in with the rest of the world. If there's little or no difference between us and the rest of the people around us, we are walking "as the Gentiles do," that is, "in the futility of their minds."

Futility of Mind

The term "futility of mind" is related to the idea presented in the book of Ecclesiastes, "Vanity of vanities ... all is vanity." It's the same Greek word used to translate that concept in Ecclesiastes, where it refers to a materialistic worldview that encourages one to eat and drink, for tomorrow we die, to get as much out of this life as possible because there is nothing else. It's that state of mind oblivious to the spiritual dimension, the mission of the soul, relationship with God, the existence of God, reward and punishment, and future redemption. Futility of mind is about finding happiness in this world by pursuing pleasure and avoiding pain. It's the selfishness of the human ego, the fool who says in his heart, "There is no God" (Psalm 14:1).

Paul describes it this way:

> They are darkened in their understanding, alienated from the life of God because of the ignorance that is in them, due to their hardness of heart. They have become callous and have given themselves up to sensuality, greedy to practice every kind of impurity. (Ephesians 4:18-19)

That's how the world lives and behaves—ignorant of the knowledge of God, and not just ignorant, but willfully ignorant and hard of heart (a term that means "unwilling to repent"). From such a perspective, life is all about satiating the appetites, "the desires of the flesh and the desires of the eyes and pride of life" (1 John 2:16). The Gentile world is obsessed with consumerism, materialism, power, wealth, sex, and prestige. These things can never satisfy the hunger of the human soul. Paul, therefore, calls the disciples of Yeshua to separate themselves from this empty value system.

Paul's words continue today to be an apt description of the pornographic secular world around us—greedy to practice every kind of impurity, celebrating indiscretion, brazen and unblushing, without shame, constantly pushing the envelope to call evil good and to call good evil. That's not us. That's not the manner of our calling.

The New Self

> But that is not the way you learned Christ!—assuming that you have heard about him and were taught in him, as the

> truth is in Jesus, to put off your old self, which belongs to your former manner of life and is corrupt through deceitful desires, and to be renewed in the spirit of your minds, and to put on the new self, created after the likeness of God in true righteousness and holiness. (Ephesians 4:20-24)

The Gentile disciples once lived according to the futility of mind that chases vanity like a man chasing the wind, but no longer. Having received the testimony of the apostolic community, primarily through the teaching of Paul and his colleagues, the Gentile disciples gave themselves to Yeshua. They died with him, putting off their old lives of egoic materialism like a person shedding an old pair of clothes. They were resurrected with him to new life, a new self, like a person putting on a new pair of clothes.

The new clothes are "created after the likeness of God in true righteousness and holiness." The "likeness of God" is that original image of God, the heavenly Adam, in whose pattern the earthly Adam was made when he was given the task of bearing God's image in this world. Adam failed in that high calling when, in futility of mind, he pursued "deceitful desires." But now, in the Messiah, the heavenly Adam and the second Adam, humanity has a new beginning and a new chance to fulfill the mission of bearing God's image. But it's not going to work if we continue to live like the rest of the world. We need to shed the old identity, die to the self, and put on the new identity, which is the life of Messiah that he now lives in and through us.

What does that mean in practical terms?

Put Away Falsehood

> Therefore, having put away falsehood, let each one of you speak the truth with his neighbor, for we are members one of another. (Ephesians 4:25)

The old man, the egoic identity, is a liar, constantly spinning and stretching the truth or just lying to protect and aggrandize himself. He's always concerned with making himself look better in the eyes of others. But that guy is dead. Take off that identity and put on the new one.

The new self in Messiah is a person of integrity and honesty. We have no desire to deceive one another because we recognize that we share a common mutual connection as members of one body. The eye does not lie to the hand; the foot does not swindle the ear. No more lies. Lies and deceit are the language of the old man who is always looking to shield himself from criticism and make excuses for his failures. We are to regard that egoic identity, so concerned with protecting and exalting the self, as dead in Messiah. There's no need to lie to protect that person any longer. Instead, we are members one of another; that single egoic sense of self and self-protection should be subsumed into the larger metaphysical reality of connection in the body of Messiah.

Anger

> Be angry and do not sin; do not let the sun go down on your anger, and give no opportunity to the devil. (Ephesians 4:26–27)

The old man, the egoic self, is easily offended, holds grudges, and seethes with anger against anyone who crosses him. His fragile ego is always getting wounded and hurt. Don't be that guy. Take that identity off. Put on the new.

Of course, we are not perfect, and people are not perfect. We will inadvertently or advertently step on one another's feelings from time to time, and there will be cause to be offended or angry. Paul gives his readers a rule of thumb for dealing with anger: Don't sleep on it, and don't carry it into the next day. The bedtime *Shema* in the Siddur contains a similar passage in which a person makes a declaration of forgiveness for anyone who has wronged him or her in any way during the day or at any time, whether in this lifetime or another. It's a beautiful text and a beautiful prayer, in keeping with the teaching of our Master regarding forgiveness of sins. The Torah warns us not to carry a grudge but to love one's neighbor as oneself. Part of this is not letting the sun go down on one's anger. If you remain angry, you give opportunity to the accuser to accuse you before the heavenly court. If you forgive others for their trespasses, your trespasses also will be forgiven, robbing the devil of the opportunity to level an accusation against you in the heavenly court.

Theft

> Let the thief no longer steal, but rather let him labor, doing honest work with his own hands, so that he may have something to share with anyone in need. (Ephesians 4:28)

The old man, the egoic self, is a thief. In the words of the sages, he is the one who says, "What's mine is mine and what's yours is mine" (*Pirkei Avot* 5:13). He covets and wants what others have, and if he can take what belongs to others without getting caught, he'll do it. That's because his identity is not in the Spirit but the material world. He's jealous and resentful, feeling that he deserves what others have. Sure, he might keep his selfishness concealed under a veneer of piety, but the reality is that he feels as though he is being mistreated unless he gets what he wants.

He's lazy, too, always coming up with excuses about why he doesn't need to work or can't work but should instead receive a handout or some credit for effort he has not made. But in Messiah, that old thief is dead. Take off that identity and put on the new one.

The new identity in Messiah does not take what does not belong to him. Instead, the new identity labors to provide for himself and others in need. Rather than being motivated to take what does not belong to him (or her), the new person in Messiah is motivated to share what belongs to him with others. In the words of the sages, he is the person who says, "What's mine is yours, and what's yours is yours" (*Pirkei Avot* 5:13).

Corrupting Talk

> Let no corrupting talk come out of your mouths, but only such as is good for building up, as fits the occasion, that it may give grace to those who hear. (Ephesians 4:29)

The old man, the egoic self, never ceases to speak corrupting talk. "Corrupting talk" does not refer to cussing or dirty jokes. (That gets mentioned later.) "Corrupting talk" refers to *lashon hara* (evil speech)—the complaining, murmuring, and malcontent spirit that feels it must air its grievances and share its gripes with listening ears. Paul refers to this as "corrupting talk" because the sages likened it to leprosy, which corrupts the flesh.

This is how the people of the world talk. They love to tear down, criticize, and complain. They love to speak evil of others, speaking behind people's backs with slander, gossip, and malicious speech. The old man, the egoic self, draws energy and vitality for itself from corrupting talk. It tastes delicious to him, like delightful morsels. He sits in the seat of scoffers and loves nothing more than to find a listening ear upon which to vent his dissatisfaction. He will tell you everything that's wrong with everything, especially what's wrong with the community, the leadership, and other members of the assembly. But in Messiah, the old man is dead. Take off that identity and put on the new one.

The new man speaks "only such as is good for building up, as fits the occasion, that it may give grace to those who hear." The new man is constantly looking for the right word of spiritual encouragement to turn the conversation into something constructive, something good, something edifying, "as fits the occasion." Rather than looking for every opportunity to spill the venom he's been storing up inside, the new man looks for the right moment to speak a word of the Spirit.

Grieving the Spirit

> Do not grieve the Holy Spirit of God, by whom you were sealed for the day of redemption. (Ephesians 4:30)

Corrupting talk grieves the Spirit of God who is within us and among us. Paul refers to the Holy Spirit as the one "by whom you were sealed for the day of redemption." To be sealed means to be marked. A scroll with a seal bore a clay mark with an insignia belonging to the sender. To be sealed with the Spirit of God means that we bear God's impression upon our being. A seal is intended to keep a scroll closed and its contents concealed until it is delivered into the hands of the recipient. Likewise, the seal of the Spirit preserves us until the day of redemption, the future Messianic Era, when the Spirit will be poured out on all flesh. Until then, the Spirit is within us and moves among us, but we risk offending the Spirit with our corrupting talk, *lashon hara*, and relentless negativity.

It reminds me of the mitzvah of the shovel:

> Because the LORD your God walks in the midst of your camp, to deliver you and to give up your enemies before

> you, therefore your camp must be holy, so that he may not see anything indecent among you and turn away from you. (Deuteronomy 23:14)

The old man, the egoic self, loves to sit around and complain, but this grieves the Spirit of God. It's offensive to the Spirit of God, as we learn from the stories in the book of Numbers. The children of Israel murmured and complained; God heard it, and he punished them. What is it that grieves the Holy Spirit? It's the words that come out of our mouths. It's how we talk about one another and how we talk about the community in general.

The old man is dead. Put off the old identity and put on the new one. How so?

Do this:

> Let all bitterness and wrath and anger and clamor and slander be put away from you, along with all malice. Be kind to one another, tenderhearted, forgiving one another, as God in Christ forgave you. (Ephesians 4:31-32)

SERMON EIGHT:

THE ONE WHO ALSO ASCENDED

(EPHESIANS 4:7–11)

An obscure midrash about Moses is concealed behind Paul's cryptic allusion to Psalm 68 in Ephesians 4:9-10. Here's an apostolic teaching about the ascension of the Messiah that likens it to Moses ascending Mount Sinai.

What does Paul mean by saying "grace was given to each one of us according to the measure of Christ's gift" (Ephesians 4:7)? You might suppose he speaks about the forgiveness of sins—Christ's gift of grace for his disciples. If so, you would expect that the same equal measure of grace should be bestowed upon everyone. But that's not what Paul is saying. He says this grace is to be doled out "to each one of us according to the measure of Christ's gift," implying that some people receive more grace than others.

It makes sense only when we remember that the word translated as "grace" should be understood as analogous to the Hebrew term *chen*, which means "favor." In the New Testament, "grace" usually refers to the favor that Messiah found in God's eyes through the merit of his righteousness and his suffering. Because Yeshua found such an abundance of favor in God's eyes, he has ample favor to share with his disciples. His disciples, in turn, rely upon the Messiah's favor for the forgiveness of sins. That's how the theology of grace works in the New Testament.

But the word "grace" does not always have that specific theological meaning. It can also refer, as it does in Hebrew, to selective favor, which favors one person above another. That's the case here. Paul indicates that some are favored with specific spiritual gifts, tasks, and roles, and he counts himself among the favored ones.

The same terminology appears in Galatians 2 where he said that the other apostles recognized "the grace that was given to me." They concluded that Paul "should go to the Gentiles and they to the circumcised" (Galatians 2:9). He used the same term in Ephesians 3 to refer to his specific calling to work as an apostle to the Gentiles: "the stewardship of God's grace that was given to me for you" (Ephesians 3:2):

> Of this gospel I was made a minister *according to the gift of God's grace, which was given me* by the working of his power. To me, though I am the very least of all the saints, *this grace was given*, to preach to the Gentiles the unsearchable riches of Christ. (Ephesians 3:7-8, emphasis mine)

In Romans 12:3, Paul again refers to his authority as an apostle to the Gentiles as "the grace given to me." This authority was given to him but not to everyone else:

> As in one body we have many members, and the members do not all have the same function, so we, though many, are one body in Christ, and individually members one of another. Having *gifts that differ according to the grace given to us*, let us use them: if prophecy, in proportion to our faith; if service, in our serving; the one who teaches, in his teaching. (Romans 12:4-7, emphasis mine)

Likewise, he says in Romans 15, "I have written to you very boldly by way of reminder, because of *the grace given me* by God to be a minister of Christ Jesus to the Gentiles" (Romans 15:15-16, emphasis mine). God favored him with this assignment as the minister to the nations, the apostle to the Gentiles.

Again, in 1 Corinthians 3, he speaks of his work as an apostle in Corinth:

> According to *the grace of God given to me*, like a skilled master builder I laid a foundation, and someone else is building upon it. (1 Corinthians 3:10, emphasis mine)

God's grace through the Messiah for the forgiveness of sins is not in view here. Paul refers instead to a specific measure of God's favor. Suffice it to say that not everyone receives this same measure of God's favor. Paul felt special because he had been singled out for a specific role, a specific task within the body of Messiah. God had favored him with this mission.

In Ephesians 4:7, he says, "But grace was given to each one of us according to the measure of Christ's gift." Again, this is not the general grace we find in Messiah for the forgiveness of sins. Instead, it's the specific favor bestowed upon an individual. What is that gift? We'll see what it is a few verses later, but first, Paul takes us on a brief midrash about the ascension of the Messiah and the Festival of Shavu'ot.

Psalm 68 and Shavu'ot

> Therefore it says, "When he ascended on high he led a host of captives, and he gave gifts to men." (Ephesians 4:8)

The quotation comes from Psalm 68, a psalm that Jewish interpretation associates directly with the first Shavu'ot at Mount Sinai. In the Apostolic Era, Psalm 68 and Psalm 29 were considered Psalms of the Day for the Festival of Shavu'ot.

We spend a long time preparing for Shavu'ot. During the forty-nine days of the Counting of the Omer that lead up to Shavu'ot, we recite Psalm 67, a harvest psalm containing forty-nine Hebrew words and predicting that God's salvation will extend to all nations. Then, on the day of Shavu'ot itself, we read Psalm 68, which makes allusions to the story of the revelation of the Torah at Mount Sinai. I believe the main point of Psalm 67 being read throughout the forty-nine days of the Omer is to point us to Psalm 68 for the day of Shavu'ot.

Tongues and Torches

Jewish tradition has richly embellished certain passages from Psalm 68 to connect them with the giving of the Torah on Shavu'ot. For example, Psalm 68:12(11) says, "The Lord gives the word; the evangelists (*HaMevasrot,*) are a great host" (my translation). The word I'm translating as "evangelists" is the Hebrew word *Mevasrot,* which literally means "proclaimers of good news." The Talmud interprets this same verse to refer to the giving of the Torah in every language: "Every single word that went forth from the Almighty divided into seventy languages" (b.*Shabbat* 88b). Thus Jewish tradition ties Psalm 68 with the story of the giving of the Torah on Shavu'ot, and apostolic tradition ties it with the story of the giving of the Spirit on Shavu'ot when the LORD gave "the word," and the disciples of Yeshua who were gathered in the Temple proclaimed the good news in every language.

Psalm 68:18 is also understood to refer to the descent of God upon Mount Sinai. It says, "The chariots of God are twice ten thousand, thousands upon thousands; the Lord is among them; Sinai is now in the sanctuary" (Psalm 68:18[17]). This is also why the story of the chariot in Ezekiel 1 became the haftarah (the portion read from the prophets) for Shavu'ot.

Ezekiel's vision of the chariot also speaks of "the appearance of torches moving to and fro among the living creatures" (Ezekiel 1:13), alluding to the passage in Exodus that says, "All the people saw the voices and the torches" (Exodus 20:18, my translation). The apostles experienced this phenomenon as "tongues of fire [that] appeared to them and rested on each one of them. And they were all filled with the Holy Spirit and began to speak in other tongues as the Spirit gave utterance" (Acts 2:3–4). So, as you can see, there's a great deal of Shavu'ot tradition invested into this psalm.

The Ascent of Moses

Several other Shavu'ot traditions are tied to Psalm 68, including a story about the specific verse Paul quotes in Ephesians 4. Here's what the verse says:

> You ascended on high, leading a host of captives in your train and receiving gifts among men, even among the rebellious, that the LORD God may dwell there. (Psalm 68:19[18])

Jewish interpretation explains that this verse describes Moses' ascent of Mount Sinai. When Moses went up the mountain to get the

Torah, he ascended into the heavenly Temple. The supernal heights of the dwelling place of God had descended to the top of the mountain. As Moses stepped onto the top of the mountain, he found himself in heaven. However, when the angels saw a mortal man of flesh and blood standing among them, they objected to his presence there, and they objected to the idea that the holy Torah should be put into the hands of human beings:

> When Moses ascended on High to receive the Torah, the ministering angels said before the Holy One, Blessed be He: Master of the Universe, what is one born of a woman doing here among us? The Holy One, Blessed be He, said to them: He came to receive the Torah. The angels said before Him: The Torah is a hidden treasure that was concealed by you 974 generations before the creation of the world, and you seek to give it to flesh and blood? "What is man that You are mindful of him and the son of man that You think of him?" (Psalm 8:5). Rather, "God our Lord, how glorious is Your name in all the earth that Your majesty is placed above the heavens" (Psalm 8:2). The Holy One, Blessed be He, said to Moses: You answer them. (b.*Shabbat* 88b)

Moses answers the angels by pointing out that the Torah is not given to angels. Commandments such as "remember the exodus when I brought you out of Egypt," and "honor your father and mother," and "rest on the Sabbath," and "You shall not murder, you shall not commit adultery, you shall not steal" do not pertain to angels. Moses wins the argument and prevails over the angels, fulfilling what it says in Psalm 8:5, "You have made him a little lower than the [angels] and crowned him with glory and honor." (The apostles associated the same psalm with the ascension and exaltation of Messiah.) In the Talmud, the story continues:

> Immediately, each and every one of the angels became an admirer of Moses and gave some gift to him, as it is stated: "You ascended on high, leading a host of captives in your train and receiving gifts [for] men, even among the rebellious, that the LORD God may dwell there" (Psalm 68:19[18]). That is to say, "In reward for the fact that they called you a mere man, you took gifts from the angels." (b.*Shabbat* 88b–89a)

In this explanation, the "host of captives" that Moses took refers to the five books of the Torah. The "gifts for men" he received are the commandments of the Torah along with spiritual secrets and spiritual gifts from the angels, which exist today as the esoteric mystical tradition. The Targum on the Psalms paraphrases the verse to say, "You ascended to the heavens, O prophet Moses; you captured captives, you taught the words of Torah, you gave gifts to the sons of men, and even the stubborn who are converted turn in repentance, and the glorious presence of the LORD God abides upon them."

Ascent of the Messiah

This explanation of the verse should be compared to a midrash on Deuteronomy 30:11–14 that explains that since Moses had already ascended to heaven to retrieve the Torah on behalf of the Jewish people, no one should say that the Torah is too difficult or too far off. It's not up in heaven; it's not beyond the sea. Instead, Moses had already done the hard work to bring the Torah near: "The word is very near you. It is in your mouth and in your heart, so that you can do it" (Deuteronomy 30:14). Paul invokes that same explanation in Romans 10:

> The righteousness based on faith says, "Do not say in your heart, 'Who will ascend into heaven?" (that is, to bring Christ down) or "Who will descend into the abyss?" (that is, to bring Christ up from the dead). But what does it say? "The word is near you, in your mouth and in your heart" (that is, the word of faith that we proclaim); because, if you confess with your mouth that Jesus is Lord and believe in your heart that God raised him from the dead, you will be saved. (Romans 10:6–9)

In other words, no one needs to ascend into the heavens to bring the Messiah down to earth or descend into Sheol to bring him up from the dead because God has already accomplished these things through Yeshua of Nazareth. The righteousness of God has already been obtained by him, just as Moses had already obtained the Torah.

In Ephesians 4, Paul makes a similar, but not identical, comparison between Moses and Messiah. Moses ascended into the heavens, defeated the angels, took the Torah captive, received gifts from the angels, and then descended to bestow these gifts upon human beings. Likewise, Messiah, who was "a little lower than the angels," has ascended to heaven to be "crowned with glory and honor" (Psalm 8:5; cf. Hebrews 2:7-9). He has taken captive spiritual authorities and has been seated "far above all rule and authority and power and dominion, and above every name that is named" (Ephesians 1:21) to fill all in all. He has received gifts to be distributed among men. Like Moses, he bestows these gifts upon human beings. Paul referred to these gifts when he said, "Grace was given to each one of us according to the measure of Christ's gift" (Ephesians 4:7).

Now we finally have enough information to read and interpret the rest of the passage.

He Who Descended

> In saying, "He ascended," what does it mean but that he had also descended into the lower regions, the earth? He who descended is the one who also ascended far above all the heavens, that he might fill all things. (Ephesians 4:9-10)

There are three valid ways to understand "He also descended into the lower regions, the earth." The first is in reference to his incarnation, as it says in John 3, "No one has ascended into heaven except he who descended from heaven, the Son of Man" (John 3:13).

The second is in reference to his death and burial, which is elsewhere referred to as a descent into Sheol and is paralleled in Romans 10.

However, many scholars suggest a third possibility. They believe that it should be understood as the descent of the Holy Spirit on the day of Shavu'ot. Yeshua is likened to Moses, who ascended to plunder heaven and acquire the gift of the Torah. Moses descended back to earth with the Torah and gave it to human beings. Likewise, Yeshua ascended to get the gift of the Spirit, and through the outpouring of the Spirit, he descended, so to speak, into the lower regions of the earth to bestow that gift on the day of Shavu'ot when the Holy Spirit was poured out on his disciples. According to that idea, one would translate the passage like this:

> In saying, "He ascended," it implies that he also had to descend [back] to the lower regions of the earth. He who

descended [to bestow the Spirit] is the same one who also ascended far above all the heavens, that he might fill all things. (Ephesians 4:9–10, paraphrased)

I don't know which interpretation best fits what Paul is getting at, but I am sure that the ascent of the Messiah refers to his resurrection from the dead and his ascent to the right hand of God. I am also confident that the gifts he obtained in heaven and bestows upon human beings are referred to here as the "grace given to each one of us according to the measure of Christ's gift" (Ephesians 4:7). What is that gift? It's the apostles, the prophets, the evangelists, the shepherds, and teachers:

> He gave the apostles, the prophets, the evangelists, the shepherds and teachers, to equip the saints for the work of ministry, for building up the body of Christ, until we all attain to the unity of the faith and of the knowledge of the Son of God, to mature manhood, to the measure of the stature of the fullness of Christ. (Ephesians 4:11–13)

This passage parallels an earlier one: "You are fellow citizens with the saints and members of the household of God, *built on the foundation of the apostles and prophets,* Christ Jesus himself being the cornerstone" (Ephesians 2:19–20, emphasis mine). In other words, Paul is speaking about the apostolic community of Jewish believers, the original apostles and the prophets of the Jerusalem community. They are the foundation. As an apostle, Paul represented this community of Yeshua's Jewish disciples to the Gentiles in Ephesus, fulfilling the role of Israel's priestly duty of ministering to the nations, "the priestly service of the gospel of God, so that the offering of the Gentiles may be acceptable, sanctified by the Holy Spirit" (Romans 15:16).

This is the "grace" that was "given to each one of us according to the measure of Christ's gift" (Ephesians 4:7). Those designated as apostles received that calling as a gift of God's favor. The Messiah obtained it for them as a spiritual gift wrested from heaven. Likewise, with the prophets, the evangelists, the shepherds, and teachers. In the next chapter, we will look at each office and see how Paul uses these titles to describe the leadership of Jerusalem's community of Jewish disciples.

They are the "gift of Messiah" to human beings, filled with the Spirit on the day of Shavu'ot. The apostolic community attributed the outpouring of the Spirit on Shavu'ot to the ascension of Yeshua. Elisha did not receive a double portion of his teacher Elijah's spirit until Elijah ascended. It all started on Shavu'ot, the day God poured out his Spirit on the disciples of Messiah: the apostles, the prophets, the evangelists, the pastors, and teachers. Before his ascension, Yeshua told his disciples, "I tell you the truth: it is to your advantage that I go away, for if I do not go away, the Helper will not come to you. But if I go, I will send him to you" (John 16:7).

Under the authority and instruction of those original apostles, prophets, evangelists, pastors, and teachers, the whole body of Messiah grew, the Messiah himself at the head. We, too, are members of the same body, tracing our spiritual ancestry back to those disciples until we all attain to the unity of the faith and of the knowledge of the Son of God, to mature manhood, to the measure of the stature of the fullness of the Messiah.

SERMON NINE:
THE FIVEFOLD GIFT
(EPHESIANS 4:11–12)

It is commonly taught that Ephesians 4:11 presents fivefold gifts of ministry for leadership and service in a congregation. A post-supersessionist perspective on the passage comes to a completely different conclusion.

In the last chapter we worked through Ephesians 4:7–11, in which the Apostle Paul presents himself to the Gentile disciples living in Ephesus as an emissary and representative of the Jewish people bringing the message of Messiah's revelation to the nations. He sees himself and his colleagues as missionaries (so to speak) acting in accordance with Israel's national destiny to be a priestly people among the nations and a light to the nations. He says regarding himself and his colleagues, "Grace was given to each one of us according to the measure of the Messiah's gift." (Ephesians 4:7)

"Grace" here refers to the favor that Paul and the other apostles enjoyed as official emissaries for the Messiah. The Messiah's gift is the anointing of the Holy Spirit upon them, a gift that Yeshua obtained through his ascension to the right hand of the Father. The gifting is the Spirit of God that rested upon Yeshua while he was among his disciples and was subsequently invested into those upon whom he poured this Spirit out.

Two similar stories from the Hebrew Scriptures illustrate the idea. In the Torah, Moses asks God to help him with the task of leadership. He selects seventy elders. The Torah says, "Then the LORD came down in the cloud and spoke to him, and took some of the Spirit that was on him and put it on the seventy elders. And as soon as the Spirit rested on them, they prophesied" (Numbers 11:25). In this way, the Spirit of the LORD that rested upon Moses was shared with the elders.

They formed the first Sanhedrin, and they represent the beginning of the chain of spiritual authority that extends through the ages all the way to the prophets and the men of the great assembly, to the sages, the Sanhedrin, the establishment at Yavneh, the Jewish courts, and to the rabbinic authority today. This spiritual authority began with the Spirit of God that rested upon Moses, but it was transferred thereafter through the laying on of hands, through discipleship, through the office, and through the title. This is why Yeshua ascribed spiritual authority to them, saying, "The scribes and the Pharisees sit on Moses' seat" (Matthew 23:2). That's not the same as claiming that scribes and Pharisees are inerrant; it's simply a concession that their authority has a spiritual basis. God's Spirit is involved in shaping Judaism and has been since the beginning.

Another similar story is that of Elijah and his disciples. When the Prophet Elijah was about to ascend, his disciple Elisha requested a double portion of the Spirit of God that rested upon Elijah. He asked Elijah to bequeath it to him. This means that all of Elijah's disciples (the school of the sons of the prophets) received a portion of the Spirit that rested upon their teacher Elijah. Elisha wanted twice the amount that the others would receive. Elijah told Elisha that the request would be granted him if he saw him ascend. Elisha saw him ascend, and the Spirit that was upon Elijah came to rest upon Elisha. God's Spirit rested upon the prophets.

The story of Yeshua's ascension and the outpouring of the Spirit on Shavu'ot uses some of the same terminology:

> Therefore it says, "When he ascended on high he led a host of captives, and he gave gifts to men." In saying, "He ascended," what does it mean but that he had also descended into the lower regions, the earth? He who descended is the one who also ascended far above all the heavens, that he might fill all things. (Ephesians 4:8–10)

The gift that he gave was the outpouring of the Holy Spirit upon the disciples who were gathered in the Temple to celebrate the Festival of Shavu'ot:

> He gave the apostles, the prophets, the evangelists, the shepherds and teachers, to equip the saints for the work of ministry, for building up the body of Christ. (Ephesians 4:11-12)

If you have ever heard this passage taught from a pulpit before, you might be familiar with the concept of "the fivefold gifts." The idea is that God distributes these various roles and titles among an assembly of disciples. Some people receive the calling to be apostles, which may be a type of church-planter or a missionary. Some receive the calling to be prophets, which may be understood as one with the gift of prophecy or as one who preaches with a prophetic type of authority. Some receive the calling to be evangelists, usually understood as those most adept at persuading others to become believers, sometimes in the context of large meetings to present the gospel, like the Billy Grahams of the world. Some are called to be shepherds, that is, pastors who care for and tend the local community. Some are called to be teachers, that is, Bible teachers. Someone who feels called to ministry just needs to figure out which job description God has best suited them to fulfill.

I will not dispute that there is a division of labor like this in the assembly of Messiah. Compare Romans 12 and 1 Corinthians 12, both of which speak of the body of the Messiah and the variety of gifts at work among its members—spiritual gifts that have been bestowed upon the disciples of Yeshua. In one passage, Paul illustrates the point by naming various titles, roles, offices, positions, and gifts within the assembly of Messiah:

> You are the body of Christ and individually members of it. And God has appointed in the [community of Messiah] first apostles, second prophets, third teachers, then miracles, then gifts of healing, helping, administrating, and various kinds of tongues. Are all apostles? Are all prophets? Are all teachers? Do all work miracles? Do all possess gifts of healing? Do all speak with tongues? Do all interpret? (1 Corinthians 12:27-30)

But that general gifting of the whole body is not what Paul is talking about in Ephesians 4:11-12. Instead, his point here must be understood in the context of what he had written previously: "You are fellow citizens with the saints and members of the household of God, *built on the foundation of the apostles and prophets*, Christ Jesus himself being the cornerstone" (Ephesians 2:19-20, emphasis mine). In other words, he's speaking about the apostolic community of Jewish believers, the original apostles, and the prophets of the Jerusalem community. They are the foundation. As an apostle, Paul represented this community of Yeshua's Jewish disciples to the Gentiles in Ephesus, fulfilling the role of Israel's priestly duty of reaching to the nations, "the priestly service of the gospel of God, so that the offering of the Gentiles may be acceptable, sanctified by the Holy Spirit" (Romans 15:16).

Some English Bibles obscure this point by omitting the definite articles and implying that these five titles are simply general categories distributed among all believers:

> He gave some as apostles, and some as prophets, and some as evangelists, and some as pastors and teachers. (Ephesians 4:11 NASB)

Correctly translated, each one should have a definite article ("the"). The gift that the Messiah took from heaven and gave to human beings is "the apostles, the prophets, the evangelists, the shepherds and teachers" (Ephesians 4:11). The definite article is significant because it implies that we are not speaking about general categories. Not just any apostles, prophets, evangelists, shepherds, and teachers are in view here, but specifically, the ones anointed and appointed from the Jerusalem assembly of Yeshua's original disciples. This passage speaks of the ones upon whom the Spirit was poured out on Shavu'ot and those appointed by them.

As we see in 1 Corinthians 12:28, Paul even ranks them: "God has appointed in the [community of Yeshua] first apostles, second prophets, third teachers."

The Apostles

> And he gave the apostles ... (Ephesians 4:11)

Not just anyone can be called an apostle. It's a measure of grace given to only a few. To be favored by God as an apostle, one had to have been one of those disciples of Yeshua to whom he appeared during the forty days between his resurrection and his ascension. During those forty days, he commissioned the apostles to serve as his witnesses, testifying to his resurrection. Simon Peter described the apostles as follows:

> "[The risen Yeshua did not appear] to all the people but to us who had been chosen by God as witnesses, who ate and drank with him after he rose from the dead. And he commanded us to preach to the people and to testify that he is the one appointed by God to be judge of the living and the dead." (Acts 10:40-43)

There were more than just twelve apostles. According to Paul, the Master appeared to more than five hundred of his disciples:

> He appeared to Cephas, then to the twelve. Then he appeared to more than five hundred brothers at one time, most of whom are still alive, though some have fallen asleep. Then he appeared to James, then to all the apostles. (1 Corinthians 15:5-7)

There seems to have been a ranking of authority in the Jerusalem community. James and the brothers of the Master stood at the top, stewarding the Master's chair at the head of the assembly. The three of the inner circle, Simon Peter and the two sons of Zebedee, James and John, are next. Mary Magdalene was over the women. The rest of the twelve were one rung lower, and after them, the seventy. After them come the rest of those men and women who saw the risen Master, ate and drank with him after he rose from the dead and received his commission to testify.

Last but not least comes Paul himself. He refers to himself as an apostle "untimely born" only because the Messiah did not appear to him until after the ascension. He says, "Last of all, as to one untimely born, he appeared also to me" (1 Corinthians 15:8).

All the apostles functioned as Yeshua's official representatives. They had the authority to speak in his name and on his behalf. That was especially true of the original disciples, the twelve and the seventy, who were all present on the day of Shavu'ot for the outpouring of the Spirit. Paul refers to them as the "chief apostles" (2 Corinthians 12:11). They were entrusted with Yeshua's teaching and his message, and they had the authority to perform miracles in his name, as it says regarding the Twelve, "[He] gave them authority over unclean spirits, to cast them out, and to heal every disease and every affliction" (Matthew 10:1). He told them, "Whoever believes in me will also do the works that I do; and greater works than these will he do, because I am going to the Father. Whatever you ask in my name, this I will do, that the Father may be glorified in the Son" (John 14:12-13). But the signs and miracles were not limited only to the chief apostles. While living in Ephesus, Paul wrote to the Corinthians, saying, "I was not at all inferior to these [chief]-apostles, even though I am nothing. The signs of a true apostle were performed among you with utmost patience, with signs and wonders and mighty works" (2 Corinthians 12:11-12).

Nevertheless, it should now be clear that "the apostles" were a specific group of Jewish believers in Yeshua—his disciples. Many of them were present in the Temple on the day of Shavu'ot when the Holy Spirit was poured out upon them. Paul said that "grace was given to each one of us according to the measure of Christ's gift" (Ephesians 4:7). To be favored as one of the apostles was a special measure of God's grace—Messiah's gift.

The Prophets

> He gave the apostles, the prophets ... (Ephesians 4:11)

Paul here refers not to the Old Testament prophets but to "the prophets" of the Jerusalem assembly—men and women from among the disciples of Yeshua invested with the gift of prophecy. The early apostolic community had a special class of prophets, Jewish men and women who had been commissioned by the Messiah as prophets in fulfillment of the words, "in those days I will pour out my Spirit, and they shall prophesy" (Acts 2:18). The Prophet Agabus and his colleagues, of whom it says, "Now in these days prophets came down from Jerusalem to Antioch" (Acts 11:27), were among them. They predicted a famine that was about to come upon the land, one that other Jewish historical accounts corroborate. It happened just as the prophets of the Yeshua community predicted.

We know that the spirit of prophecy was very much at work in the first generation of Yeshua's disciples. We see it in the book of Acts, but I also think of the story about the flight to Pella. A tradition of the early Jewish believers explains that before the First Jewish-Roman War, a prophecy in the Jerusalem community of Yeshua-followers issued a warning to flee the city and withdraw to the Transjordanian Decapolis city of Pella. The community received a sign on Shavu'ot that year, and they heeded the warning. They withdrew from Jerusalem and relocated to Pella. When the Jewish Revolt broke out later that year, the Gentiles in all but a few of the Decapolis cities turned against their Jewish populations and slaughtered them. Pella was among those where the Jewish community survived.

Prophets don't always predict the future. To prophesy means to speak on behalf of a deity; while that might include a prediction, it also might not. The gift of prophecy is not limited only to people officially commissioned as prophets. Not everyone with the gift of prophecy qualified for this role. Paul rhetorically asks, "Are all apostles? Are all prophets?" (1 Corinthians 12:29). To be favored as one of the prophets was a special measure of God's grace.

Other disciples who joined the community later, as well as individuals among the Gentile communities of Yeshua's disciples, also received the gift of prophecy, but Paul does not include them in this specific designation of "the prophets."

The Evangelists

> He gave the apostles, the prophets, the evangelists ... (Ephesians 4:11)

"The evangelists" here refers not to just anyone with a knack for winning converts and persuading people to believe in Yeshua. It refers to the proclaimers of the good news from the Jerusalem community of Yeshua's original disciples. The title "evangelist" seems to be derived from Psalm 68:12(11), which says, "The Lord gives the word; the evangelists are a great host" (my translation). As I explained above, the psalm (which is the Psalm for the Day of Shavu'ot) uses the word *Mevasrot*, which literally means "proclaimers of good news." The Talmud interprets this same verse to refer to the giving of the Torah in every language: "Every single word that went forth from the Almighty divided into seventy languages" (b.*Shabbat* 88b).

The book of Acts refers to the evangelists as those who went out from Jerusalem proclaiming the Master:

> Now those who were scattered because of the persecution that arose over Stephen traveled as far as Phoenicia and Cyprus and Antioch, speaking the word to no one except Jews. But there were some of them, men of Cyprus and Cyrene, who on coming to Antioch spoke to the Hellenists also, preaching the Lord Jesus. And the hand of the Lord was with them, and a great number who believed turned to the Lord. (Acts 11:19-21)

Chief disciples of the apostles carried the title "evangelist" as well. For example, the twelve apostles appointed seven servants, "men of good repute, full of the Spirit and of wisdom" (Acts 6:3). The apostles laid hands on them, commissioning them to act on their behalf as apostles of the apostles. These included Philip, who is referred to as "Philip the evangelist" (Acts 21:8). Likewise, Paul appointed Timothy as his agent over the assembly in Ephesus, and he said to him, "Do the work of an evangelist, fulfill your ministry" (2 Timothy 4:5). The evangelists are the direct agents of the apostles.

That's not to say that other disciples who joined the community later, including some disciples among the Gentile communities, did not also evangelize and proclaim the good news, but Paul does not include them in this specific designation of "the evangelists." The original evangelists were those favored disciples of Yeshua who received the Spirit on Shavu'ot in Acts 2 and went out from Jerusalem, or, as in Timothy's case, those who became direct agents of the apostles.

The Shepherds and Teachers

> He gave the apostles, the prophets, the evangelists, the shepherds and teachers ... (Ephesians 4:11)

The shepherds and teachers are others from among the original disciples of Yeshua, probably also among those who received the outpouring of the Spirit on Shavu'ot. This is where we get the title "pastor," which literally means "shepherd." However, the original shepherds and teachers were not just anyone with the gift of pastoring or teaching; they were Jewish disciples of Yeshua commissioned to teach and shepherd the community of Yeshua, as when Yeshua said to Simon Peter, "Feed my sheep." Apparently, Paul had in mind specific Jewish believers acting in these roles as representatives of the Jewish believers in Jerusalem. He probably had in mind his own colleagues and traveling companions. That's not to say that other disciples who joined the community later, including some disciples among the Gentile communities, did not also become pastors and teachers, but Paul does not include them in this specific designation.

None of these categories are mutually exclusive. It's possible to belong to several. Paul might have considered himself as belonging to all five categories. Both Paul and Barnabas seem to qualify as apostles, prophets, and teachers. We also meet Simeon Niger, Lucius of Cyrene (Luke), and Manasseh, who were teachers and prophets in the community of disciples that formed at Antioch (Acts 13:1).

To recapitulate, Paul tells the Gentiles living in Ephesus that God favored specific individuals from the original community of Jewish disciples by designating them with authority to serve the body of Messiah as the apostles, the prophets, the evangelists, the shepherds, and the teachers. Those are the five. Contrary to the traditional view, this passage does not refer to fivefold ministry gifts generally distributed among Yeshua followers such that every assembly of Yeshua might expect to have some who are apostles, some who are prophets, some who are evangelists, and some who are shepherds and teachers. That seems self-evident regarding the category of apostles, but Lionel Windsor's commentary *Reading Ephesians & Colossians after Supersessionism* makes a compelling case that all five categories are best understood as descriptions of the offices of specific individuals within the original community of Jewish disciples—not general giftings to be anticipated in all Yeshua communities.

Windsor emphasizes the continuity between the first part of Ephesians and this section. Remember that the first three chapters of Ephesians lay out Paul's teachings about the distinction between Israel and the nations, between the Jewish disciples and the Gentile disciples. This discussion of the five offices naturally continues that discussion in that these five offices—the apostles, the prophets, the evangelists, the shepherds, and teachers—represent the Jewish community and the Jewish religion to the nations. They are fulfilling their role of being a light to the nations, introducing the world to the one God, the God of Israel, and his Messiah. They are the Messiah's gift to human beings, a gift he obtained by ascending like Moses into heaven and taking it from the angels. Paul counts himself among that select group of chosen ones when he says, "Grace was given to each one of us according to the measure of Christ's gift" (Ephesians 4:7). They represent Israel and the Jewish people to the nations. It's their job to equip the saints for the work of ministry, for building up the body of Messiah.

SERMON TEN:
A LAMP THAT LIGHTS MANY LAMPS
(EPHESIANS 4:11–14)

We discover how the gift of the Holy Spirit was transmitted through the disciples of Yeshua, through the apostles, the prophets, the evangelists, teachers, and pastors who first received it during the outpouring that took place on Shavu'ot.

The flame of a single candle can light many candles without suffering any diminishment of its own brightness. Rashi cites a midrash on Numbers 11:17 that uses this illustration to describe how the Spirit of the LORD that rested upon Moses could be transferred to the seventy elders without diminishing Moses' own spiritual endowment:

> To what can Moses be compared at that moment? He was like to a light that is placed in a candlestick at which everybody lights his lamps and yet its illuminating power is not the least diminished. (Rashi on Numbers 11:17, cf. *Sifre Bamidbar* 93)

> Just as a man who kindles a thousand flames from one does not lessen the first in communicating light to the others, so God did not diminish the grace imparted to Moses by the fact that he communicated of it to the seventy. (Theodoret)

An oil lamp can light many oil lamps without its own flame suffering diminishment. Likewise, when it came time to appoint a successor, God told Moses, "Take Joshua the son of Nun, a man in whom is the Spirit, and lay your hand on him" (Numbers 27:18). Moses did so, and he transferred the Spirit and authority God had invested in him to Joshua through the laying on of hands.

This idea of transmitting the Spirit of God is pertinent to the story of the ascension, the story of the outpouring of the Spirit, and also to our studies in Ephesians 4 regarding the gift that Messiah attained in his ascension: "The apostles, the prophets, the evangelists, the shepherds and teachers, to equip the saints for the work of ministry" (Ephesians 4:11-12).

I want to test a hypothesis about this text.

> Hypothesis: The gift of the Holy Spirit was transmitted through the disciples of Yeshua, through the apostles, the prophets, the evangelists, teachers, and pastors who first received it during the outpouring that took place on Shavu'ot.

The idea is that the disciples present that day on Shavu'ot to receive the outpouring of God's Spirit then became the initial vectors through which the Spirit of the LORD was transmitted to subsequent generations of Yeshua's disciples. They are "the apostles, the prophets, the evangelists, the teachers and pastors" to whom Paul refers. Like lamps lighting other lamps by passing the gift of flame from wick to wick, the apostles spread out into the world, from Jerusalem to Judea, to Samaria, and the ends of the earth, transmitting the Holy Spirit. To test the hypothesis, we will examine a series of ten incidents involving the transmission of the Holy Spirit.

Incident One: Immersion of Yeshua

> When Jesus was baptized, immediately he went up from the water, and behold, the heavens were opened to him, and he saw the Spirit of God descending like a dove and coming to rest on him; and behold, a voice from heaven said, "This is my beloved Son, with whom I am well pleased." (Matthew 3:16-17)

Yeshua himself is the initial flame that ignites the other lamps. The Spirit of God descended to rest upon him in full measure at his immersion in the Jordan. That's not to say that he was the first person ever to receive an endowment of God's Spirit, but all previous prophets, seers, poets, craftsmen, sages, kings, and holy men received only a portion of that endowment. From the least to the greatest of them, they received only a measure of the Spirit of God, whereas Yeshua received the Spirit without measure. God lavished his Spirit upon his Son as if to say, "You are my Son in whom my Spirit delights. Today I have begotten you."

Before his ascension, Yeshua bequeathed the Spirit of God that rested upon him to his disciples. On the eve of his ascension, he appeared in their midst in Jerusalem, and he said to them, "'Peace be with you. As the Father has sent me, even so I am sending you.' And when he had said this, he breathed on them and said to them, 'Receive the Holy Spirit'" (John 20:21-22). He told them, "John baptized with water, but you will be baptized with the Holy Spirit not many days from now" (Acts 1:5). He commissioned them as witnesses and apostles, saying, "You will receive power when the Holy Spirit has come upon you, and you will be my witnesses in Jerusalem and in all Judea and Samaria, and to the end of the earth" (Acts 1:8).

Incident Two: Outpouring in the Temple

> When the day of Pentecost arrived, they were all together in one place. And suddenly there came from heaven a sound like a mighty rushing wind, and it filled the entire house where they were sitting. And divided tongues as of fire appeared to them and rested on each one of them. And they were all filled with the Holy Spirit and began to speak in other tongues as the Spirit gave them utterance. (Acts 2:1-4)

Ten days after the ascension, on the day of Shavu'ot, something extraordinary happened. Like a lamp that lights many lamps, Yeshua distributed the Spirit of God that rested upon him among his disciples. That transference of Spirit can be compared to the story of Elijah and Elisha, where the disciples of the prophets declared, "The spirit of Elijah rests on Elisha" (2 Kings 2:15). The outpouring of the Spirit upon the apostles signified the beginning of a new era.

This by no means indicates that the Holy Spirit had never before been active. New Testament readers sometimes mistakenly assume that before the outpouring of the Spirit in Acts 2, nobody experienced the Holy Spirit. This is a troubling premise. It implies that Christians have greater spiritual endowment than men like Abraham, Moses, David, and the prophets. Abraham spoke with God, and God spoke to him. Moses was the greatest of the prophets. David received the Holy Spirit when Samuel anointed him, and he spoke by the Holy Spirit when writing the Psalms. All the prophets prophesied by means of the Holy Spirit, the "Spirit of Messiah within them" (1 Peter 1:11). It would be arrogant to suppose that believers in Yeshua have the Spirit and such men did not.

On the contrary, the Holy Spirit of God was active in the lives of men and women long before the days of the apostles. The term "Holy Spirit" is merely a circumlocution for the Old Testament term "Spirit of the LORD." God's Spirit remains active in Israel, even among people of Jewish faith who have not yet discovered the identity of the Messiah.

In that case, what was so extraordinary about the outpouring of the Holy Spirit upon the believers? What does the Gospel of John mean when it says that "the Spirit was not yet given, because Jesus was not yet glorified" (John 7:39)? The outpouring of the Spirit upon the believers refers to a unique investment of God's Spirit in that he distributed the same Spirit that had rested upon Yeshua to each of his disciples. Similarly, when Elijah ascended, his disciple Elisha received a double portion of the Holy Spirit that anointed him. After Elijah's ascension, Elisha walked in a special anointing of God's Spirit. So too, the seventy elders in Numbers 11 received a special anointing of God's Spirit that had been upon Moses. In Acts 2, the disciples of the Master received an outpouring of the Holy Spirit, a special share in the anointing of the Messiah. They are henceforth called "the body of Messiah" because the Spirit that rested upon Yeshua's human body now rests upon this corporate body of his disciples. They have become Messiah on earth, so to speak—the image of God.

A Sign of the Kingdom

Peter explains the significance of the moment in reference to the Messianic Era. He interpreted the outpouring as a fulfillment of a prophecy uttered by Joel:

> This is what was uttered through the prophet Joel: And in the last days it shall be, God declares, that I will pour out my Spirit on all flesh, and your sons and your daughters shall prophesy, and your young men shall see visions, and your old men shall dream dreams; even on my male servants and female servants in those days I will pour out my Spirit, and they shall prophesy. (Acts 2:16-18)

The prophets predicted a unique endowment of God's Spirit in the Messianic Age. "I will pour out my Spirit on all flesh," the LORD promised (Joel 2:28). The messianic outpouring of the Holy Spirit brings the exalted revelation of God that people in the kingdom will enjoy. "They shall all know me, from the least of them to the greatest" (Jeremiah 31:34).

This Messianic-era endowment of the Holy Spirit will not only reveal the knowledge of God but also will transform human beings, quenching the rebellious sin nature and inspiring obedience: "I will put my Spirit within you, and cause you to walk in my statutes and be careful to obey my rules" (Ezekiel 36:27). When John says, "the Spirit was not yet given," he alludes to these Messianic-era endowments of the Spirit.

The Down Payment

However, a problem emerges. How does the outpouring of the Spirit on a small collection of Yeshua's disciples fulfill the prophecy that predicts a universal outpouring of the Spirit on all of humanity? It doesn't. Instead, the idea is that the outpouring of the Spirit upon the disciples began a process that will culminate in the universal outpouring of the Spirit. The apostles who received the outpouring on Shavu'ot were to become the vectors of transmission that would eventually infect all of humanity with the revelation of God's Spirit.

According to John, the Spirit had not yet been given because the Messiah was not yet glorified. The glorification of the Messiah refers, on the one hand, to his resurrection and ascension, and on the other hand, to his advent in glory in the Messianic Era.

After Yeshua's resurrection and ascension, a portion of the Spirit was distributed to his disciples on Shavu'ot as a deposit against the full principal yet to be paid out in the Messianic Era. Notice how Paul explains that the Holy Spirit is given as a pledge, a guarantee, a down payment against the future outpouring of the Spirit:

> It is God who establishes us with you in Christ, and has anointed us, and who has also put his seal on us and given us his Spirit in our hearts as a guarantee. (2 Corinthians 1:21–22)

> He who has prepared us for this very thing is God, who has given us the Spirit as a guarantee. (2 Corinthians 5:5)

Therefore, the Holy Spirit on the disciples should be understood as the Spirit of the LORD that rested upon Yeshua. This same Spirit has now been imparted to his disciples in the outpouring at Shavu'ot in anticipation of the general outpouring, which will be universal, uniting all things in the Messiah. The goal of the outpouring is a universal enlightenment, at which point the Spirit of the LORD that was upon Yeshua will come to rest upon all humanity. Then all things will be reconciled into Yeshua. This is the ultimate destiny of the nations and all of humanity: to be absorbed into the body of the Messiah on earth. Then the Son of Man ("the Human Being") will be all in all because all humanity will be members of his body.

Incident Three: A Second Outpouring

> When they had prayed, the place in which they were gathered together was shaken, and they were all filled with the Holy Spirit and continued to speak the word of God with boldness. (Acts 4:31)

The third incident occurs in Acts 4. By then, the community of Yeshua's disciples had significantly grown, and the Spirit was active through the apostles. When the religious leadership prohibited the apostles from further testifying about Yeshua, they met for prayer. God's Spirit again shook the place in which they were gathered, again filled them with the Holy Spirit, and again enabled them "to speak the word of God with boldness." This corresponds to what Yeshua had said:

> When they deliver you over, do not be anxious how you are to speak or what you are to say, for what you are to say will be given to you in that hour. For it is not you who speak, but the Spirit of your Father speaking through you. (Matthew 10:19-20)

This story (the third incident) implies that the Spirit of God filled the apostles and the disciples of Yeshua with special endowment on occasion. Being filled with the Spirit is not a static experience. It includes exceptional moments that might be characterized as spiritual recharges.

After this, we read that "many signs and wonders were regularly done among the people by the hands of the apostles" (Acts 5:12). It does not say that all disciples of Yeshua were performing signs and wonders regularly, but the apostles did so. The apostles explained, "We are witnesses to these things, and so is the Holy Spirit, whom God has given to those who obey him" (Acts 5:32).

Incident Four: Appointment of the Seven

> Therefore, brothers, pick out from among you seven men of good repute, full of the Spirit and of wisdom, whom we will appoint to this duty ... These they set before the apostles, and they prayed and *laid their hands on them*. (Acts 6:3-6, emphasis mine)

The apostles spread the message throughout Jerusalem and into Judea. The community of disciples grew so rapidly that they found themselves unable to administer the whole assembly. The apostles appointed seven men to act as their representatives in the administration of the community. This story should be compared to the story of Moses appointing the seventy elders in Numbers 11 to assist with the administration of the community. The apostles selected men from among the disciples of Yeshua who were already "full of the Spirit and of wisdom," and they "laid their hands on them" to commission them as their agents. This incident illustrates the mechanism of laying on of hands as an investiture and act of commissioning. It was a rite considered pertinent to "the elementary doctrine of Christ" (Hebrews 6:1) and a transference of spiritual power.

Incident Five: Samaria

> Now when the apostles at Jerusalem heard that Samaria had received the word of God, they sent to them Peter and John, who came down and prayed for them that they might receive the Holy Spirit, for he had not yet fallen on any of them, but they had only been baptized in the name of the Lord Jesus. Then they *laid their hands on them and they received the Holy Spirit.* (Acts 8:14-17, emphasis mine)

Incident five is the story of how the apostles brought the Holy Spirit out from Jerusalem and Judea to Samaria.

After the death of Stephen, persecution against the disciples scattered the Yeshua community abroad. Philip, one of the seven, took refuge in a Samaritan city where he began to raise up disciples of Yeshua among the Samaritans. But he was not able to transmit the Spirit himself.

The apostles in Jerusalem sent Peter and John to investigate the reports of Samaritan disciples. Peter and John found that Philip had immersed Samaritan disciples under the authority of the name of the Master, but the Samaritan disciples had not experienced the spiritual manifestations of God's Spirit as the Jewish disciples had.

Peter and John laid hands on the disciples and prayed for them "that they might receive the Holy Spirit." The apostles are depicted transmitting the Spirit they received at Shavu'ot, not unlike Moses laying hands upon Joshua and the elders. The Spirit fell upon the Samaritan disciples. Simon Magus was so impressed that he sought to obtain the same power—the power to convey the Holy Spirit through the laying on of hands.

Incident Six: Paul and Ananias

> So Ananias departed and entered the house. *And laying his hands on him* he said, "Brother Saul, the Lord Jesus who appeared to you on the road by which you came has sent

me so that you may regain your sight and be filled with the Holy Spirit." (Acts 9:17, emphasis mine)

Incident six involves a disciple of Yeshua named Ananias, one of the original disciples who were present in the Temple for the outpouring of the Spirit on the day of Shavu'ot. He had since relocated to the Syrian city of Damascus. The Master appeared to him in a vision and told him to go to a particular house, lay hands upon Paul of Tarsus, and pray for him to receive the Spirit. He found Paul still fasting in the aftermath of his encounter with Yeshua, still blinded from the light. Ananias laid hands on him. Paul's vision returned, and he received the Holy Spirit. The story illustrates the principle of the original disciples serving to transmit the Spirit to subsequent disciples.

Incident Seven: Cornelius and Peter

> While Peter was still saying these things, the Holy Spirit fell on all who heard the word. And the believers from among the circumcised who had come with Peter were amazed, because the gift of the Holy Spirit was poured out even on the Gentiles. For they were hearing them speaking in tongues and extolling God. (Acts 10:44-46)

Incident seven involves the household of Cornelius the Centurion in the city of Caesarea. As Peter testified about Yeshua to the Gentiles gathered there, the Holy Spirit fell upon them. He did not even need to lay hands on them, and he probably would not have done so because he and the rest of the apostles did not anticipate transferring the Spirit to Gentiles. Nevertheless, that's what his presence in the home of Cornelius accomplished, thereby moving a step closer to the fulfillment of the prophecy about God's Spirit being poured out "on all flesh." Peter asked, "Can anyone withhold water for baptizing these people, who have received the Holy Spirit just as we have?" (Acts 10:47). In this way, the apostles moved the Spirit from Jerusalem to Judea, to Samaria, and out to the ends of the earth.

Peter later explained the significance of the moment to the other apostles back in Jerusalem:

> As I began to speak, the Holy Spirit fell on them just as on us at the beginning. And I remembered the word of the

> Lord, how he said, "John baptized with water, but you will be baptized with the Holy Spirit." If then God gave the same gift to them as he gave to us when we believed in the Lord Jesus Christ, who was I that I could stand in God's way? (Acts 11:15-17)

When the rest of the apostles heard about how the Spirit had crossed over the divide between Jews and Gentiles, they dropped their objections. They blessed God, observing, "Then to the Gentiles also God has granted repentance that leads to life" (Acts 11:18).

Incident Eight: The Laying on of Hands over Timothy

> This charge I entrust to you, Timothy, my child, in accordance with the prophecies previously made about you ... Do not neglect the gift you have, which was given you by prophecy when the council of elders laid their hands on you. (1 Timothy 1:18, 4:14)

Incident eight involves the immersion, laying on of hands, and transfer of the Spirit to Paul's Jewish disciple Timothy. Timothy is described as "A disciple... the son of a Jewish woman who was a believer" (Acts 16:1). Paul was apparently present at Timothy's immersion and the laying on of hands. In this story we see that the laying on of hands was a standard part of the ritual for receiving a new disciple, most probably because it symbolized the transference of the Holy Spirit like the flame of one candle igniting the wick of another.

Incident Nine: Twelve Disciples of John

> When Paul had laid his hands on them, the Holy Spirit came on them, and they began speaking in tongues and prophesying. (Acts 19:7)

Incident nine involves twelve disciples of John the Immerser. On arriving in Ephesus, Paul encountered twelve Jews in the synagogue who identified themselves as disciples of John the Immerser. Paul asked them if they had received the outpouring of the Holy Spirit. They replied that they were unaware of what he was speaking about. Paul realized that although they were disciples of John, they did not hear about Yeshua. John had only baptized them. He told them, "John baptized with the baptism of repentance, telling the people to believe in the one who was to come after him, that is, Yeshua." He persuaded them to become disciples of Yeshua. They agreed to transfer to Yeshua's school. This time they were immersed in the authority of Yeshua's name. Paul laid hands on them and prayed for them. "The Holy Spirit came on them, and they began speaking in tongues and prophesying."

In this story, we see that Paul was serving in his capacity as an apostle, transmitting the outpouring of the Holy Spirit to other Jews.

Incident Ten: The Ephesian Disciples

Paul served as a vector for the transference of the Spirit, just like the other apostles. But as he passed the flame, he did not limit himself to Jewish disciples. He also passed the Spirit to the Gentile disciples of Yeshua in Ephesus. Speaking to the Gentile disciples in Ephesus, Paul indicated that as members of the Jewish people, he and his colleagues (the apostles, the prophets, the evangelists, the teachers, and pastors) transmitted this anointing of the Spirit to the Gentile disciples of Yeshua:

> In him you [Gentile disciples] also, when you heard the word of truth, the gospel of your salvation, and believed in him, were sealed with the promised Holy Spirit, who is the guarantee of our inheritance until we acquire possession of it, to the praise of his glory. (Ephesians 1:13-14)

Toward Heavenly Adam

The endowment of the Spirit is a guarantee, a pledge on the Messianic Era, "the redemption of God's own possession," the people of Israel. But it's also a down payment on the outpouring of the Spirit on all flesh. It is the gift that the Messiah obtained to be given to human beings, to be passed through the apostles and those who originally received the Spirit. He received the Spirit at the Jordan. He passed it to his original school of Jewish disciples. They passed it on to those who followed in Jerusalem, Judea, Samaria, and ultimately to the ends of the earth—to Jews, to Samaritans, and ultimately to all nations.

The Spirit didn't come upon people in isolation, but only under the investment of the body of Messiah, through the laying on of hands and in conjunction with immersion in Messiah's name. This is not to limit God or deny the outliers such as Eldad and Medad or the story of the unknown exorcist who was commanding spirits in the Master's name. However, at least during the Apostolic Era, the ordinary way to receive this gift was through the apostles or through those who had received the anointing by them. They transferred the Holy Spirit like one lamp lighting many lamps, and those lamps lighting others, but none were diminished in the process. The goal of the process was to ignite the whole world, lighting up the whole earth with the brilliant light of God's revelation, one human being at a time. This was the work of "the apostles, the prophets, the evangelists, the shepherds and teachers, to equip the saints for the work of ministry, for building up the body of Christ" (Ephesians 4:11-12) toward that eventual goal when the Spirit will be upon all flesh and all humanity will be joined together into the messianic identity—the metaphysical body of the heavenly Adam.

The spiritual life they conveyed also belongs to us who are heirs of this process that has been preserved by faith through the hands of those who have clung to the confession of Yeshua before us. If so, let us be diligent to walk by the Spirit and transmit this gift to those who come after us, not letting its light go out of the world with us.

SERMON ELEVEN:
THE CHILDREN OF LIGHT
(EPHESIANS 5:1–20)

Why does Paul tell the Gentile disciples in Ephesus that they must no longer live as Gentiles? In what way are Gentile disciples of Yeshua supposed to live like Jews? Paul offers his readers practical guidance for their new life with God's people.

In chapter 4 of the book of Ephesians, Paul spoke about walking in a manner worthy of our calling as disciples. He warned the Ephesian Gentile disciples that they must "no longer walk as the Gentiles do" (Ephesians 4:17). In chapter 5, Paul continues his discourse on righteous living with practical instructions that distinguish between Israel and the idolatrous world of the nations from which the Ephesian disciples have come. If the Gentile disciples are to walk in a manner worthy of their calling, they must no longer live like idolaters. Paul refers to the people of the world and the idolatrous nations as the sons of disobedience and the children of darkness. He refers to the Jewish people as the holy ones (saints) of Israel and to the disciples of Yeshua as the children of God and the children of light.

The idolatrous world of Paul's day corresponds to today's secular world. They aren't that different. The darkness of the idolatrous world and the darkness of the secular world are the same: ignorance of God. The children of God, on the other hand, walk in the light of God's revelation.

Imitators of God

> Therefore be imitators of God, as beloved children. And walk in love. (Ephesians 5:1-2)

Paul says that if we want to be considered sons and daughters of our Father in heaven, we should imitate God in how we treat others. That means walking in love. The imitation of God is the meaning of the English word "godliness." The Torah refers to it as "walking in God's ways."

In the Torah, Moses says, "And now, Israel, what does the LORD your God require of you, but to fear the LORD your God, to walk in all his ways, to love him, to serve the LORD your God with all your heart and with all your soul" (Deuteronomy 10:12). The sages asked, "What does it mean to 'walk in all his ways'? How can a human being be expected to walk in the ways of the Almighty?" The explanation is that it means imitating God and walking in godliness:

> Just as He clothes the naked, as it is written [in Genesis 3:21], "The LORD God made garments of skin for Adam and his wife, and clothed them," so too should you also clothe the naked. The Holy One, blessed be He, visited the sick, as it is written [in Genesis 18:1], "Now the LORD appeared to him by the oaks of Mamre" [while he was still recovering from circumcision], so too should you also visit the sick. The Holy One, blessed be He, comforted mourners, as it is written [in Genesis 25:11], "After the death of Abraham, that God blessed his son Isaac," so too should you also comfort mourners. The Holy One, blessed be He, buried the dead, as it is written [in Deuteronomy 34:6], "And He buried him in the valley in the land of Moab," so too should you also bury the dead. (b.*Sotah* 14a)

In Ephesians 5:1, where Paul tells his readers to imitate God "as beloved children," he specifically refers to forgiving each other for shortcomings and sins. "Be kind to one another, tenderhearted, forgiving one another, as God in Christ forgave you. Therefore be imitators of God, as beloved children" (Ephesians 4:32-5:1). When I find it difficult to forgive my debtors and those who have transgressed against me, I need to remember that I rely upon God's forgiveness of my own sins and shortcomings in Messiah. If I desire God's forgiveness, it is incumbent upon me to forgive others. This is what it says in *Midrash Sifre* regarding the mitzvah of walking in the ways of God:

> Just as the Holy One, blessed be He, is called merciful, so you should be merciful; just as He is called gracious, so you should be gracious; just as He is called righteous, so you should be called righteous; just as He is called devout, so you should be devout. (*Sifre* on Deuteronomy 10:12)

Sacrifice of Love

Paul summarizes the concept with the words, "Walk in love":

> Walk in love, as Christ loved us and gave himself up for us, a fragrant offering and sacrifice to God. (Ephesians 5:2)

There is no higher calling, no higher mitzvah, no higher form of godliness than to treat our fellow human beings with love. Yeshua says, "Greater love has no one than this, that someone lay down his life for his friends" (John 15:13), and he models the principle of sacrificial and selfless love for others in laying down his own life. Paul compares the Messiah's willing death on behalf of others to a sacrifice offered up to God on the fires of the altar, to which the Torah refers as "a fragrant aroma to the LORD."

Likewise, in imitation of Messiah, we sacrifice our own self-interest on behalf of others as an act of love. God receives that setting aside of the will and setting aside of the self as if it were a sacrifice offered to him on his altar. When we forgive others for the wrongs that they have done to us, God receives that gesture as a divine act of worship on par with the sacrifices offered in the Temple.

This principle of walking in love summarizes the manner of conduct for a disciple of Yeshua.

Two Different Worlds

> But sexual immorality and all impurity or covetousness must not even be named among you, as is proper among saints. (Ephesians 5:3)

The apostle enjoins the disciples in Ephesus to adopt Jewish standards of conduct and piety, conforming their behavior to "what is proper" among the holy ones. He refers here to the wide discrepancy that existed between the moral norms and standards of the Jewish world and the norms and standards of the idolatrous Gentile nations of the time. The Roman world celebrated impurity, greed, covetousness, sensuality, and sexual immorality. It was a world that celebrated personal ambition and the acquisition of power. It was a world dedicated to elite debaucheries, a world swimming in a sea of immorality. This was the world of Nero's Rome, a world that would make even Hollywood blush.

The Jewish world, on the other hand, looked prudish by comparison because the Jewish people conducted themselves according to the biblical values of modesty, discretion, morality, marital fidelity, and the high standards of the Torah. A greater contrast between worlds can hardly be conceived. Paul refers to it as the contrast between light and darkness.

When the Gentile disciples in Ephesus became part of the same body with the Jewish disciples of Yeshua, they, too, became saints, holy ones, set apart from the rest of the world. Therefore, it was not appropriate for them to behave like the rest of the world. For the rest of the people living in Ephesus and Asia Minor, immorality, impurity, and greed were the common, everyday values. But among the disciples of Yeshua, there shouldn't even be a mention of such things—not even a suspicion of their presence.

The same sharp divide should exist today between the disciples of Yeshua and the secular world. Sexual immorality, impurity, and greed should not be found among those who call themselves by our Master's holy name. A few years ago, we saw a social upheaval called the #MeToo movement. It started when women began coming forward with reports of being sexually manipulated by men who occupied positions of authority over them in the workplace. No one was surprised. Many objected that it was the way of things. That's just the way the world behaves and always has behaved. The powerful take advantage of the weak. Men take advantage of women. That's the way the world has always worked.

But the people of God are supposed to be different. That's why it was such a disappointment to see so many prominent pastors and religious figures exposed to the world as predators and seducers. Victims came forward with reports of how their pastors and religious leaders had taken advantage of them. Immorality, impurity, and greed were named among the so-called people of God. It was embarrassing and a *chillul HaShem*—a desecration of God's holy name. (It became even more embarrassing when the people who traditionally champion family values turned against the victims and became the defenders of immorality, impurity, and greed as if these things were men's inalienable rights.) God forbid that such things should even be mentioned in association with disciples of our Master.

Conversation of the Saints

> Let there be no filthiness nor foolish talk nor crude joking, which are out of place, but instead let there be thanksgiving. (Ephesians 5:4)

Paul contrasts the conversation of the saints with that of the people of the world. In the Midrash, the sages point out how even the conversation of the servants in Abraham's household centered on godliness, and even the lowly servants received revelations through angels.

The world speaks the language of filthiness, folly, cruelty, obscenity, and crude jokes. The people of the world clutter their conversation with profanity, and their perverse sense of humor sullies both the mouth of the one who speaks and the ear of the one who hears. That's fine for the people of the world, but it's inappropriate for the people of God.

Paul invites his readers to sanctify themselves from the nations by replacing the filthy talk, foul language, and obscenities that pass for normal conversation with words of thanksgiving and gratitude. With our words, we can elevate or lower both the one speaking and the one listening.

Sons of Belial

One might mistakenly suppose that these rules of conduct are merely a matter of cultural difference and Jewish custom—nothing more than suggested standards of behavior. On the contrary, Paul sounds deadly serious. He warns the disciples in Ephesus that if they behave like idolaters, they will face the same fate as idolaters:

> For you may be sure of this, that everyone who is sexually immoral or impure, or who is covetous (that is, an idolater),

> has no inheritance in the kingdom of Christ and God. (Ephesians 5:5)

Idolaters have no inheritance in the Messianic Era. Neither will those who walk in their ways or imitate their culture. Paul warns the Ephesian disciples that it's not sufficient to call themselves disciples if there is no difference between them and the idolatrous world. The same is true for us. If we share the immorality, impurity, covetousness, consumerism, and greed that characterizes the secular world, we should expect no inheritance in the Messianic Era. Many today would object and say, "But surely we are saved by grace, and our sins are forgiven!"

Paul replies:

> Let no one deceive you with empty words, for because of these things the wrath of God comes upon the sons of disobedience. Therefore do not become partners with them. (Ephesians 5:6-7)

We dare not persist in the ways of disobedience while expecting to receive the reward of obedience. The term "sons of disobedience" translates the Biblical Hebrew idiom "sons of Belial." If we partake of the pleasures, vices, and sinful indulgences enjoyed by the sons of disobedience, we can expect to also partake in the wrath God allots to the sons of Belial.

Sons of Light

Paul concedes that before they became disciples of Yeshua, the Ephesian disciples were numbered among the sons of disobedience, but that was no longer the case:

> For at one time you were darkness, but now you are light in the Lord. Walk as children of light. (Ephesians 5:8)

The sectarian literature in the Dead Sea Scrolls uses this same terminology, dividing the world into children of light and children of darkness. The Dead Sea Scrolls anticipate a future apocalypse and final battle between light and darkness, waged by the children of light and the children of darkness. Paul similarly uses the terminology to contrast the people of God (Israel and the Gentile disciples) against the idolatrous world (the nations).

Light and darkness metaphorically represent good and evil, but in this case, they also symbolize knowledge and ignorance. In the previous chapter, Paul characterized the idolatrous world as "darkened in their understanding, alienated from the life of God because of the ignorance that is in them" (Ephesians 4:18). Like them, the disciples in Ephesus were at one time "separate from Christ, excluded from the commonwealth of Israel, and strangers to the covenants of promise, having no hope and without God in the world" (Ephesians 2:12). Through the message of the gospel, however, they were enlightened to the revelation of the one God, the God of Israel. With that enlightenment and revelation came responsibility. They were no longer in the darkness of ignorance and must no longer live as the children of darkness do. Instead, the disciples had become "light in the Lord" and must henceforth "walk as children of Light."

The Fruit of Light

> For the fruit of light is found in all that is good and right and true, and try to discern what is pleasing to the Lord. (Ephesians 5:9-10)

No longer living in the darkness of ignorance like their idolatrous neighbors, it now fell to the Gentile disciples of Yeshua in Ephesus to walk as the children of light, trying to learn "what is pleasing to the Lord," namely, the pursuit of goodness, righteousness, and truth. Paul mixes his metaphors. The "fruit of light" is all that is good and right and true. If we are children of the light, we should be bearing a harvest of goodness, righteousness, and truth. Therefore, a disciple of Yeshua asks himself or herself, in every situation, "Is this pleasing to the LORD? Is this good? Is this right? Is this true?"

This is the standard by which we are to conduct ourselves. It's a sort of litmus test you can apply to your life. You can ask yourself these questions about the company you keep, the friends you are hanging out with, the places you are going, the party you are attending, the things you are doing, the things on which you spend your money, the entertainments you are watching, the things you are reading, the people who are influencing you, the movies, the music, the websites, your social media feed, and the way that you interact with others. In all things, in all these situations and places, with all these people and friends, you should be asking yourself, "Is this good? Is this right? Is this true? Is this pleasing to the LORD?"

How would a former idolater from Ephesus know what is good, right, true, and pleasing to the LORD? Where can these new disciples find the meaning of goodness? Where will they find the standards of righteousness? Where will they find the revelation of truth? The same place that we will find them: in the Scriptures of Israel, in the Torah of Moses, and in the words of the Master transmitted through his apostles, the revelation of God to human beings.

The Fruit of Darkness

The fruit of the light is everything good, right, and true. What is the fruit of darkness? We don't really need a list. We know the fruit of darkness, and we are to have no part in it:

> Take no part in the unfruitful works of darkness, but instead expose them. For it is shameful even to speak of the things that they do in secret. But when anything is exposed by the light, it becomes visible, for anything that becomes visible is light. (Ephesians 5:11-14)

Light dispels darkness. We should not need a list of prohibited behaviors, and it shouldn't be necessary to discuss "the unfruitful works of darkness" because, when exposed to the light, darkness vanishes. For disciples of Yeshua, "It is shameful even to speak of the things that [the idolaters] do in secret." Paul has in mind the vices and the entertainments of the Roman world. The banquets and symposiums, the drinking halls, the flute players, the slave girls and slave boys, the orgies, the theaters, the games, the spectacles, the stadiums, the gross indulgence in immorality and every vice. It is shameful for a disciple to even speak of such things. Such things should not be named among us. If we are of the light, it should be completely obvious that we don't participate in those activities or dabble in that world.

The Light of Messiah

We are of the light because the light of the Messiah has shined upon us, which is to say that we have experienced the revelation of God that comes through Yeshua:

> Therefore it says, "Awake, O sleeper, and arise from the dead, and Christ will shine on you." (Ephesians 5:14)

In Ephesians 5:14, Paul quotes a short passage from an unknown source. Joseph Good suggests that Paul might have been quoting from an early Rosh HaShanah liturgy regarding the sounding of the shofar. Just as the shofar of Messiah is destined to raise the dead slumbering in their tombs, likewise, the shofar should awaken our slumbering souls from the coma of sin to shake off their lethargy and repent. This corresponds to what Maimonides said about the voice of the shofar at Rosh HaShanah:

> It is as if the shofar is saying, "Wake up, sleepers from your sleep, and you who slumber, arise. Consider your deeds, repent, remember your Maker." To those who forget the truth and are distracted by empty pursuits the entire year, to those who devote their energy to vanity and emptiness which will not benefit or save, the shofar says, "Look to your souls. Improve your ways and your deeds and let every one of you abandon his evil path and thoughts." (Maimonides, *Hilchot Teshuvah* 3:4)

Use Your Time Wisely

Maimonides says, "Consider your deeds ... Look to your souls." Paul says,

> Look carefully then how you walk, not as unwise but as wise, making the best use of the time, because the days are evil. Therefore do not be foolish, but understand what the will of the Lord is. (Ephesians 5:15-17)

He reminds his readers that time is short. He says, "The days are evil," meaning that these are troubled times, and the end is surely near.

We don't have any time to waste. The time to repent is now. It doesn't work to plan on becoming godly sometime in the future. For the disciple of Yeshua, who knows that there is a coming judgment at which he or she must give an account before the throne of God, every minute is precious.

A clever businessman carefully invests his limited resources only into merchandise that will bring him a good return. Our limited resource is our time. There's only so much time in a day, in a week, in a year, in a lifetime. When it runs out, it's gone. We should be making the best use of what we have left by investing it into those things that will bring the best return, and that is to "understand what the will of the Lord is." Torah, mitzvot, goodness, righteousness, and truth.

Drunk and Disorderly

> Do not get drunk with wine, for that is debauchery, but be filled with the Spirit. (Ephesians 5:18)

Ephesians 5:18 often gets quoted as if it is a New Testament prohibition on alcohol consumption. It's not. But neither should its warning be disregarded. It's a boundary we should be careful not to cross. If you drink at all, if alcohol is in your life, you are in danger. Alcohol is an addictive drug, and there's a basic rule of human biology and physiology that says if you take an addictive drug in sufficient quantity often enough and long enough, you will get addicted. I don't need to lecture about the dangers of alcohol. Suffice it to say that alcohol, in any form, is a dangerous drug that causes a disproportionate amount of sorrow in the world.

It was no different in the Roman world, in which the highlight of the idolatrous life was a night of alcohol-fueled revelry with all its associated indulgences. In Galatians 5, Paul lists out the indulgences one might anticipate while out on a bender or a night on the town in the Roman world: "Sexual immorality, impurity, sensuality, idolatry, sorcery, enmity, strife, jealousy, fits of anger, rivalries, dissensions, divisions, envy, drunkenness, orgies, and things like these I warn you, as I warned you before, that those who do such things will not inherit the kingdom of God" (Galatians 5:19–21). That's a snapshot of the Roman world, a grocery list of options for evening activities.

Have things changed so much since then? The secular world has the same ambition, and more than ever, our society considers alcohol to be the elixir of life. Debauchery is the goal. Dissipation is the destination. Debauchery means overindulgence and gluttony. Dissipation is addiction and substance abuse. The Greek word *asotia*, translated here as "debauchery," means wastefulness. It's the idea that you had enough wine in that wineskin to last you a week, and you drank it all in one go.

The life of debauchery and drunkenness is not for disciples. Alcohol should not hold sway over us as it does over the secular world. This is supposed to be one of the defining differences between them and us. If we drink as much or more than the secular world, something is wrong.

Psalms, Hymns, Spiritual Songs

> Be filled with the Spirit, addressing one another in psalms and hymns and spiritual songs, singing and making melody to the Lord with your heart. (Ephesians 5:18-19)

Our goal in life is not to get hammered and have such a good time partying that we don't remember it the next morning. Instead of the intoxication of alcohol, a disciple of Yeshua should be seeking the exhilaration that comes from being filled with the Spirit of God. Instead of a night of rowdy drinking songs and bawdy entertainment common to the symposiums of the idolatrous world, the disciples of Yeshua are "addressing one another in psalms and hymns and spiritual songs, singing and making melody to the Lord with your heart, giving thanks always and for everything to God the Father in the name of our Lord Jesus Christ" (Ephesians 5:18-20).

With these words, Paul sought to paint a picture of an alternative world, one with a completely different set of values from the world to which the Gentiles of his day were accustomed. It's also a different world from the one to which the secular people of our day are accustomed. It's like the difference between light and dark.

In the world of the children of light, our common language is supposed to be the language of psalms, hymns, and spiritual songs. The "psalms" Paul had in mind are the Psalms of David, but the early believers also wrote their own psalms in imitation of David's. The word "hymns" is better translated as "odes," a popular genre of lyrical poem or song written to celebrate some celebrity, athlete, hero, political leader, deity, or idea. The early believers wrote odes about Messiah. You can read a collection of them in the *Odes of Solomon*. "Spiritual songs," I believe, refer to wordless melodies like the Chasidic *niggunim*, which are, in themselves, supposed to be imbued with a portion of the spirit of prophecy.

The Children of Light

> Giving thanks always and for everything to God the Father in the name of our Lord Jesus Christ. (Ephesians 5:20)

Instead of a society of people devoted to getting smashed and wallowing together in the muck of human depravity, Paul paints a picture of a community dedicated to exalting the Messiah and lifting one another spiritually higher. It's a community characterized by a spirit of gratitude in which the watchword is thanksgiving. These people are animated with gratitude for the goodness that God has shown them through the Messiah. Their world is one of *Baruch HaShem* ("Bless the LORD"), and every occasion is an opportunity to offer a blessing to God in thanksgiving for his goodness. There's a *brachah* ("blessing") for everything.

In his letter to the disciples of Colossae, Paul repeats this idyllic depiction of a community of Yeshua's disciples interacting with one another in reciting the words of the Master, teaching the Scriptures, encouraging one another in godliness, and delighting together in song and thanksgiving:

> Let the word of Christ dwell in you richly, teaching and admonishing one another in all wisdom, singing psalms and hymns and spiritual songs, with thankfulness in your hearts to God. And whatever you do, in word or deed, do everything in the name of the Lord Jesus, giving thanks to God the Father through him. (Colossians 3:16-17)

These people are not like the rest of the world. What's happening here isn't normal. Disciples of Yeshua are a completely different breed of human beings.

SERMON TWELVE:
A PROFOUND MYSTERY
(EPHESIANS 5:21–33)

*Moving beyond the Jew-Gentile distinction,
Paul considers other relationships
affected by the Messiah, starting with
the profound mystery of marriage.*

During the forty days before Yom Kippur, God's people take account, creating a *Cheshbon HaNefesh*, an accounting of our own souls, searching out our hearts, as King David said, "Search me ... try me ... and see if there be any grievous way in me" (Psalm 139:23-24). We make what rectifications and repairs we can, offering restitution when necessary and working toward reconciliation wherever possible. Ordinarily, for most people, most of the work needs to be done in our closest relationships. Those we love the most tend to be the ones we hurt the most. That's why living at peace with one another in a community is so difficult. Not because we hate each other, but because we love one another. Because we are a family. That's why living at peace with your family is so difficult. Not because you hate one another, but because you love one another and are so invested in one another.

In Ephesians 5, Paul speaks about these types of relationships, particularly the marriage relationship. He refers to marriage as a "profound mystery." By that remark, he does not mean that "men are from Mars and women are from Venus" or that "you can't live with them and can't live without them." By referring to marriage as a "profound mystery," he invokes the language of Jewish mysticism. A "mystery" is an esoteric secret on the level of *sod*, the deepest level of biblical interpretation.

The Heavenly Man

Paul did not write the Epistle to the Ephesians to offer marital counsel. The principal concern behind Paul's letter to the Ephesians pertains to the symbiotic relationship between Israel and the nations. This relationship finds expression in the seemingly dichotomous poles of unity and distinction within the school of Yeshua's disciples. Paul describes the body of Messiah as a spiritual entity composed of many different parts. The various parts come together to constitute one metaphysical entity, but the parts are not identical. The various parts of the body have their unique roles and functions, but they share in the common unity of the collective entity to serve as the physical presence of Messiah on earth until his return. This is to teach us the principle of unity and differentiation. Oneness does not entail a loss of individual identity. Oneness is not sameness:

> As it is, there are many parts, yet one body. (1 Corinthians 12:20)

Paul describes the body as "one new man," likening us to a single human being. It's not just a convenient metaphor; it has theological significance pertaining to the resurrection of the dead. The spiritual essence, which is our sense of self, our *neshamah*, lacks distinction and definition until it becomes associated with a human body. We derive individuality, distinction, identity, and personality through our association with our human body. These are gifts that the human body's limitations bestow upon the otherwise limitless and unbounded spirit. Compressed into a limited awareness and forced into identification with a finite human body, our spirits take on shape and definition, so to speak. They become differentiated.

This is the reason for the future resurrection of the dead. The physicality of the human body anchors man's otherwise undefined spiritual aspect, lest we be reabsorbed into the Light from which we were birthed and in which there is neither shadow nor variation. We do not seek a state of nirvana where our ego ceases to be. Instead, we are to retain distinction, differentiated even in unity with the Source, even in the World to Come. Therefore, resurrection is the central idea of the salvation of the soul. Without resurrection, the soul's individuality is lost and reabsorbed into the Light.

Distinction Theology in the Body of Messiah

These are the higher mystical ideas knocking around in Paul's head as he works out the shape of the assembly of Messiah on paper in the book of Ephesians. Paul believes that these esoteric ideas, which are hallmarks of Pharisaic cosmology, find expression in this world through the resurrection of the physical body of Yeshua of Nazareth and his ascension to the Father, a precursor of the future resurrection of the righteous. Meanwhile, until then, his school of disciples remains here as his representatives on earth to stand in for him. No single disciple can take his place or claim to be the Son of God, but we are all elevated to the level of sons and daughters by kinship with him, as members of the same spiritual family with the same Father. Together, we become the Messiah on earth. That's what it means to be members of the body of Messiah. In the physical body of Messiah on earth, there remains physical distinction. Paul expresses the same concept in Galatians in these words:

> For as many of you as were baptized into Christ have put on Christ. There is neither Jew nor Greek, there is neither slave nor free, there is no male and female, for you are all one in Christ Jesus. (Galatians 3:27-28)

In this saying, Paul does not discount the distinctions between the Jews and Gentiles, between slave and free, and between male and female. He does not blur the boundaries between the nations or between the genders, nor does he attempt to diminish the sober social reality of slavery in the Roman world. Instead, he appeals to a higher sense of unity that ought to transcend distinctions of nation, gender, and class. That higher sense of unity is derived from our common and shared identity in Yeshua.

On this basis, Paul argues in all of his epistles that Jewish and Gentile disciples should offer one another mutual respect, dignity, and honor, affirming each other's unique callings and submitting to one another in love. Likewise, husbands should love their wives and treat them with the honor and dignity befitting a co-heir of salvation, and wives should submit to their husbands and grant them honor and respect. Children should honor and obey their parents, and parents should not disregard the dignity of their children. Slaves should serve their human masters honestly and diligently as if they labored for Yeshua, their true Master. Slave owners should not mistreat their slaves or deal with them harshly, remembering that they are brothers in Messiah. All this is the outworking and natural application of distinction theology.

Submit to One Another

These are the types of distinctions Paul has in mind when he offers us this idyllic snapshot of the community of Messiah:

> Address one another in psalms and hymns and spiritual songs, singing and making melody to the Lord with your heart, giving thanks always and for everything to God the Father in the name of our Lord Jesus Christ, submitting to one another out of reverence for Christ. (Ephesians 5:19–21)

When he says that we should submit to one another "out of reverence for Messiah," it should be understood to mean, "Submit to one another as if you were submitting to the Messiah."

Paul wants Jewish and Gentile disciples to submit to one another, outdoing one another in according honor to each other, each one looking to the other as if the other were the Messiah himself. The principle applies not just to relationships between Jews and Gentiles within the body of the Messiah but to all of us with one another. The rule of thumb is that we should offer deference to our brother or our sister in Messiah as we would for the Messiah himself. This calls for a high level of humility.

Subduing the Ego

If you ever feel like your ego is bruised, if you feel insulted, if you feel that you have not received the respect that you deserve, if your feathers get ruffled, this is the work of the Spirit indicating areas in your life where you have yet to apply this principle of "submitting to one another out of reverence for the Messiah." It calls *not* for a total abnegation of the ego, which is the same as the disappearance of the individual, but rather for a conquest of the ego. God does not seek the dissolution of the self or the individual, as some Eastern religions do. Instead, as the Baal Shem Tov said, our job is to subdue the evil inclination and bring it into the service of God and the love of God along with our good inclination.

Imagine a community governed by such a principle, in which no one is on the warpath to defend the self or prop up the ego. Where no one feels the need to assert power over another, and no one has an ego to bruise or feelings to hurt. That's a picture of the kingdom. This is what Yeshua envisioned when he spoke of taking the lower seat, of the least being greatest, the last being first, the first being last, and "whoever would be great among you must be your servant, and whoever would be first among you must be your slave, even as the Son of Man came not to be served but to serve, and to give his life as a ransom for many" (Matthew 20:26–28). This concept of "submitting to one another" as if submitting to the Messiah is utterly disruptive to an honor-based society. It's disruptive to us. It's utterly contrary to the normal human tendency.

We go just the opposite direction, wanting others to submit to us, serve our needs, acknowledge our rank, and bestow flatteries to prop up our egos. Facebook created a platform that allowed people to find affirmation for their egos in the form of "likes" and thumbs-ups and other social media accolades, launching a whole new universe of self-absorption. Such a combination is utterly addictive to the ego—more addictive than heroin: a steady drip of bite-sized morsels of social approval and validation.

The self is insatiable. The more you feed the self, the hungrier it becomes. People try to quench their inner pain and sense of inadequacy by slathering the wounded ego with self-aggrandizement, power, position, prestige, possessions, and whatever else makes them feel important. Others continuously apply and reapply the balm of self-pity, blame, and resentment, bathing their wounded egos in bitterness and victimization. However, neither remedy works. We can see how this toxic stew of self-absorption has the potential to sour every human relationship, especially our relationships with those closest to us. That's human dysfunction.

What's the solution? The solution is to find our identity in the new man, which is Messiah, in whose body each of us has a function and a role to play. We need not concern ourselves with our own sense of self because each of us belongs to a greater self. We defer one to another within this greater self, submitting one to another as if to the Master. "The eye cannot say to the hand, 'I have no need of you,' nor again the head to the feet, 'I have no need of you'" (1 Corinthians 12:21).

Husbands and Wives

Paul extends this principle to address family relationships, and he offers a few words to address the marital relationship between a husband and a wife:

> Wives, submit to your own husbands, as to the Lord. For the husband is the head of the wife even as Christ is the head of the church, his body, and is himself its Savior. (Ephesians 5:22-23)

It's easy to perceive Paul's instructions to women as patriarchal and a little chauvinistic by today's standards. But they're not intended that way. Instead, Paul seeks to lift the relationship between a man and his wife out of dysfunction to a spiritual plane of mutual submission modeled on the relationship between Yeshua and his disciples. Women were not treated well in the Roman world, and wives had few rights. Judaism looked positively progressive and nearly egalitarian by comparison with the rest of the world.

Judaism introduced the Bible's view of women to the pagan world—a view where husbands and wives were deemed equal and opposite partners, like two halves of a single being. In fact, that's the traditional Jewish interpretation of the creation of human beings. The first male and female were severed halves of the same being, the same creature. From the Bible's perspective, women are not property. They have rights and dignity and protections under the Torah. They cannot be used and discarded.

In Paul's view, every home reflects the union of Messiah and his disciples, which is itself a microcosm of the union of God and Israel and, ultimately, of God and all humanity. Accordingly, every home is a spiritual unit in the greater spiritual unity and part of a spiritual hierarchy that starts with God, who is the head of the Messiah, who is the head of the disciple, who is the head of his wife, who is head of the household, the children, and the servants.

This material is well-covered in the FFOZ book *Adam Loves Eve*, and I'm not going to reproduce those long discussions about how to negotiate a marriage here. I don't want to get distracted by the controversy around the passage or by pastoral concerns for fixing marriages. However, a few words are necessary.

Her Mitzvah

First, notice that Paul addresses this directive to women and not to men. When he says, "Wives, submit to your husbands as to the Master," he is speaking not to husbands but to wives. Men wrongly have felt as if this directive, and many similar directives in the New Testament, grant them permission to spiritually bully their wives and force them to submit to their will and whim. That's not the case at all. It's her mitzvah and her prerogative, not his. It's not his job or responsibility to make her submit. It's not really even his business. He remains bound by the previous principle, "submitting to one another out of reverence for Christ." When Paul turns to the husbands to address them and their role in the relationship, he does not say, "Force your wives to submit to you." Instead, he tells them to love their wives as Messiah loves his disciples. Likewise, in the sister epistle of Colossians, Paul enjoins married men, "Love your wives, and do not be harsh with them" (Colossians 3:19).

Biblical Headship

Paul says, "For the husband is the head of the wife even as Christ is the head of the church, his body, and is himself its Savior." The Torah explains that when a man clings to his wife, the two will become one flesh, that is, a new, single creature. This is why the New Testament can, on the one hand, refer to the disciples of Yeshua as "the bride of Messiah," and, on the other hand, describe the disciples of Yeshua as "the body of Messiah." A man's bride becomes his own self when he leaves his family and cleaves to her to create a new family. That's the biblical model. Husband and wife join to create a new identity that is compared to a new physical creature, "one flesh."

The man is to be the head of this one-flesh new creature. The woman is the body of the creature. In a similar passage, he says, "I want you to understand that the head of every man is Christ, the head of a wife is her husband, and the head of Christ is God" (1 Corinthians 11:3). This means that when a man is properly attached to his wife, he functions as her spiritual head, just as the Messiah is his spiritual head, and God is the spiritual head of Messiah. This idea of "headship" implies leadership and authority, but in this equation, it also implies completing a spiritual circuit between heaven and earth, where the human family reflects the divine family.

The Bible models a husband who loves his wife. Paul tells us that men are to emulate the Messiah in their love for their wives. He says, "Husbands, love your wives, as Christ loved the church and gave himself up for her" (Ephesians 5:25), a sentiment that evokes the image of a man crucified to the self on behalf of the marriage. This is sacrificial love. It allows no bullying; it does not force one's will on another. Instead, the biblical husband nourishes and cherishes his wife. One cannot cherish a person and at the same time disregard her wishes, opinions, preferences, and dignity. Christlike headship calls for servanthood. The Master considers heavy-handed authority and lording it over others as something one might expect of idolaters, but this kind of egoism is unworthy of his disciples.

In Paul's view of the marriage relationship, the husband is the head and the leader, which makes him the servant according to the kingdom's principles of inversion. Yeshua's disciples are taught to lead by servanthood, "for the Son of man came not to be served but to serve." The husband is to deal with his wife according to how the Master deals with his disciples and ultimately with all of Israel.

Respective Obligations

According to what Paul says here in Ephesians, women have two obligations to their husbands: to defer to them and honor them. What does it mean for a woman to honor her husband? We can derive that from Jewish law regarding the commandment to honor one's father and mother. It means that she doesn't contradict him, insult him, or embarrass him publicly. She doesn't appropriate his position, take his seat, or usurp his authority. She looks after him. She takes care of him.

The wife is told to defer to her husband and honor and respect him. But she is not told to love him.

Husbands have the much more difficult task of loving their wives. From this perspective, love is not merely affection or fond feelings but rather self-sacrifice, service, providing for her, and nurturing her. It's the taller order of the two, the more difficult of the two. Whereas she is called upon merely to defer to his leadership and offer him some civility and dignity, he is called upon to sacrifice his very self on her behalf, loving her as the Messiah loves his disciples.

The Cleansing

> Husbands, love your wives, as Christ loved the church and gave himself up for her, that he might sanctify her, having cleansed her by the washing of water with the word, so that he might present the church to himself in splendor, without spot or wrinkle or any such thing, that she might be holy and without blemish. (Ephesians 5:25-27)

The cleansing and washing of water with the word borrows imagery from ritual purification and immersion. In Jewish tradition, the bride goes through a ritual immersion for purification before her wedding. This is what Yeshua does for his disciples "by the washing of water with the word," that is, his message and his teaching. He sanctifies, cleanses, and prepares his disciples for a metaphysical union through his teachings.

Because the Messiah cleaves to his disciples, he is able to spiritually cleanse them through the merit and virtue of his own righteousness and suffering. This is the forgiveness of sins that we find through the authority of his name. Like a husband who grants his name and legal identity to his wife, Messiah grants his righteous identity, "splendor, without spot or wrinkle or any such thing," to his disciples so that we "might be holy and without blemish."

Love Your Wife as Yourself

> In the same way husbands should love their wives as their own bodies. He who loves his wife loves himself. (Ephesians 5:28)

Paul juxtaposes several different ideas in these words. The Torah teaches that the husband is to cleave to his wife so that they become, as it were, one new creature:

> Therefore a man shall leave his father and his mother and hold fast to his wife, and they shall become one flesh. (Genesis 2:24)

In Paul's analogy, the Messiah is the man, the Heavenly Adam, who leaves the Father to cleave to his disciples so that we become one new man with him at the head. It's the metaphysical man about which we have been speaking. Again, this is why Paul can speak of the community of Yeshua's disciples on the one hand as the bride of the Messiah and on the other hand as the body of the Messiah. Because a man leaves his father and mother to cleave to his wife and becomes with her a new entity, a new creature: "For neither circumcision counts for anything, nor uncircumcision, but a new creation" (Galatians 6:15).

This is the idea behind his theology of the body of the Messiah.

However, it's not just theological mysticism. It has a practical application. Paul says, "In the same way husbands should love their wives as their own bodies. He who loves his wife loves himself." This is the marital application of the commandment that says, "You shall love your neighbor as yourself" (Leviticus 19:18). A man's closest neighbor is his wife. The Bible calls her "a neighbor who cleaves closer than a brother" (Proverbs 18:24). Paul explains that the commandment to "love your neighbor as yourself" especially applies to one's wife. He combines the commandment with Genesis 2:24:

> Therefore a man shall leave his father and his mother and hold fast [cleave] to his wife, and they shall become one flesh. (Genesis 2:24)

By becoming a new creature with his wife, the husband discovers that she is himself. Their identities have merged. As Adam said, "This at last is bone of my bones and flesh of my flesh." (Genesis 2:23). In other words, "She is me." We are the same creature. So Paul tells husbands, "Love your wife as yourself because she is yourself":

> For no one ever hated his own flesh, but nourishes and cherishes it, just as Christ does the church. (Ephesians 5:29)

This passage alludes to a verse from Isaiah about giving charity and providing for the needy:

> Is it not to share your bread with the hungry and bring the homeless poor into your house; when you see the naked, to cover him, and not to hide yourself from your own flesh? (Isaiah 58:7)

The rabbis interpreted the words "your own flesh" to mean not just your close relatives but specifically your wife. She is "his own flesh." She is the husband's first responsibility. He must share his bread with her, bring her into his home, clothe her, protect her, and provide for her.

A Profound Mystery

Paul's instruction is drawn from the very biblical and Jewish idea that a man joined to his wife becomes one flesh with her. Therefore, his love for her fulfills the commandment to love his neighbor as himself because she is actually himself. He sees in marriage a divine and spiritual union, a fractal—a repeating pattern on a different scale—of the spiritual realities that exist higher up on the spiritual hierarchy. Marriage uniquely illustrates the idea of distinction within unity. Within the body of Messiah, there are distinct members with distinct roles and functions:

> As in one body we have many members, and the members do not all have the same function, so we, though many, are one body in Christ, and individually members one of another. (Romans 12:4-5)

Just as a husband and wife are one in marriage, yet remain differentiated one from another within the marriage, so too, everyone within the body of the Messiah participates in an overarching unity despite the differentiation of the members:

"Therefore a man shall leave his father and mother and hold fast to his wife, and the two shall become one flesh." This mystery is profound, and I am saying that it refers to Christ and the church. (Ephesians 5:31-32)

At the same time, this profound mystery has a simple, practical application. Paul concludes the thought on that practical application. Yes, it's a profound mystery, and he is speaking metaphorically about the Messiah and the community of his disciples—"However, let each one of you love his wife as himself, and let the wife see that she respects her husband" (Ephesians 5:33).

SERMON THIRTEEN:
CHILDREN, OBEY YOUR PARENTS
(EPHESIANS 6:1–4)

Children fall under the Torah of their parents until adulthood. There's no formula guaranteeing godly children, but here are a few pastoral tips from Ephesians 6.

> Children, obey your parents in the Lord, for this is right. (Ephesians 6:1)

The book of Ephesians is primarily about the relationship between Israel and the nations. Prior to the proclamation of the good news about Yeshua, there was no relationship. The Gentiles were far off, strangers and aliens, without God and without hope, foreigners to the covenants of promise and outside of the commonwealth of Israel. That changed with the introduction of the good news about Yeshua. Now the apostles, prophets, teachers, and evangelists of the Yeshua-believers represent Israel on a mission to bring God's revelation to the nations. The Gentile disciples of Yeshua represent the first fruits of that mission to the nations.

The first several chapters of the epistle describe this new and unprecedented relationship. Paul describes the union of Jewish and Gentile disciples into the assembly of Messiah in metaphysical terms as "one new man." He describes how the dividing wall that once kept Jews and Gentiles separate has been removed by the Messiah. He explains that the Jewish disciples received the Spirit and were given the responsibility of serving the nations as apostles, prophets, teachers, and evangelists. In the Epistle to the Ephesians, Paul speaks about the unity of the Jewish people and Gentile disciples without abandoning the distinction between Israel and the nations. In other writings, he categorizes that distinction as analogous to that of a male and female, or of slave and free, while pointing out that the various categories all share the same criteria for participation in the kingdom and the World to Come: Messiah Yeshua:

> There is neither Jew nor Greek, there is neither slave nor free, there is no male and female, for you are all one in Christ Jesus. (Galatians 3:28)

> Here there is not Greek and Jew, circumcised and uncircumcised, barbarian, Scythian, slave, free; but Christ is all, and in all. (Colossians 3:11)

The distinctions remain in place, but all are saved by faith in the Messiah. In the kingdom, there is no difference in criteria for salvation.

After his discussion about the relationship between Israel and the Gentile disciples (Ephesians 1-4), Paul transitions to discussing the implications of the new union in Messiah, specifically as it applies to three other types of relationships:

- Husbands and wives (5:22-33)
- Children and parents (6:1-4)
- Slaves and masters (6:5-9)

The new identity found in Messiah transforms these relationships, just as it has transformed the relationship between Jews and Gentiles in Messiah. Paul presents rules governing each relationship to explain how the new identity in Messiah impacts it.

Not coincidentally, Jewish law makes a distinction between these categories as well. Three blessings in the morning prayers at the beginning of the Siddur distinguish between Jew and Gentile, male and female, slave and free.

- Blessed are you, LORD our God, King of the universe, who has not made me a woman.
- Blessed are you, LORD our God, King of the universe, who has not made me a Gentile.
- Blessed are you, LORD our God, King of the universe, who has not made me a slave.

These three blessings are unfortunately formulated in such a way as to sound offensive, misogynistic, racist, and classist. Believe it or not, that's not the actual intention of these three infamous blessings. The liturgy was not intended to give Jewish men a pat on the back every morning for not being Gentiles or women. Instead, these blessings are supposed to remind a Jewish man that he belongs to God and has no exemptions from the obligations of the Torah.

A woman, a Gentile, and a slave are all exempt from certain commandments of the Torah. For example, a woman need not wear tzitzit, don tefillin, pray at the fixed times of prayer, or perform other commandments specifically incumbent upon a Jewish male. A Gentile need not observe the Sabbath, the calendar, or the strict dietary laws. A slave has no rights of his own and is therefore exempt from the commandments he cannot perform because he is under his master's control. Therefore, the three blessings are intended to distinguish these categories of people and remind the Jewish male that he has no exemptions to the Torah as others do. He is God's slave. These three blessings are not supposed to be anti-Gentile, anti-female, or anti-slave. Instead, they are intended as offerings of thanksgiving to God for one's specific obligations to the Torah.

It's not coincidental that while discussing the relationship between Israel and the nations and the distinction between Jewish and Gentile disciples, Paul goes on to discuss these additional categories in which occur similar distinctions regarding one's respective obligations to the Torah.

Husbands and wives are described as "one flesh," but their roles differ dramatically. Husbands must love their wives sacrificially, but wives must submit to their husbands "as to the Master." Likewise, children and parents share a close union but with different roles, privileges, and responsibilities—children must honor and obey their parents, and parents must instruct their children in the discipline of discipleship and godliness. Slaves and masters are both fellow servants of "their Master in heaven."

It's worth pointing out that the epistle discusses one category of relationship that doesn't appear in the formula of the three blessings but still follows the same pattern. There is no blessing in the Siddur that says, "Blessed are you ... who has not made me a child." That's because, in fact, God did make all of us as children. Everyone begins life as a child. Nevertheless, this category fits the pattern of distinguishing between those who are obligated to the whole Torah and those who are not. A child under the age of puberty is not obligated to the commandments as an adult is. That's the point of the "bar mitzvah," which means "son of the commandment." At the age of thirteen, a boy becomes officially obligated to observe the Torah as an adult.

For example, before becoming a bar mitzvah, a boy is not required to wear tzitzit, don tefillin, pray at the appointed times, recite the Shabbat *Kiddush*, or fast on Yom Kippur. Children are exempt from many of the commandments. One might wonder, "What rules must a child observe?" Paul explains that children are obligated to obey their parents: "Children, obey your parents in the Lord, for this is right" (Ephesians 6:1). To the child, the parents carry the authority of the Torah. Moreover, children are specifically obligated to the commandment of honoring their parents.

Before entering into further discussion on Ephesians 6, it's worth emphasizing that Paul is still working within these legal categories. Israel and the nations retain their distinction, but in Messiah, they are joined into one metaphysical body—the body of Messiah. Males and females retain their distinction, but in marriage, they are joined into one new identity as "one flesh." Therefore, husbands should love their wives as the Messiah loves the assembly, and wives should honor their husbands and defer to their authority. Adults and children retain their distinction, but children should obey their parents, and parents should raise their children in the discipline and instruction of the Master. Slaves and masters retain a legal distinction, but in Messiah, slaves should serve their masters as if serving Messiah, and masters should treat their slaves with dignity and respect as fellow servants of Messiah.

Honor Your Father and Mother

> Children, obey your parents in the Lord, for this is right. "Honor your father and mother" (this is the first commandment with a promise), "that it may go well with you and that you may live long in the land." (Ephesians 6:1-3)

Paul binds the Gentile disciples in Ephesus with the commandment to "honor your father and mother." Jewish law does not consider this commandment to be an obligation for Gentiles. The sages did not include the commandment to honor one's mother and father in the list of seven laws commanded to the son of Noah. Why? The justification for excluding the commandment to honor one's parents from the universal Noachide laws is never stated explicitly. However, one could presume that a Gentile's parents were idolaters and that honoring them would involve allegiance to their idolatrous faith and practice, participation in idolatrous rituals, and possibly even veneration of the dead in the form of ancestor worship.

Paul had a different perspective. He wanted Gentile disciples to preserve relationships with their idolatrous families if possible. For example, he encouraged disciples married to unbelieving spouses to remain with those spouses if they could (1 Corinthians 7:14-16). The apostles always weighed the commandments and assessed them under the criteria of the commandment, "Love your neighbor as yourself" (Leviticus 19:18). The apostles considered any commandment that could be construed to fall under that broad categorical commandment to apply universally to both Jews and Gentile disciples:

> For the commandments, "You shall not commit adultery, You shall not murder, You shall not steal, You shall not covet," and any other commandment, are summed up in this word: "You shall love your neighbor as yourself." Love does no wrong to a neighbor; therefore love is the fulfilling of the law. (Romans 13:9-10)

> For you were called to freedom, brothers. Only do not use your freedom as an opportunity for the flesh, but through love serve one another. For the whole law is fulfilled in one word: "You shall love your neighbor as yourself." (Galatians 5:13-14)

A Story from the Talmud

Even though the sages considered Gentiles free of the obligation to honor their parents, they described it as praiseworthy for Gentiles to do so. A story from the Talmud describes a delegation of sages from the Sanhedrin attempting to buy a precious stone from a non-Jewish gem merchant in Ashkelon. They needed the gem for the high priest's breastplate, and they were willing to pay an extraordinary price. The gem merchant refused to even show them the precious stone despite the generous offer. He explained that his father kept the key to the safe under his pillow, and seeing that his father was at that time sleeping, he would not disturb him even for such a fortune. The sages took this story as instructive, saying, "If this is how one who is not obligated to honor his parents behaves, how much more so is it incumbent upon Jews to honor their parents."

Another Story from the Talmud

The Talmud refers to the commandment of honoring one's parents as one of the weightiest commandments in the Torah. It contrasts and compares it with one of the least of the commandments, "you shall not take the mother with the young" (Deuteronomy 22:6). The Talmud points out that the Torah offers the same reward for both commandments: "That it may be well with you and that you may prolong your days." On this basis, Rabbi Yehudah said, "Be as scrupulous observing a small commandment as you are observing a great commandment for you do not know what the reward of each is" (m.*Avot* 2:1).

Paul refers to this as the "first commandment with a promise," which should be understood as an allusion to reward in the kingdom and the World to Come. A story in the Talmud raises an anecdotal objection to the notion that keeping a particular commandment can guarantee an individual reward in this lifetime:

> A father said to his son, "Climb up the tree and send away the mother bird and bring me the young birds." The son climbed the tree, drove off the mother bird, and took the young from the nest, [thereby keeping both the commandment of honoring his father and the commandment of driving away the mother bird]. As he climbed back down to his father, he fell

to his death. In what way did it go well with him? In what way were his days prolonged? Instead, the words "that it may be well with you" refer only to the day that all is wholly well, and the words "that you may prolong your days" refer only to the day that is wholly long. (b.*Kiddushin* 39b)

The Discipline and Instruction of the Master

> Fathers, do not provoke your children to anger, but bring them up in the discipline and instruction of the Lord. (Ephesians 6:4)

Children are duty-bound to obey and honor their parents, but parents are not licensed to treat children harshly or heavy-handedly. Fathers are warned against provoking their children. They are not to regard their children as their property. Instead, they are to accord their children the dignity of a fellow human being and fellow child of God. Parents are told to raise their children "in the discipline [musar] and instruction of the Master," teaching their children the words of Yeshua and the obligations of discipleship. The reference to "discipline ... of the Master" in Ephesians 6:4 refers to discipleship to the Master, not punishments for misbehavior.

Jacob and Esau

In the Torah portion Toldot, Isaac and Rebekah are desperate to have children. They try for twenty years. Isaac stands opposite Rebekah and prays for her. Why do they want children so badly? Because they need sons to carry on the Abrahamic legacy and to inherit the promises God gave to Abraham. They want children so they can transmit their faith to a new generation. After all, God chose Abraham only because he saw that Abraham would pass his faith on to his children:

> For I have chosen him, that he may command his children and his household after him to keep the way of the LORD by doing righteousness and justice, so that the LORD may bring to Abraham what he has promised him. (Genesis 18:19)

Likewise, the Torah commands the Jewish people to teach the commandments to their children: "You shall teach them diligently to your children" (Deuteronomy 6:4). Paul extends this obligation to Gentile disciples when he tells them to raise their children in the discipline and instruction of the Master. The parent is thus enjoined to correct his or her children and guide them on the straight and narrow path that leads to life. A disciple of Yeshua must not raise his or her children as King David raised Absalom and Adonijah:

> His father had never at any time displeased him by asking, "Why have you done thus and so?" (1 Kings 1:6)

Yet, despite our best efforts, kids don't always make the same choices in religion and morality that we have made. Many of us did not make the same choices that our parents made. This is illustrated well by Jacob and Esau. The twins wrestle in the womb. We don't understand why they are wrestling until they are born. Then we see that they are polar opposites in nature. One is hairy; one is smooth. Esau is a man of the field; Jacob is a perfect man, staying at home. Esau seeks to satisfy his appetites, chasing soup and Hittite girls. Jacob is looking for the spiritual inheritance of Abraham.

Nature vs. Nurture

> When Rebekah had conceived children by one man, our forefather Isaac, though they were not yet born and had done nothing either good or bad—in order that God's purpose of election might continue, not because of works but because of him who calls—she was told, "The older will serve the younger." As it is written, "Jacob I loved, but Esau I hated." (Romans 9:10-13)

Psychologists debate the roles of nature and nurture in the development of human personality, character, and behavior. The story of Jacob and Esau demonstrates that the ultimate outcome of a human being is not based on nature or nurture. Both boys shared the same genetic material, being twins and sons of Isaac and Rebekah. Both shared the same nurture, being raised in the same home by the same family at the same time. So what accounts for the big difference between Jacob and Esau? It turns out that they were entirely different people.

From the moment of conception, the souls that come to inhabit these bodies are already people. The personalities are already there.

Yes, we can influence them. Hopefully, we can persuade them toward godliness and discipleship. But they will make their own decisions in life. We can't make decisions for people. Children are not formless lumps of clay ready to be shaped by our hands. They are individuals in possession of their own unique souls—transcendent and heavenly beings.

Parents take too much credit for themselves when their children meet or exceed their expectations. Likewise, parents blame themselves too much when their children disappoint their expectations.

Tips for Raising Disciples

There's no formula to guarantee that you will raise godly children. But here are a few tips for mom and dad if you want to raise kids that stay in faith.

1. Teach your children to honor their parents.

Part of keeping children in the faith and raising them to lead godly lives involves teaching them to honor you. A child who honors his parents will naturally be reluctant to disappoint his or her parents' expectations and therefore reluctant to abandon the faith and stray into godlessness. But how do you teach your children to honor you?

If you want your children to honor you, you should model that by demonstrating utmost reverential honor for your own parents. Both sets of parents. Children learn through imitation. When they see how you honor your parents, they will imitate your model.

A father cannot teach his child to honor him by demanding honor. Neither can a mother teach her child to honor her by demanding to be honored. Instead, we teach our children to honor us by honoring our parents and our spouses. When a child observes his mother honoring his father and vice versa, then the child learns the art of honoring father and mother. Only the mother can teach a child to honor the father. Only the father can teach the child to honor the mother.

The sages say that Esau had one great redeeming quality despite his wickedness and self-indulgences: He honored Isaac. No son ever honored his father as Esau honored Isaac. However, he failed to honor his mother, Rebekah. In contrast, Jacob honored his mother, but he failed to show proper honor to his father. The story might have been different if Isaac had taught Esau to honor Rebekah and Rebekah had taught Jacob to honor Isaac.

2. *Teach your children to honor their religion.*

> A son honors his father, and a servant his master. If then I am a father, where is my honor? And if I am a master, where is my fear? (Malachi 1:6)

Children must be taught the fear of the LORD. This is accomplished only by modeling the fear of the LORD. If you want your children to stay in your religion, you need to show them that you yourselves honor your religion. When at all possible, it's important for both parents to share the same faith and be on the same page about their observance. Both parents need to present the same set of values and expectations regarding religious devotions. Disagreements over matters of faith and practice should never occur in front of the children. Talk them through privately, but parents should always present a consolidated approach to faith.

Moreover, religious upheaval, such as switching churches or switching religions, is not good for kids. Consistency is key. If we show our children that we are free to leave our religion to explore another, they may well follow our example.

3. *Teach your children to honor their community of faith.*

Engage in your religious faith and participate to the fullest extent, both in public and private, at your place of fellowship and also at home. Never speak dismissively of the religious values of your faith community. Beware of dismissing "traditions of men" or communicating to your children that religious observances are only for the pious but not for you.

Don't disparage your place of worship, your spiritual leaders, your teachers, or their teachings in front of your children. Beware the afterservice critique of the pastor's sermon or the rabbi's talk. Your children are listening, and they are absorbing your disrespect. Don't expect them to respect their religious leaders if you do not respect yours.

We have all seen this happen enough times to understand the pattern. The kids in families where the parents are unhappy with their place of worship don't grow up and find a congregation that suits them better. More often, they want nothing to do with religion at all. They want to stay far away from the religion that brought so much unhappiness into their parents' homes.

4. *Provide your children with godly peers.*

It's essential to provide your children with godly peers, preferably from your community of faith or one affiliated with it. But don't assume other children from your faith community are godly peers. Look for friends who will reinforce your values.

It's especially important to provide opportunities for your children to mix with godly peers of the opposite gender. Rebekah was disgusted when Esau married Hittite girls, but he was already forty years old, and his parents had done nothing to provide him with a wife. Realizing their mistake, they sent Jacob to Aram to find a wife from among Rebekah's family.

If our children learn to honor their parents, their religion, their religious community, and to find friends and potential spouses among godly peers, they will have a better chance of remaining within the fold of our faith. For those of you raising children: good luck. Best wishes. God's blessings. However, I think it is also helpful to remember that you don't own them. They don't belong to you. They've been entrusted to you for safekeeping and lent to you for a little while. For those brief few years, we do our best. But every single one of them is an individual with a unique soul and a unique path.

SERMON FOURTEEN:
SERVANTS AND MASTERS
(EPHESIANS 6:5–9)

Apostolic directives for slaves and their owners in the Roman world have modern implications for discipleship today. Ephesians 6 teaches principles for distinction theology, discipleship, and the service of God.

Once, it happened that Rabbi Yehudah HaNasi (Judah the Prince) needed to send a letter to the Roman Emperor. He called in his secretary, Rabbi Assef, and said, "I need you to write while I dictate a letter to the emperor." Rabbi Assef sat down and wrote the salutation: "From Rabbi Yehudah the Prince to our Lord the Emperor Antonious." Rabbi Yehudah read what Assef had written, tore it up, and threw it away. "Why did you do that? What's wrong with that?" Assef asked. Rabbi Yehudah said, "It should say, "To our Lord, the emperor from your servant Yehudah." Don't put my name in front of his name, and don't call me Judah the Prince when talking to the emperor; call me Judah your servant."

Rabbi Assef didn't like this. He complained, "Rabbi Yehudah, why are you lowering your dignity? Why would you humble yourself when writing to an idolater like the Roman emperor? Why not put your name first? And why not call yourself the Nasi, the prince, because that is what you are to the sages? And why debase yourself and call yourself the emperor's servant?" Rabbi Yehudah HaNasi replied, "Am I better than my forefather Jacob? When he sent his servants out to meet Esau on the road, he sent them with a message. He told his servants, "When you see Esau, thus shall you say to my lord Esau, 'Thus says your servant Jacob.'"

The Servant of the LORD

The story of Abraham sending his servant Eliezer on a mission to Haran to obtain a spouse for his son Isaac was programmatic for the apostles. The apostles took their sense of mission and their mode of prayer in their Master's name from this story. Just as Eliezer identified himself only as the servant of Abraham (i.e., the slave of Abraham), they always identified themselves as "servants of Yeshua" (i.e., "the slaves of Yeshua"). The distinction between servant and slave does not exist in Biblical Hebrew. The Hebrew word *eved* gets translated into our English Bibles as either "servant" or "slave," but this is an artificial distinction. It means slave. An *eved* is a human being owned by someone else.

Why do we refer to Yeshua as "Master?" This is the title by which a slave addresses his owner. Yeshua said, "A slave is not above his master, nor is a disciple above his teacher. You call me master and teacher, and rightfully so, for so I am." Though he himself came among us as one who serves, we are, in relation to him, as his servants, moreover, as his slaves. Think of his many parables in which he compares himself to a man who goes away on a journey and leaves his slaves in charge of his affairs and household. We are to understand ourselves as Yeshua's slaves.

This is similar to what God said regarding all the children of Israel. He said, "They are my servants, whom I brought out of the land of Egypt; they shall not be sold as slaves" (Leviticus 25:42). This explains why Isaiah refers to the nation of Israel as the *eved HaShem*, "the servant of the LORD," a title that he also applies to the Messiah, the King of Israel, as the chief "slave of the LORD."

The Service of the LORD

Moreover, the service of the LORD, which is the worship of the LORD, is called *avodah*, a Hebrew word ordinarily used to describe the service rendered by an *eved*, a slave. You can hear the root word *eved* inside the word *avodah*. It's the service a slave renders to his or her master.

In the Bible and in Judaism, the daily prayers and the observances of the Torah, particularly the ceremonial, ritual, liturgical, and Levitical observances, are generally and collectively referred to as the *avodah*—that is, "the service." We also translate it as "worship." But that's why we speak of a "worship service" as a service. One engaged in worship is engaged in the service of the king, serving a master.

Exemptions from the Avodah

In our previous studies in Ephesians, I pointed out that every Jewish male has this status of *eved HaShem* ("slave of the LORD") in that he has no exemptions from the service (*avodah*) of the LORD. He is responsible for the Torah's ceremonial, ritual, liturgical, and Levitical observances. This is why the daily prayers require every adult Jewish male to acknowledge every morning that he is not a woman, not a Gentile, and not a slave—that is, not a slave to someone else. All those categories of people have exemptions from the *avodah*. So do children under the age of *bar/bat mitzvah*.

We saw how the Epistle to the Ephesians addresses these differences. The first several chapters address the distinctions between the Jewish people and the Gentile disciples, emphasizing their unity as one new metaphysical identity in Messiah without losing sight of the differentiation between Jews and Gentiles along the way. The emphasis is put on unity and mutual submission despite differences. The Gentile disciples are said to be being built together with the Jewish disciples on the foundation of the prophets and the apostles. This new identity has implications for the Gentile disciples. While not making them Jewish, it imposes a higher moral standard derived from the Scriptures of Israel, which Paul makes clear in his discussions on living as children of light.

After his discussion about the relationship between Israel and the Gentile disciples (Ephesians 1-4), the epistle goes on to talk about the other distinctions in obligation to the service of God: women, children, and slaves, three classes of people who enjoy some level of exemptions to the *avodah*.

The new identity found in Messiah transforms each of these relations, just as it has transformed the relationship between Jews and

Gentiles in Messiah. Paul presents rules governing each relationship to explain how the new identity in Messiah impacts it.

Husbands and wives are described as "one flesh," but their roles differ dramatically. Husbands must love their wives sacrificially, but wives must submit to their husbands "as to the Master." Likewise, children and parents share a close union but with different roles, privileges, and responsibilities—children must honor and obey their parents, and parents must instruct their children in the discipline of discipleship and godliness. Finally, he addresses the implications for slaves and their masters.

As Yeshua himself said, "No one can serve two masters." Therefore, a slave is considered exempt from the *avodah* because he is not the master of his own time and decisions. He belongs to a competing master. In practical terms, this means that a Jewish slave was not required to pray at the set times of prayer, offer prescribed sacrifices, don tefillin or tzitzit, or undertake many of the various other obligations of Jewish law unless his master required it of him. This is also why God doesn't want his people to be slaves to others. They are his slaves.

Slavery in the Roman World

It's important to point out that we are not discussing biblical slavery as spelled out in the Torah. Those laws, which discuss the obligations of Jewish slave-owners in possession of Jewish slaves, essentially reduce slavery to a six-year term of indentured servanthood, after which the slave must be released and even compensated for his labors. That's not the type of slavery in view here. That's not how Roman slavery worked. Roman slavery was real slavery, and it was common.

In Ephesians, Paul is speaking about slavery as it existed in the Roman world.

This is not the first time Paul invokes the Roman institution of slavery. Earlier in the epistle, we discussed the concept of manumission within a Roman household. Paul used that institution as a helpful metaphor to explain a Gentile disciple's role in the kingdom when juxtaposed against the national identity of Israel. He compared Gentile disciples within the family of Israel to the household servant, or slave, in a Roman household, who has gone through manumission to become an honorary member of the family. In some cases, such a slave was allowed to take the family's surname and, through that process, obtain Roman citizenship. Paul's parents, or perhaps his grandparents, may have gone through that very process back in Tarsus, and that's probably how Paul obtained citizenship. It also explains his association with the Synagogue of the Freedmen in Jerusalem. "Freedmen" is a term used to describe former slaves.

In the Roman economy, slaves were considered property. Roman law protected the rights of slave-owners, but it accorded no legal personhood to a slave. Even though manumission was a possibility, it rarely happened. Most slaves would never be freed. Without legal protections, slaves were subject to any type of corporal punishment or torture their masters might impose, and if a slave-owner killed his slave, that was his business. Slaves were also used for sex. In the Roman world, prostitutes were almost always slaves.

In first-century Italy, about 40 percent of the population were slaves. Across the rest of the empire, the numbers were somewhere around 15 percent. That doesn't mean everyone had slaves. Only the elite upper class owned slaves. However, they had lots of them. It's not a surprise that many of the disciples in Paul's communities were slaves, or even that some were owners of slaves. (The Epistle to Philemon deals directly with that issue. Philemon, a disciple of Yeshua in Colossae, owned a slave named Onesimus who escaped to Rome, where he became a disciple under Paul's influence.) With all this background on slavery in place, we are ready to look at the next few verses of Ephesians 6.

Masters according to the Flesh

> Slaves, obey your earthly masters with fear and trembling, with a sincere heart, as you would Christ. (Ephesians 6:5)

The apostle directs slaves to obey their "earthly masters." The Greek term translated "earthly masters" is more literally translated as "masters according to the flesh," i.e., your "physical masters." Paul's need to distinguish one's master as a "physical master" implies the existence of a "spiritual master." He reminds the disciples in slavery that their earthly masters are not their real masters. Instead, they are slaves to Yeshua—their spiritual master.

This is similar to Yeshua's saying about persecution: "Do not fear those who kill the body but cannot kill the soul. Rather fear him who can destroy both soul and body" (Matthew 10:28). Paul directs the disciples in slavery to obey their earthly masters sincerely and devoutly, "with fear and trembling," as if they were serving the Messiah himself, who, in turn, is the *Eved HaShem*, "the Slave of the LORD." In this way, Paul reconciles the difficulty raised by the teaching of Yeshua that "no one can serve two masters, for either he will hate the one and love the other, or he will be devoted to the one and despise the other" (Matthew 6:24). By serving the earthly master to honor the heavenly master, the believing slave casts his full allegiance with Yeshua.

Fear and Trembling

> Slaves, obey your earthly masters with fear and trembling, with a sincere heart, as you would Christ, not by the way of eye-service, as people-pleasers, but as servants of Christ, doing the will of God from the heart, rendering service with a good will as to the Lord and not to man. (Ephesians 6:5–7)

In slave-owning cultures, the lazy slave is proverbial. The typical slave shirks his duties and responsibilities and only makes a show of working hard while under direct observation. The Master's parables refer to slaves misbehaving when their masters are absent. The proverbs of Jewish wisdom literature encourage slave-owners to impose strict measures: "By mere words a servant is not disciplined, for though he understands, he will not respond" (Proverbs 29:19).

It's easy to understand why a slave would attempt to do as little as possible. He has no incentive to work hard or show himself to be industrious since his efforts will benefit only his master. A slave could not be expected to do more than the barest minimum he or she was forced to do.

Paul calls slaves who are also disciples to adopt a higher standard of service. They are to work "not by the way of eye-service," a reference to direct supervision. In keeping with the Master's teachings about going the extra mile and exceeding what is required of us, Paul calls upon slaves to show themselves responsible and diligent even in the absence of direct supervision. They are not to act as "people-pleasers"; instead, they are to remember that they are slaves of Messiah. Therefore, they should carry out their duties as if for Yeshua. The instructions invoke the story of Joseph, who performed his service in the house of Potiphar with such excellence and diligence that Potiphar elevated him to head of the household: "So he left all that he had in Joseph's charge, and because of him he had no concern about anything but the food he ate" (Genesis 39:6). (The story of Joseph also sets the limits of the slave's submission. Joseph refused to capitulate to the demands of Potiphar's wife. In the biblical worldview, a slave need not feel compelled to consent to sexual coercion.)

A disciple's higher-level work ethic that exceeds expectations has practical implications in today's workplace. The disciple of Yeshua should be among the highest caliber of employees, working with alacrity, diligence, integrity, and attention to detail. I once met a housepainter who worked with his son painting houses in Minneapolis. Before he started work on a house, he told me that he would always tell his son, "This house belongs to Jesus, and that's who we are working for." Then they would give the job their best effort as if serving their heavenly Master, the Messiah. That's how a disciple should set about fulfilling the duties of his or her employment.

If so, how much more so should the same principle apply to our service of the Messiah, who says, "Why do you call me 'Master, Master,' and not do what I tell you?" (Luke 6:46). With fear and trembling, we should serve Yeshua—not playing religious games but exercising genuine, honest, sincere, heartfelt submission to our heavenly Master. Our discipleship should be real and not a charade. We should not act one way in private and another in public; instead, we should always conduct ourselves knowing that his eyes are ever upon us.

Recompense from the LORD

> Knowing that whatever good anyone does, this he will receive back from the Lord, whether he is a slave or free. (Ephesians 6:8)

Paul encourages slaves to serve their earthly masters "with fear and trembling" as a component of their fear of the LORD. The "fear of the LORD" is the knowledge that God exists and that he rewards righteousness and punishes wickedness. Those who conduct themselves in a God-fearing manner according to the fear of the LORD have confidence that ultimately, their actions in this lifetime, whether good or bad, receive recompense. There is a reward for righteousness and a punishment for sin, whether in this life or the next.

In the Torah, Joseph might have complained that there was no reward for the good service he rendered to his earthly master. He served Potiphar with fear and trembling and ended up in prison on false charges. But the story wasn't over yet, and neither is our story over yet. Knowing this, that there is compensation to be paid out by God for all the good we do, we can serve our earthly masters cheerfully and with a pure heart, regardless of how well they might reward us or how they mistreat us. If this principle applies to the workplace, how much more so to the service of our heavenly Master.

Their Master and Yours

> Masters, do the same to them, and stop your threatening, knowing that he who is both their Master and yours is in heaven, and that there is no partiality with him. (Ephesians 6:9)

Having addressed the slaves, Paul turns to address the believing slave-owners on the other side of the relationship. He tells the slave-owners to "do the same to them," meaning that they should treat their slaves with integrity, honesty, purity, and goodwill, both in public and private. They should keep in mind that God is watching them and will recompense them for the good or evil they do to their slaves. The apostle points out that spiritually speaking, both the slave-owner and the slave share the same heavenly Master.

This principle adjures the slave-owner to treat their slaves not as property but as fellow human beings. They are to grant them dignity, remembering that the distinction between slave and master exists only in this world. In the sight of heaven, all men are equal, and before God, there is no partiality.

This directive to slave-owners has practical implications for how we treat those in our employ and anyone occupying a lower social station than ourselves. It also has ramifications for the distinction between Jews and Gentiles, which, ultimately, is the theme of the epistle to the Ephesians.

No Distinction

> There is no partiality with him. (Ephesians 6:9)

The Greek translated as "there is no partiality with him" could be more literally translated to read that with God, there is no "respect of faces." This turn of phrase hearkens back to Peter's initial revelation in the household of Cornelius, where he used the same term in his surprising declaration: "Truly I [now] understand that God shows no partiality, but in every nation anyone who fears him and does what is right is acceptable to him" (Acts 10:34-35). That revelation became the theological basis for welcoming Gentiles into the school of Yeshua's disciples and granting them standing in the kingdom. It's the origin of Paul's frequently repeated axiom about the equal standing of Jewish and Gentile disciples before God:

> There is neither Jew nor Greek, there is neither slave nor free, there is no male and female, for you are all one in Christ Jesus. (Galatians 3:28)

> Here there is not Greek and Jew, circumcised and uncircumcised, barbarian, Scythian, slave, free; but Christ is all, and in all. (Colossians 3:11)

> There is no distinction between Jew and Greek; for the same Lord is Lord of all, bestowing his riches on all who call on him. For "everyone who calls on the name of the Lord will be saved." (Romans 10:12-13)

Yet, as regards this world ("according to the flesh"), such distinctions do remain in place, and these relationships still need to be navigated, even for Yeshua-believers. It's possible to be a believing slave or a believing slave-owner as long as one acknowledges that their real Master is the Messiah. In that regard, they are equals, and there is no distinction between them. In terms of this world ("according to the flesh"), however, there remains a distinction, just as there remains a distinction between children and adults and between husbands and wives and between Jews and Gentiles concerning their respective roles and obligations in Messiah.

Slaves of the Messiah

Ultimately, the lesson regarding slaves and masters teaches us that we are not to see ourselves as our own masters. To be your own master is to be a slave to sin and self, as our Master says, "Everyone who practices sin is a slave to sin" (John 8:34). Bob Dylan puts it succinctly in his song, "Gotta Serve Somebody." One who lives for himself or herself, serving himself or herself alone, has a cruel and relentless taskmaster. It's a life of slavery to the evil inclination.

The apostles teach us that we do not serve ourselves. Instead, we are slaves of the Messiah. The Messiah owns us, bought and paid for. Therefore, we endeavor not to do our own will but his will (even as he sets aside his will for the sake of his Father's), whether we be slave or free in this world ("according to the flesh"), child or adult, male or female, Jew or Gentile. We all share a common Master. We are servants of Messiah, fellow bondservants with the apostles and disciples, and slaves to righteousness.

SERMON FIFTEEN:
NOT AGAINST FLESH AND BLOOD
(EPHESIANS 6:10–12)

Stand against the schemes of the devil and learn about spiritual warfare in Ephesus. Here's the real story behind the "armor of God" in Ephesians 6 and the meaning of "the devil's schemes."

> Finally, be strong in the Lord and in the strength of his might. (Ephesians 6:10)

Beginning with the word "finally," Ephesians 6:10 indicates that our study in the Epistle to the Ephesians is wrapping up. We have "finally" come to the end of the epistle. Almost. It says, "Finally, be strong in the Lord and in the strength of his might." These words, coming at the conclusion of the epistle, should remind us of Moses' final words to Israel and to Joshua, in which he frequently repeated the admonition, "Be strong and courageous." In the last days of his life, Moses encouraged Israel to "be strong and courageous" because he knew they would face war as they went into the land of Canaan. He did not want them to shrink back, as their fathers had done a generation earlier, and abandon the land. Likewise, Paul knew that the disciples in Ephesus faced war—not a physical war of flesh and blood, but a spiritual war.

Don't forget about the context in Ephesus. Remember the story of the riot: "Great is Artemis of the Ephesians." Ephesus was a spiritual warzone because Ephesus belonged to Artemis, i.e., Diana. The temple of Artemis at Ephesus was considered one of the seven wonders of the world, and the many-breasted idol of Artemis at the center of the temple was said to have fallen from the sky. When Paul's teaching led to Gentile idolaters in Ephesus abandoning Artemis and turning to worship the God of Israel, their defection inspired a riot in which the citizens of the city turned against the Jewish population and several Jews were nearly killed. Paul was forced to flee, and he could never return to Ephesus. So he knew that there is real spiritual warfare in Ephesus. In anticipation of future conflicts, he told the Ephesian disciples, "Be strong in the Lord and in the strength of his might."

The Armor of God

> Put on the whole armor of God, that you may be able to stand against the schemes of the devil. (Ephesians 6:11)

The passage about the "armor of God" brings us into some familiar territory. If you grew up in a Bible-teaching church as I did, you encountered this passage frequently. You probably heard many teachings about the armor of God. Many of us from an evangelical or charismatic background may be over-familiar with the passage. It's popular in teachings about "spiritual warfare." That over-familiarity can sometimes be an obstacle to reading the New Testament from a Jewish perspective. If you grew up in Messianic Judaism, on the other hand, this passage might be all new to you, but it shouldn't be. It's one of those that should be underlined and highlighted in your Bible:

> Put on the whole armor of God, that you may be able to stand against the schemes of the devil. For we do not wrestle against flesh and blood, but against the rulers, against the authorities, against the cosmic powers over this present darkness, against the spiritual forces of evil in the heavenly places.
>
> Therefore take up the whole armor of God, that you may be able to withstand in the evil day, and having done all, to stand firm. Stand therefore, having fastened on the belt of

truth, and having put on the breastplate of righteousness, and, as shoes for your feet, having put on the readiness given by the gospel of peace.

In all circumstances take up the shield of faith, with which you can extinguish all the flaming darts of the evil one; and take the helmet of salvation, and the sword of the Spirit, which is the word of God, praying at all times in the Spirit, with all prayer and supplication. (Ephesians 6:11-18)

A New Subject

Is this a new subject? As Paul launches into this discussion on spiritual warfare and girding oneself for battle, it seems as if he is introducing a totally new topic unrelated to the preceding discussion. But that doesn't make a lot of sense. Paul's letters are never collections of random thoughts. There's always some type of internally consistent logic organizing his discussions. Furthermore, he introduces this seemingly new subject with the word "finally," indicating that he has come to some type of conclusion based on the previous discussion.

Remember that this entire letter is about the same thing Paul always talks about: namely, the inclusion of Gentile disciples in the kingdom and the working through of the parameters of their relationship to Israel, the Torah, and the Jewish people. I think I've demonstrated that the text of the epistle is concerned with explaining the inclusion of the Gentile disciples, their unity with Israel in Messiah, and the resulting implications for their lives. It's some of Paul's most explicit teachings on the subject of what I call "distinction theology." This includes all the passages about the commonwealth of Israel, the one new man, the dividing wall of partition, the spiritual Temple, and the rest of Paul's metaphors. It's reasonable to ask what spiritual warfare and the armor of God have to do with that subject. It seems to have nothing to do with the relationship between Jews and Gentile believers in Messiah. However, although the transition sounds like an abrupt shift to a new subject, it's not. It's the same idea, the same concerns, and the same subject.

The Schemes of the Devil

Paul warns the disciples to arm themselves against "the schemes of the devil." The English word "devil" is really a mistranslation of the Greek *diabolos*, a word that literally means "accuser." In other words, it's the Greek equivalent of the Hebrew word *satan*, the accuser of the brethren.

> Devil = Satan = Adversary = Accuser

What are the "schemes" of the devil? The phrase alludes to Genesis 3:1, where it says, "Now the serpent was more crafty (*arum*) than any other beast of the field." The Hebrew word translated by the ESV as "crafty" could also be rendered as "clever," "shrewd," or "scheming." According to Jewish lore, the serpent in the garden was possessed by Satan when he schemed to deceive Adam and Eve. Yeshua alludes to Genesis 3:1 when he warns his disciples to avoid falling into the hands of persecutors by being "wise as serpents and innocent as doves" (Matthew 10:16). He's not referring to divine wisdom. He's talking about being clever enough to stay one step ahead of those who wanted to harm them. We could translate Genesis 3:1 to say, "The serpent was more scheming than any other animal."

Ephesians 6 is not the only place Paul refers to the devil's schemes. It's an idea he invokes frequently. According to Paul's idea, the schemes of Satan and his many snares take place primarily in the realm of interpersonal relationships.

We Are Not Ignorant of His Schemes

For example, previously in the epistle, Paul warned his readers, "Do not let the sun go down on your anger, and give no opportunity to the devil" (Ephesians 4:26–27). By retaining anger against one who has offended or sinned against us, we ally ourselves with the Satan, who seeks to bring his accusations against that person. Paul asks us to forgive everyone before we go to sleep so that the accuser has no basis for bringing his charges against the one who has offended us. Jewish liturgy prescribes the same exercise in the form of the so-called *Bedtime Shema*, a recitation of the *Shema* intended to literally fulfill the injunction, "when you lie down" (Deuteronomy 6:7). The recitation is prefaced with a legal declaration offering forgiveness and exoneration to anyone who has sinned against you:

> Master of the Universe, behold I forgive and pardon anyone who angered me, or antagonized me or who sinned against me, whether relating to my body, or my money, or my honor, or anything that belongs to me, whether done accidentally, or willingly, unintentionally or intentionally, or whether with words, whether with actions, whether in this present incarnation, whether in another incarnation—any person of Israel. And may no person be punished because of me. (*Bedtime Shema*)

Paul said, "We are not ignorant of [Satan's schemes]." From Paul's perspective, unforgiveness toward a person gives the devil opportunity against that person—that's the devil's scheme. For that reason, Paul legally forgives those who sin against him, and when he does, he invokes the presence of the Messiah as a witness:

> But one whom you forgive anything, I forgive also; for indeed what I have forgiven, if I have forgiven anything, I did it for your sakes in the presence of the Messiah, so that no advantage would be taken of us by Satan, for we are not ignorant of his schemes. (2 Corinthians 2:10-11 NASB)

It should be clear that in Paul's mind, the schemes of the devil function in the sphere of interpersonal relationships. Satan invests his energy in destroying our relationships with one another. This explains why the writings of the apostles focus on the command of love for one another and so frequently admonish us with the commandments about "one to another." It also explains why we are so frequently and relentlessly beset with attitudes of unforgiveness and bitterness, contention and agitation, and why there are always people in a community who take an unholy delight and perverse satisfaction in stirring up trouble and fueling contention. In 1 Timothy 6:4-5, Paul warns about fellow believers who have "an unhealthy craving for controversy and for quarrels about words, which produce envy, dissension, slander, evil suspicions, and constant friction among people who are depraved in mind and deprived of the truth." Yes, that sounds familiar.

Ostensibly, we should be the most loving people in the world; after all, we are the only people with an absolute mandate to love everyone—especially one another—as the Master loved us. Moreover, Yeshua himself said that the mark that distinguishes us as his disciples from every other people on earth is supposed to be our love for one another. So how can it be that disciples of Yeshua are beset with such inner animosity at work within our communities? It's the work of Satan.

Whenever my father faced trouble in the churches he led in the form of contentious people who fought with him, fought with one another, or otherwise disrupted the peace, he would remind himself, "We do not wrestle against flesh and blood." Before letting feelings of resentment or animosity dictate his attitude toward an individual, he would say to himself, "My enemy is not Mr. So-and-so; it's the devil."

The real spiritual battleground is not in demonic possession and exorcism (though I do not discount those situations or question their reality) but in how we treat one another. Solomon said, "The wise woman builds her house, but the foolish tears it down with her own hands" (Proverbs 14:1 NASB). It is almost always the case, both in the home and in the community, that the real danger comes not from outside but from within. This is the work of Satan, and we need to recognize it for what it is, and not join his team or give him an opportunity.

Not against Flesh and Blood

> For we do not wrestle against flesh and blood, but against the rulers, against the authorities, against the cosmic powers over this present darkness, against the spiritual forces of evil in the heavenly places. (Ephesians 6:12)

What does the phrase "We do not wrestle against flesh and blood" remind us of? If we are reading Ephesians from a Jewish perspective, it should remind us of the story of Jacob, who wrestled an assailant who was not of flesh or blood. Of course, a cursory reading of the Torah might lead us to conclude that the assailant Jacob wrestled was the Angel of the LORD, as Jacob himself said, "I have seen God face to face" (Genesis 32:30), but the sages object to that interpretation. The story is not about Jacob's struggle with God; it's about Jacob's struggle with Esau. Jacob had been wrestling with his twin brother since before he and Esau were born.

The story of Jacob wrestling the angel comes in the context of the culmination of that narrative thread. It occurred as Jacob prepared to face off with Esau. He was afraid of facing his brother. He knew that Esau intended to kill him. He knew that Esau had come out with armed men and was on his way, at that very moment, to kill him. He had done what he could to prepare. He had divided his family into two camps in the hope that one might escape the sword of Esau. He had thrown himself on God, praying for God's help. That night, in the darkness, the wrestling match took place. So who does the angel represent? It represents Esau, and the struggle with the angel represents Jacob's struggle.

On this basis, Jewish tradition identified the angel with whom Jacob wrestled as "the angel of Esau"—not just Esau's guardian angel, but the angelic prince appointed over the nation of Edom (i.e., the nation founded by Esau). From that perspective, the idea is that Jacob needed to wrestle with and defeat the spiritual force behind Esau before he could be reconciled to Esau. Because he won the spiritual wrestling match, the battle was already over by the time he encountered Esau. Rather than killing him, Esau embraced him, and the brothers were reconciled. Jacob declared, "Seeing your face is like seeing the face of God." According to this interpretation, the spiritual battle is about personal relationships.

Principalities

It's obvious that Paul had the story of Jacob's encounter with the angelic prince of Edom in mind when he said, "We wrestle not against flesh and blood, but against principalities" (Ephesians 6:12 KJV). I prefer the King James Version's word "principalities" because it's a better translation of Paul's intent. In Judaism, the angel with whom Jacob wrestled is called the Prince of Edom (*Sar Esav*). The "principalities" against which we struggle are such angelic princes.

The idea is derived from the book of Daniel. In that story, Daniel received a troubling vision he did not understand. He prayed to God, asking for the interpretation of the vision. Heaven dispatched the angel Gabriel to bring Daniel the interpretation, but it took a long time for Gabriel to arrive. When he finally did arrive, he apologized to Daniel for his tardiness. He said, "The prince of the kingdom of Persia withstood me for twenty-one days, but Michael, one of the chief princes, came to help me, for I was left there with the kings of Persia" (Daniel 10:13).

The Prince of Persia is the angelic prince over the nation of Persia. At that point in the Daniel story, Persia had just defeated Babylon, meaning that Daniel had fallen under the power of the Persians. Gabriel had to cut through the angelic defenses of the Principality of Persia to reach Daniel and deliver the message. He would not have been able to reach Daniel if the archangel Michael (one of the chief princes) had not come to his assistance.

Judaism teaches that each of the seventy nations is under the authority and administration of an angelic prince, but Israel is the LORD's portion. That idea is derived in part from the Torah portion Vayigash, which counts the seventy sons of Jacob who go down into Egypt. The Torah says, "All the persons of the house of Jacob who came into Egypt were seventy" (Genesis 46:27). A critical textual variant in Deuteronomy correlates that number with the number of angelic princes assigned over the nations. Compare Deuteronomy 32:8-9 as it appears in the New American Standard, the English Standard, and the Greek Septuagint (LXX):

- When the Most High gave the nations their inheritance, when He separated the sons of man, He set the boundaries of the peoples according to the number of the sons of Israel. For the LORD's portion is His people; Jacob is the allotment of His inheritance. (NASB)

- When the Most High gave to the nations their inheritance, when he divided mankind, he fixed the borders of the peoples according to the number of the sons of God. But the LORD's portion is his people, Jacob his allotted heritage. (ESV)

- When the Most High divided the nations, when he separated the sons of Adam, he set the bounds of the nations according to the number of the angels of God. (LXE)

When the Septuagint version says, "according to the number of the angels of God," it's almost certainly translating a Hebrew version of Deuteronomy that read, "according to the number of the sons of God." A version of Deuteronomy from the Dead Sea Scrolls says precisely that. But the Masoretic Text of the Hebrew prefers to alter the expression "sons of God" to "sons of Israel." This explains the discrepancy between the New American Standard and the English Standard versions. However, in the days of the apostles, the reading was probably "sons of God," a term the Bible regularly uses to describe the angels. Moreover, the apostles regarded the Septuagint as a reliable witness, and they employed it regularly.

Judaism derives the idea that humanity is divided into seventy nations directly from the table of nations in Genesis 10, which charts the descendants of Noah's three sons. According to the traditional Jewish interpretation of Deuteronomy 32:8-9, God assigned each of the seventy nations to an angelic prince, but he retained Israel, the seventy-first nation, as his own. The archangel Michael stands for Israel as his representative (the name Michael means "Who is like God?"). Other than Michael, the other angelic princes over the nations are not exactly good angels. They are the false gods of the nations, which according to first-century Jewish thought, were the idolatrous gods worshiped by the Gentiles.

The Heavenly Sanhedrin

The idea of the seventy angelic princes presiding over the nations is also derived in part from Psalm 82, in which the gods are said to form a heavenly Sanhedrin. According to this idea, the Sanhedrin on earth, with seventy members, corresponds to the heavenly Sanhedrin, just as the Temple on earth is a shadow and reflection of the heavenly and angelic Sanctuary. This is the older, ancient Near East meaning of Psalm 82, in which God is depicted as rebuking the angelic principalities for the injustices that they have perpetrated upon the nations:

> *A Psalm of Asaph.* God has taken his place in the divine council; in the midst of the gods he holds judgment: "How long will you judge unjustly and show partiality to the wicked? Selah. Give justice to the weak and the fatherless; maintain the right of the afflicted and the destitute. Rescue the weak and the needy; deliver them from the hand of the wicked."
>
> They [the gods] have neither knowledge nor understanding, they walk about in darkness; all the foundations of the earth are shaken. I said, "You are gods, sons of the Most High, all

> of you; nevertheless, like men you shall die, and fall like any prince."
>
> Arise, O God, judge the earth; for you shall inherit all the nations! (Psalm 82)

At the conclusion of the psalm, the LORD removes the corrupt administration of false gods and takes over the nations himself. He takes the nations as his inheritance, elevating them to a status originally unique to Israel: "Jacob his people, Israel his inheritance" (Psalm 78:71). The psalm predicts a regime change in which the authority over the nations is transferred from the false gods over to the LORD. This worldview also explains how it is that Satan has possession over the nations and was able to offer them to Yeshua in the third temptation:

> Again, the devil took him to a very high mountain and showed him all the kingdoms of the world and their glory. And he said to him, "All these I will give you, if you will fall down and worship me." (Matthew 4:8–9)

Paul speaks about the seventy angelic princes over the nations when he warns his readers that they are in a struggle against "the rulers, against the authorities, against the cosmic powers over this present darkness, against the spiritual forces of evil in the heavenly places" (Ephesians 6:12). He's talking about the spiritual powers over the Gentile nations. This is also why he urges the Ephesians to be strong and put on the armor of God. He knows that the spiritual powers over the nations are not happy with the defection of the Gentile disciples. They will make war against them, trick them, trap them, deceive them, turn them against one another, and especially turn them against the Jewish people. Paul has prophetically foreseen a coming apostasy.

Earlier in his career, not long after he had to flee Ephesus, he arranged a rendezvous with the elders of the Yeshua-believing communities in Ephesus. Since it was impossible for him to go to Ephesus, he arranged the meeting in nearby Miletus. The elders of the Ephesian communities made the trip to meet with him, and he bade them farewell. He knew, through prophecy, that he would never again see them. He warned them about a coming spiritual battle that would take place in their communities and an apostasy that would draw disciples away:

> I know that after my departure fierce wolves will come in among you, not sparing the flock; and from among your own selves will arise men speaking twisted things, to draw away the disciples after them. Therefore be alert, remembering that for three years I did not cease night or day to admonish every one with tears. (Acts 20:29-31)

Eternal Purpose of God

It should now be clear that this discussion of spiritual warfare relates directly to the earlier content in the Epistle to the Ephesians. It's not just a collection of random thoughts at the end of the letter. It's the whole point of the letter.

As Paul persuaded Gentiles in the ancient world to abandon their allegiance to their idolatrous gods and cast their allegiance with the God of Israel, he incurred the displeasure of the idolatrous gods. The Gentile disciples were contested property. The gods of the nations claimed that they belonged to them and were under the authority of the kingdom of darkness. But God was redeeming them, stealing them away from the false gods, and adding them to his own portion.

The same thing happened in the story of Israel's redemption from Egypt. God used the redemption of Israel as a judgment against all the gods of Egypt and as a means to establish his reputation among the nations. This is made explicitly clear in the literal reading of the Exodus narratives: "So that they will know my name ... I will bring judgment on all the gods of Egypt." Paul taught that the redemption of Israel was merely a first step in God's war with the false gods. Through the work of the Messiah, the LORD now redeems the nations, too, stealing them away from the false gods. Paul believed that this was God's mysterious purpose and sovereign plan for world domination from the beginning. According to Paul, God uses the salvation of the Gentile disciples to flaunt his wisdom and sovereign power before the principalities, rulers, and authorities in the heavenly realms:

> To me, though I am the very least of all the saints, this grace was given, to preach to the Gentiles the unsearchable riches of the Messiah, and to bring to light for everyone what is the plan of the mystery hidden for ages in God who created all things, so that through the church [i.e., the assembly of

Yeshua] the manifold wisdom of God might now be made known to the rulers and authorities in the heavenly places. This was according to the eternal purpose that he has realized in Christ Jesus our Lord, in whom we have boldness and access with confidence through our faith in him. (Ephesians 3:8–12)

Paul refers to this cosmic plot twist as "the mystery of the gospel." It's the salvation of the whole world. For the sake of this mystery, Paul was willing to endure humiliation and imprisonment as a casualty of the ensuing spiritual war. Satan's forces were doing everything they could to hold on to their Gentiles. The spiritual forces to whom the nations belong were reluctant to let their property go, so the devil schemed about how best to attack the disciples. Paul believed there was a spiritual war going on between the powers of darkness over the nations and the powers of heaven. This is why he told the Gentile disciples in Ephesus, "At one time you were darkness, but now you are light in the Lord. Walk as children of light" (Ephesians 5:8).

From this, we learn that spiritual warfare is real. It happens in all our congregations all the time. We should be more careful about whose side we are on in this spiritual battle. When we raise accusations against our brothers and sisters or against the community or stir up trouble and dissension, we are speaking on behalf of the devil and granting him opportunity. That's tragic.

It's not a battle against "flesh and blood." That's part of the deception. That's Satan's scheme. When he turns us against one another, he wins. The battle is against the rulers, against the authorities, against the cosmic powers over this present darkness, and against the spiritual forces of evil in the heavenly places. Make sure you are on the right side.

SERMON SIXTEEN:
ARMAGEDDON AND THE ARMOR OF GOD
(EPHESIANS 6:13-24)

A discussion on the armor of God in its biblical and eschatological context: the final battle with the nations, which is called Gog and Magog and the battle of Armageddon.

As Paul persuaded Gentiles in the ancient world to abandon their allegiance to their idolatrous gods and cast their allegiance with the God of Israel, he incurred the displeasure of the idolatrous gods. The Gentile disciples were contested property. The gods of the nations claimed that they belonged to them and were under the authority of the kingdom of darkness. But God was redeeming them, stealing them away from the false gods, and adding them to his own portion, as it says at the end of Psalm 82:

> "You are gods, sons of the Most High, all of you; nevertheless, like men you shall die, and fall like any prince." Arise, O God, judge the earth; for you shall inherit all the nations! (Psalm 82:6-8)

According to Paul, God used the redemption of the Gentile disciples to flaunt his wisdom and sovereign power before the principalities, rulers, and authorities in the heavenly realms, just as he used the redemption of Israel from Egypt to flaunt his power in front of the Egyptian gods:

> [This is] the plan of the mystery hidden for ages in God who created all things, so that through the church [i.e., the assembly of Yeshua] the manifold wisdom of God might now be made known to the rulers and authorities in the heavenly places. This was according to the eternal purpose that he has realized in Christ Jesus our Lord. (Ephesians 3:9-11)

The gods of the nations are actively fighting to hold on to their possessions and thwart the efforts of the assembly of Yeshua. So Paul tells us to "put on the whole armor of God, that you may be able to stand against the schemes of the devil." The "schemes of the devil" are primarily at work in interpersonal relationships. Unforgiveness, bitterness, dissensions, discord, quarrels, fights, factions—that's the real spiritual warfare in which we are engaged. The fight is not against one another or against other disciples of Yeshua or against the Jewish people. It's not against flesh and blood at all; it's against these unseen spiritual beings and powers.

The Evil Day

> Therefore take up the whole armor of God, that you may be able to withstand in the evil day, and having done all, to stand firm. (Ephesians 6:13)

In view of the spiritual warfare in which the disciples are engaged, Paul urges them to gird themselves in "the whole armor of God." They are to prepare so that they can stand firm in *the evil day*. Not an evil day, but *the evil day*. What is the evil day? You won't find it marked on your calendar, but the prophets spoke about it. The "evil day" is a component of the broader term "the day of the LORD." The evil day generally refers to the travails before the final redemption and specifically to the battle of Gog and Magog, at which the seventy nations will unite to turn against Israel (Ezekiel 38-39). It's the last battle, also called Armageddon (Revelation 16:16). It's the beginning of the day of judgment that will usher in the end of the age and the Messianic Era.

The book of Revelation speaks about Gog and Magog with reference to "all nations" falling under Satan's deceptions, falling into his schemes, and joining in with his campaign against Israel. The prophecy in the book of Revelation says:

> [Satan] will come out to deceive the nations that are at the four corners of the earth, Gog and Magog, to gather them for battle; their number is like the sand of the sea. (Revelation 20:8)

Paul warned the Gentile disciples about "Satan's schemes" because he knew Satan's endgame. He knew that Satan would deceive the nations. The devil schemes to divide us and fracture us, but his ultimate scheme is to turn the nations, including the Gentile disciples of Yeshua from the nations, against the nation of Israel.

The principalities and powers hope to enlist the Gentile disciples as recruits in their war against the Jewish people. This explains the otherwise baffling history of Jewish-Christian relations. It explains the spiritual significance of the last two thousand years of Christian anti-Semitism. It explains why the nations wage a ceaseless war against Israel and the Jewish people. It explains the Holocaust and where we stand even today with anti-Israel sentiment, rising anti-Semitism, and the shocking rise of anti-Semitic nationalism in our own country. We are careening on the edge of a terrible plunge.

We need to take Paul's warnings seriously, and as disciples, we need to prepare today for the evil day, making sure that we have done all that can be done to stand firm, lest we step into Satan's snares and fall prey to his schemes.

Messiah at War

In the war of Gog and Magog, there are only two sides: the right side and the wrong side. We don't want to be on the wrong side. When this battle finally comes, it will not go well for the nations. Why? Because God is going to fight on behalf of his people in the person of the Messiah.

Jewish interpretation considers Psalm 2 to be a prophecy of the final battle. The psalm depicts the nations and the peoples of the earth plotting against the Messiah. The kings of the earth and the ruling principalities conspire together to throw off God's kingdom. The enmity of the nations erupts in the war of Gog and Magog. The LORD installs the

Messiah in Zion to fight the nations. He declares to the Messiah, "You are my Son; today I have begotten you. Ask of me, and I will make the nations your heritage, and the ends of the earth your possession. You shall break them with a rod of iron and dash them in pieces like a potter's vessel" (Psalm 2:7-9).

The messianic prophecies in Isaiah concur. The Messiah's rod of iron with which he shatters the nations is to be the word of his mouth:

> He shall strike the earth with the rod of his mouth, and with the breath of his lips he shall kill the wicked. Righteousness shall be the belt of his waist, and faithfulness the belt of his loins." (Isaiah 11:4-5)

The Messiah declares that the words of his mouth have become a weapon of war: "He made my mouth like a sharp sword" (Isaiah 49:2).

A prophecy in Isaiah depicts the Messiah entering the land of Israel from the east. He comes like a blood-red sunrise over Edom. His garments are stained red from treading down nations in his wrath. He explains, "Their lifeblood spattered on my garments, and stained all my apparel. For the day of vengeance was in my heart, and my year of redemption had come" (Isaiah 63:3-4). In Zechariah 14, after the Messiah's feet touch the Mount of Olives, he deploys the sword of his mouth and the iron rod by smiting the nations that have come to conquer Jerusalem. The Messiah smites the armies of the nations with a plague.

All these prophecies of Messiah at war with the nations converge in Revelation 19:15:

> From his mouth comes a sharp sword with which to strike down the nations, and he will rule them with a rod of iron. He will tread the winepress of the fury of the wrath of God the Almighty.

As the Messiah gears up for the epic battle against the enemies of Israel, he armors himself with righteousness, salvation, vengeance, and zeal:

> He put on righteousness as a breastplate, and a helmet of salvation on his head; he put on garments of vengeance for clothing, and wrapped himself in zeal as a cloak. According to their deeds, so will he repay, wrath to his adversaries,

repayment to his enemies; to the coastlands he will render repayment. (Isaiah 59:17-18)

Along similar lines, the *Wisdom of Solomon* depicts the LORD arming himself to go to war against the nations:

> He shall take to him his jealousy for complete armour, and make the creature his weapon for the revenge of his enemies. He shall put on righteousness as a breastplate, and true judgment instead of an helmet. He shall take holiness for an invincible shield. His severe wrath shall he sharpen for a sword, and the world shall fight with him against the unwise. Then shall the right aiming thunderbolts go abroad; and from the clouds, as from a well-drawn bow, shall they fly to the mark. And hailstones full of wrath shall be cast as out of a stone bow, and the water of the sea shall rage against them, and the floods shall cruelly drown them. Yea, a mighty wind shall stand up against them, and like a storm shall blow them away. (*Wisdom of Solomon* 5:17-23)

As the Apostle Paul urged his disciples to prepare for the coming evil day, he armed them for the battle with images from these apocalyptic prophecies about the Messiah at war in the last battle:

> Stand therefore, having fastened on the belt of truth [Isaiah 11:5] and having put on the breastplate of righteousness [Isaiah 59:17] and, as shoes for your feet, having put on the readiness given by the gospel of peace [Isaiah 52:7] ... the shield of faith [*Wisdom* 5:19] ... the helmet of salvation [Isaiah 59:17], and the sword of the Spirit [Isaiah 49:2]. (Ephesians 6:14-17)

The specific function of the various items and the relationship to a particular virtue is probably not as important as the broader theme of identifying oneself with the Messiah as he goes to war. In his first letter to the disciples in Thessalonica, Paul urged them to "put on the breastplate of faith and love, and for a helmet the hope of salvation." It's the same general idea, but the associations are fluid. Instead of a breastplate of righteousness, it's a breastplate of faith and love, and the shield of faith is absent.

The Flaming Darts

> In all circumstances take up the shield of faith, with which you can extinguish all the flaming darts of the evil one. (Ephesians 6:16)

Satan's attacks come in the form of fiery arrows. The metaphor alludes to the imagery of Psalm 120, which depicts "lying lips" and a "deceitful tongue" as "a warrior's sharp arrows with glowing coals" (Psalm 120:4). Satan's "flaming darts" strike in the form of verbal attacks, evil speech, slander, character assassination, malicious talk, gossip, and abusive language. Words are like fiery arrows launched in a spiritual war. Make sure you aren't the one shooting them.

"The tongue is a fire ... set on fire by hell" (James 3:6). The wise soldier does not attempt to return fire under a barrage of flaming arrows. Rather, he takes shelter under his shield. Paul said that faith in God is the best shield against such assaults. In any case, if we know that the "flaming darts of the evil one" consist chiefly of evil speech, slander, and malicious talk, we should check ourselves to make sure that we are not the ones responsible for shooting the flaming darts on Satan's behalf.

The Sword of the Spirit

> The sword of the Spirit, which is the word of God. (Ephesians 6:17)

All the aforementioned items of gear from the armory of spiritual warfare are defensive in nature. The only weapon in the kit is the "sword of the Spirit, which is the word of God." The same imagery appears in the Epistle to the Hebrews:

> For the word of God is living and active, sharper than any two-edged sword, piercing to the division of soul and of spirit, of joints and of marrow, and discerning the thoughts and intentions of the heart. (Hebrews 4:12)

This is the sharp sword that issues from the mouth of the Messiah to strike down the nations. There's some wordplay at work in the image of a sword coming out of the Messiah's mouth. In the Hebrew Bible, the cutting edge of a sword is called "the mouth of the sword," and the sword is said to devour flesh as a mouth. The Hebrew word for a two-edged sword could be literally translated as "two-mouthed," and the same holds true in the Greek. The sword that issues from the Messiah is the "word of God," a term that can broadly apply to any message from God, but in the narrow sense, it should be understood as the Torah, the Prophets, the Writings, and the teaching of Yeshua.

Recall that when Satan came out to tempt the Master, Yeshua replied only with quotations from the Torah. The Torah was in his mouth. He wielded the Torah as the sword of the Spirit.

The Scriptures are referred to as a sword issuing out from the mouth because the Word of God, in those days, was memorized. It was supposed to be "in your mouth" as you repeated it for the sake of memorization and discussion. Once memorized, it was "in your heart" or "on your heart" (Deuteronomy 6:6). "What does it say? 'The word is near you, in your mouth and in your heart' (that is, the word of faith that we proclaim)" (Romans 10:8, quoting Deuteronomy 30:14).

The Word of God serves as an effective weapon against our enemy so long as it resides in our mouths and in our hearts.

Pray in the Spirit

> Praying at all times in the Spirit, with all prayer and supplication. (Ephesians 6:18)

Paul called upon the disciples in Ephesus to wage a spiritual war against Satan and the principalities, powers, and spiritual authorities in heavenly places. In addition to the spiritual armor that they must gird on, they have the weapon of God's Word in their mouths. Moreover, they have the powerful weapon of prayer in their mouths. Paul reminded them to pray continuously, at all times, and not just at formal times of prayer. In the inner person (the spirit), the disciple should make every effort to maintain a continual ongoing conversation with God. No weapon on earth is more powerful than sincere prayer. In spiritual battles, we wrestle not against flesh and blood, but we prevail by the Word of God and by prayer.

Mystery of the Gospel

> To that end, keep alert with all perseverance, making supplication for all the saints, and also for me, that words may be given to me in opening my mouth boldly to proclaim the mystery of the gospel, for which I am an ambassador in chains, that I may declare it boldly, as I ought to speak. (Ephesians 6:19-20)

In conclusion, Paul reminded his readers to pray also for him and "for all the saints," that is, "the holy ones"—the Jewish disciples and all the brothers and sisters in Messiah. He specifically asked that God might inspire him with a bold spirit and eloquent words to convey the mystery of the gospel to those who would listen. "This mystery is that the Gentiles are fellow heirs, members of the same body, and partakers of the promise in the Messiah Yeshua through the gospel" (Ephesians 3:6). Paul considered himself the steward and the ambassador of that particular revelation. While under house arrest in Rome and awaiting a trial before Nero, Paul considered himself to be "an ambassador in chains" for the sake of the proclamation of that mystery. After all, it was the message of Gentile inclusion that got him into trouble in the first place, beginning with his arrest in Acts 21.

Mail Call

> So that you also may know how I am and what I am doing, Tychicus the beloved brother and faithful minister in the Lord will tell you everything. I have sent him to you for this very purpose, that you may know how we are, and that he may encourage your hearts. (Ephesians 6:21-22)

Tychicus of Ephesus carried the letter from Rome along with a stack of Paul's mail to other communities in Asia Minor. Tychicus was one of the Gentile delegates that Paul brought with him to Jerusalem before his arrest (Acts 20:4). When news of his imprisonment in Rome reached them, the Ephesian disciples sent Tychicus to Rome carrying greetings, letters, gifts, and news from the congregations in Ephesus and other communities around Asia Minor.

Tychicus remained with Paul in Rome for a short while before returning to Asia Minor with Onesimus (Colossians 4:7-9). He carried several epistles for the disciples in Ephesus and the Lycus Valley. In the same mailbag, Tychicus carried Paul's letters to the congregations at Colossae and Laodicea and a piece of personal correspondence to a disciple in Colossae named Philemon.

The Epistle to the Ephesians concludes:

> Peace be to the brothers, and love with faith, from God the Father and the Lord Jesus Christ. Grace be with all who love our Lord Jesus Christ with love incorruptible. (Ephesians 6:23–24)

www.ingramcontent.com/pod-product-compliance
Lightning Source LLC
Chambersburg PA
CBHW070135080526
44586CB00015B/1700